REREADING LITERATURE
Thomas Hardy

REREADING LITERATURE
General Editor: Terry Eagleton

W. H. Auden
Stan Smith

William Blake
Edward Larrissy

Emily Brontë
James H. Kavanagh

Geoffrey Chaucer
Stephen Knight

Charles Dickens
Steven Connor

Thomas Hardy
John Goode

Ben Jonson
Peter Womack

John Milton
Catherine Belsey

Alexander Pope
Laura Brown

William Shakespeare
Terry Eagleton

Alfred Tennyson
Alan Sinfield

Virginia Woolf
Rachel Bowlby

Thomas Hardy
The Offensive Truth

John Goode

Basil Blackwell

Copyright © John Goode 1988

First published 1988

Basil Blackwell Ltd
108 Cowley Road, Oxford, OX4 1JF, UK

Basil Blackwell Inc.
432 Park Avenue South, Suite 1503
New York, NY 10016, USA

British Library Cataloguing in Publication Data

Goode, John, 1939–
    Thomas Hardy: the offensive truth—(Rereading literature)
    1. Fiction in English. Hardy, Thomas,
    1840–1928 – Critical studies
    I. Title   II. Rereading literature
    823'.8
    ISBN 0–631–13954–0
    ISBN 0–631–13953–2 Pbk

Library of Congress Cataloging in Publication Data

Goode, John, 1939–
    Thomas Hardy: the offensive truth
    Bibliography: p.
    Includes index.
    1. Hardy, Thomas, 1840–1928—Criticism and
interpretation.   I. Title.   II. Series.
PE4754.G66   1988   823'8   88–5021
ISBN 0–631–13954–0
ISBN 0–631–13953–2 (pbk.)

Typeset in 11 on 12 pt Baskerville
by Columns, Reading
Printed in Great Britain by Billing & Sons Ltd, Worcester

Contents

Editor's Preface

'The village atheist brooding and blaspheming over the village idiot' was how G. K. Chesterton portrayed Thomas Hardy; and Chesterton was not the only contemporary of Hardy to be rattled by his resolute refusal of false consolation. Hardy's fiction violates the Arnoldian imperative that art should be edifying; and since the middle class have always found pessimism somewhat unnerving, its critics have struggled hard to 'contain' Hardy as a gauche autodidact, the purveyor of a homespun, crackerbarrel wisdom who had grown a little too big for his literary boots. His 'clumsy' provincialism and 'bucolic' quaintness could be patronized by a James or a Woolf; but they are unsettlingly mixed in with an undeniably sophisticated artistry, and his work thus calls into question the distinctions between 'fine writing' and popular culture, the local and the global, high tragedy and wry, deflating irony. It proved necessary, then, either to suppress him altogether from the 'great tradition' of English fiction (F. R. Leavis), or to argue with bland implausibility that comedy was his true home (John Bayley).

John Goode's extraordinarily subtle, original readings of Hardy's novels take no pains to render them more palatable by ransacking the texts for messages of social hope. Goode's Hardy is the dark, bitter Hardy; but this pessimism is less some ponderously metaphysical habit of mind than the astonishing realism of a mind which, by the end of its imaginative trek, has seen coldly through the major ideological institutions of its society. It lays bare a condition in which desire is unintegrated and unappeased; in which experience and institution, or agency and structure, thwart one another at every turn; and in which there takes place an implacable negation of learning, labour and love. In the teeth of Victorian repressiveness, the Hardy of *Far from the Madding Crowd* enacts a kind of 'gospel of the body'; but this is no facile libertarianism, for by the time of *The Woodlanders* this gospel will be seen to send unmarried mothers to the workhouse, and Tess Durbeyfield will finally refuse to acknowledge her body as her own.

Goode's study is sensitively alert to Hardy's fiction less as 'representations' than as transformative practice, disruption, intervention, texts which refuse to stay still within their frames and which often enough meditate on the act of writing as a metaphor of their preoccupations. By the time of *Jude the Obscure* – a novel, in Goode's phrase, 'simply not fit for consumption' – Hardy will have carried this subversive, experimental practice of fiction to an extreme limit. Goode's book is richly freighted with allusions to Victorian historical and intellectual life, placing Hardy in the context of such contemporaries as William Morris; and it is this contextualization which allows the full, astonishing force of Hardy's radicalism to emerge, as it has rarely done previously in literary criticism. That this is a radicalism of gender as well as class is a theme which Goode keeps steadily in the foreground throughout. It will be less possible, after this illuminating account, to 'contain' a novelist whose work, as Goode shows, is always on the point of breaking through its own containing forms.

Terry Eagleton

To Magdi Yacoub FRCS

'After so many deaths I live and write'
George Herbert

1 A Scientific Game

The last years have been years of demolition. Because faith
and belief were getting pot-bound, and the Temple was made
a place to barter sacrifices, therefore faith and belief and the
Temple must be broken. This time art fought the battle,
rather than science or any new religious faction. And art has
been demolishing for us; Nietzsche, the Christian religion as
it stood; Hardy, our faith in our own endeavour; Flaubert,
our belief in love. Now, for us, it is all smashed, we can see
the whole again. We were in prison, peeping at the sky
through loop-holes. The great prisoners smashed at the loop-
holes, for lying to us. And behold, out of the ruins leaps the
whole sky.

D. H. Lawrence, on *Georgian Poetry 1911–1912*[1]

He perceived that he was 'up against' the position of having
to carry on his life not as an emotion, but as a scientific game;
that he was committed by circumstances to novel-writing as a
regular trade, as much as he had formerly been to
architecture.

F. E. Hardy, *Life of Thomas Hardy 1840–1928*[2]

The Writing Age

In the seventh chapter of Hardy's third novel, *A Pair of Blue Eyes*,
Stephen Smith, who is actually the son of a local artisan, enters the
class-conscious rectory with a letter of recommendation which
makes it possible to suppose him a sophisticated urban stranger.[3]
Soon he reveals that though he has learnt how to play chess from a

book, he has never played a game. And though he can cap the rector's Latin quotes, it is not with the voice of the accepted (though, of course, entirely arbitrary) pronunciation of the schools because he has learnt it by post. Later he will admit that he has never learnt horse-riding, though for a member of the rural middle class this would seem a more useful accomplishment than chess (or Latin) because 'there are so many other things to be learnt in this wide world that I didn't trouble about that particular bit of knowledge' (7). In short, though he has learning, he does not have education. His bits of knowledge do not add up to an organic whole. It is a distinction familiar to readers of texts as widely different as *Mansfield Park* and *Hard Times*. But it is a distinction whose effect, in this novel, is first of all reversed and secondly made to serve an entirely different function. For the values which Stephen does not possess, in spite of his learning, are mere snobbery and elusiveness, and he is about to represent young love at loggerheads with parental stupidity. Bitzer appears as Romeo. More importantly, Stephen glosses himself as a symptom of a process defined, appropriately, by his closest friend, whom he has hardly ever seen but who has taught him for years by letter. 'The speaking age,' Henry Knight has told him, 'is passing away, to make room for the writing age.'

Writing is at the very root of Hardy's self-consciousness.[4] Its vocabulary, as we shall see, pervades his novels with the authority of a dead metaphor. Texts, letters, verbal signs motivate innumerable changes of narrative. In his final novel, writing, as a drawing on a signpost or the reprinting of the Greek transcription of the New Testament, appears non-phonetically, as a signification on its own rather than as the representation of sound. It is on the face of it a negation. The writing age is an age of dislocation. In *Desperate Remedies*, Cytherea Graye advertizes for a job in the local newspaper, and confronts her printed name as a more material existence than her own (II. 1). When, in *A Pair of Blue Eyes*, the rector complains that he has been misled by the letter of recommendation (which he quotes from), Elfride replies:

> 'Professional men in London . . . don't know anything about their clerks' fathers and mothers. They have assistants who come to their offices and shops for years, and hardly even know where they live. What they can do – what profits they can bring the firm – that's all London men care about.' (9)

The negation turns into something else. Not a new value, but rather a shift from what they *are* to what they can do, what men mean to the firm. She is talking about urbanization, and it is equally a condition of Hardy's fiction that he is urbanized – the third chapter of the *Life* which is the one that launches him on his career resonantly begins: 'On Thursday, April 17, 1862, Thomas Hardy started *alone* for London.' Alone for London comes to mean writing. The written is a mode of access to the culture and a career. If it is a form of displacement it is also, as Stephen's lugubrious relationship with his entirely unsentimentalized parents makes clear, an escape from a structure of oppression. Not, of course, that writing is a utopian liberation. It is a mode of insertion, but not one in which one's *whole being* is a given.

Hardy is, of course, by no means the first author whose life is made through writing. However, he is the first major writer to articulate writing itself as a career *and* as a disruptive presence. And this is why he seems more modern than Victorian. I will first suggest a model, then try to illustrate it by further analysis of *A Pair of Blue Eyes*, and then try to define the initial stages of a project which will be the unfolding of this, the writing age.

Hardy's two most distinguished petty bourgeois predecessors are Dickens and George Eliot. Both work entirely through the project of the written. Both evolve a prose style which exposes and deletes the *voices* of authority, the centres of power and conventional wisdom in their novels by the imitation of the languages of those centres. Both, however, go beyond this decentring to the formation, out of their own success, of a new or reformed authority. Both become *influences* in their own time. If both in their different ways explode the voices Carlyle sought to recover, it is by the institution of the new voice as the industrial middle class or the new intelligentsia. For Hardy there can be no treaty with the world he addresses through writing. On the contrary the only development for Hardy is from self-conscious appeasement (a scientific game) to open confrontation (the offence he was willing to let 'come out of truth' in the Preface to *Tess of the d'Urbervilles*).

However, in turning from architecture to literature as a profession, Hardy turned not to fiction (which he thought of as a trade) but to poetry.[5] Was not the profession of literature after all most eminently represented by Tennyson and Browning? And this immediately puts him at an entirely different interface in terms of language from that occupied by Dickens and Eliot. For not only does poetry, more obviously than prose, represent the authority of the voice (since it incorporates additional features of phonetic representation such as metre and rhyme and poets are closer to priests and prophets) but also *the* poetry of the age was the high point and end point at once of the poet's public role. The dynamic of Tennyson and Browning is to do with the *use of authority* – that is the tension between what is *true* and what is *beneficial*. We should no more foreclose on them than we should on Dickens and Eliot except in order to see the space left by their preoccupations which is entered by the other two most important of Hardy's literary predecessors, Morris and Swinburne. Hardy starts to write poetry in the wake of the controversy they generate, which is specifically a strategy of writing. That is, they publically disrupt the culture in which they are inserted by rewriting its writings. They erase its authority by showing, for example, that Sappho's poetic energy derives from her sexuality or Guenevere's nobility from her adultery. That is the key to the differentiation. They disrupt the culture in which they are *already inserted*. They do not have to enter it as Dickens and Eliot do, because they are poets and thus do not have to manipulate a popular form and because, as it happens, neither of them are *petty* bourgeois. Hardy *enters* the culture, by writing, that is writing gives him access. He learns the rules from books. But he enters it as a *poet* claiming his own voice, which turns out to involve the rejection of the given voice of poetry.

The forty or so poems Hardy wrote in 1866–7, while the furore over Swinburne and Morris was raging, record again and again his alienation from poetic values. 'Hap', for example, begins by rejecting the Byronic concept of a vengeful fate and replaces it with 'crass casualty' which relegates not only the circumstances but also the desires of the individual to the merely arbitrary: 'How arrives it love lies slain / And why unblooms the best hope ever had.' 'Unblooms' is the most transitive verb of the poem and it openly derides the idea of anthology ('anthos' = flower). And if many other poems, such as 'At a Bridal', are about nature's indifference, some too are about the failure of human passion to sustain contact or sympathy: 'A Confession to a Friend in Trouble' and the 'She to Him' sonnets register the transience and unreliability of human feelings which thus no more confer meaning on experience than chance. They record the experience of the insignificance of experience, deleting the voice that speaks through them.[6]

The best poem of these years, 'Neutral Tones', presents this as a *dialectical* process. It reworks a common motif of romantic lyric – a recalled moment of love, defined within a natural landscape and seen in the perspective which has grown up since. Memory, love, nature, growth – all these poetic instruments of continuity are systematically undermined. The landscape is not only loaded with death – white sun, starving, sod, grey leaves – but alienated: 'and the sun was white as though chidden of God'. The winter day is not thus a moment in time but a bitter stasis. The undermining of human values continues in the description of the human relationship. Her eyes look at him as though they rove 'over tedious riddles of long ago' and when they speak it is not to communicate but in an aggressive game about what they each lose by love. Memory is unsupportive, language separating, and this is intensified in the vivid transformation of her smile, 'the deadest thing / Alive enough to have strength to die', into a momentary death-mask grin which foreshadows the annihilation of their relationship. The last stanza moves into the present where the *keen* lessons of the interim that love deceives *shape* this moment in the past, not with any new significance but with an empty echo of the opening, in which the allegorical simile, 'as though chidden' is re-presented as fact, 'God curst'. On the other hand, the material image loses definition – grey becoming greyish.

But it does not rest in that dilemma. The one word, 'shaped', ensures that its demolition of lyric values is a vivid lyric, a totally achieved image, distanced and powerful, not only of death in life, a frozen memory, but life in death, a God-curst but defiant beauty. Modernity is already not only ordeal but opportunity. The example of Swinburne and Morris makes that possible, but Hardy cannot stay there (nor, of course, could they). He cannot even make a living that way. Writing is his way out of his place, but it requires writing that shows what he can do and brings profit to the firm. Actually it is not Stephen Smith who shows this, but his articulate mentor, who enters *A Pair of Blue Eyes* in chapter 13 and turns the whole novel into something other than the story of romantic love thwarted by parental snobbery.

However, the story he transforms is already mutated by the writing age into an aesthetic variant of that romance. For the gap between learning and accomplishment, which is at once Stephen's ticket of admission and his notice not to trespass, involves an equivalent shift of gender roles by which Elfride, who has to let him win at chess and rides while he walks beside her, becomes *La belle dame sans merci* while remaining intact. The blue eyes must become a double-edged enigma, angelic and hypnotic, above all an *absence*: 'a misty and shady blue, that had no beginning or surface . . . As to her Presence it was not powerful' (1). She is explicitly contrasted with a real *belle dame* who would have enough 'presence' to pervade a banquet hall. You look into her eyes, not at them – they are not the achieved sign of a constructed sexuality. Stephen constructs her into something she is not by the default of his own incomplete (disorganic) construction. It is Knight who will provide the polarity that defines (differentiates) her. He will let *her* win at chess. But his first reaction to her is to turn her into a text, a note for an article on 'the artless arts' (18), and before he meets her, he reviews her novel.[7] Knight is a presence replacing the lack represented by Stephen, creature of the writing age, but the presence does not diminish the dominance and priority of the written.

On the contrary, Knight speaks the writing age. To explicate this paradox is to understand the starting point of Hardy's fictional project. He not only reflects the writing age as Stephen does, he names it and is himself the instrument of its institutionalization, whose starting-point is the acknowledged gap between knowledge and writing (17). He is introduced by Hardy with a phrase from the last chapter of Ecclesiastes, 'he set in order many proverbs', which in context is about the preacher who has sought acceptable words but who nevertheless has by truth provided goads and thus raises the problem of the tension between the truth and what is needed. At his most critical, Knight radically challenges a basic conventional wisdom: 'For a sensation of being profoundly experienced serves as a sort of consolation to people who are conscious of taking wrong turnings' (19). But at his most introspective, he retreats to a self-deleting irony that strikes the heart of his intellectual role: 'I plod along, and occasionally lift my eyes and skim the weltering surface of mankind lying between me and the horizon, as a crow might; no more.' (13) It mocks the critical project which Arnold advocated to stop the immaturity of romanticism from growing up into the despair of modernism – seeing life steadily ('I plod along') and seeing it whole ('as a crow sees'). The Victorian sage has become the man of letters, knowing the worst and trying to calculate how much knowledge is good for the world. Knight is not Arnold or Ruskin, who both transcribed an authoritative voice within a very exploratory prose. He is more like Horace Moule and Leslie Stephen, who manned the journals which were both openings and editorial folds.[8]

This means that he is not Hardy either but the way in which he is not Hardy is crucial. In his important lecture 'The Hero as Man of Letters', Carlyle has already, before Hardy is born, said/written that if you invent writing, Democracy is inevitable – the true university is a Collection of Books.[9] Thus the immediate effect of the writing age is to give access to knowledge for those who are excluded from a predominantly phonetic culture which uses writing merely as transcription and makes this access unlimited, for you can read a book how and when and as little or as often as you like. So Knight liberates Stephen. Equally, however, it becomes very important to authorize the written (one way being to maintain anonymity, which gave the weight of the journal as institution to the judgements advocated – this was a debated issue when Hardy started writing). Characteristically, Carlyle, having seen the radical potential of writing, beats a hasty retreat into a lamentation for the disorganic infidelity of the man of letters. Knight will finally occupy the ideological stance of Elfride's father. This should not blind us, however, to the significance of the text Knight is forced to read on our behalf – the fossil record which takes away the possibility of a transcendent meaning granted by the *origin*.

Knight's cliff-hanging ordeal is what everybody reads *A Pair of Blue Eyes* for and yet it is not enough to note that it exists (after all Hardy had written poems with the same import).[10] It takes over the whole thematic weight of the novel and yet is precisely marginalized and it is this double process which we need to attend to. Notice how Hardy very carefully prepares us. Returning from Ireland where he has watched himself falling in love with the images recollected of the absent Elfride, Knight has a journey 'along a road by neutral green hills', through a landscape marked by the casualness of the natural world – the blue sea glimpsed through gaps flecked with 'a few *dashes* of white', the fresh water spouting from an '*occasional* crevice and *pattering* down upon broad green leaves'. The 'unkempt locks of heather' and the bramble which swings into mid-air *snatching* at their headdresses like a claw remind us of a struggle for survival which has no pattern. Later in the same chapter, when he picnics with Elfride and her parents, there is an atmosphere of dreary passivity in which all may watch their stone dining table washed by the incoming sea: the *neutral* green and blue tongues of water slid up slopes, and were metamorphosed into foam by a *careless* blow. Such images of blind and meaningless change accompany the avoidance of the feelings between them in the chapter which precedes the fall. Momentarily, swinging against the cliff face, he is in the presence of a personalized loneliness. The confrontation with a fossil which closes up time before him brings the whole desolate store of evolution into his mind. At first inexorability is compounded by meaninglessness. The next stage in Knight's perception is to share the primitive view of nature as a person with a curious temper distributing kindnesses and cruelties in lawless caprice. The only consolation for him here is that life renounces its habitual indifference and seems to be more hostile in what appears to be an echo of Tennyson's great poem; he feels that 'pitiless Nature had then two voices and only two', but unlike Tennyson's voices they do not oppose one another as the voice of realistic despair and the voice of affirmed love, but only as the voice of the wind and the moan of the sea.

Nevertheless that invocation of Tennyson, who is quoted with some frequency in this text and specifically at the head of the chapter which inaugurates this ordeal (21) is important. For Tennyson's second voice is the voice of hope emanating from the vision of love in the young family he watches going to church. Hardy gives us a significantly transformed version of this dialectic which takes us straight to the heart of his fictional programme. Knight's ordeal is analysed with astonishing vividness to which only a much closer analysis than mine would do justice, and it is the overwhelming image of the book. But the chapter in which it is most fully described is headed 'a woman's way'. The only ray of hope for Knight is his faith in Elfride: for Love is faith, and faith like a gathered flower will *rootlessly* live on. I stress rootlessly, because the possibility of love is not, for Knight, part of the organic picture. On the contrary, immediately after this the sun shines; but not with any positive significance – rather as a mocking nightmare like a red face looking with a drunken leer. Absurdly, Knight decides that he is too intelligent to die, and then that all he can do is to renounce the desire to live. The appearance of Elfride at this point disrupts the logical sequence of his experience, exactly as the dawn and the family disrupt Tennyson's dark night of the soul. But note that in Hardy it is not love *in conjunction* with the natural world, but love as disrupter of it. What saves Knight is, with comic poignancy, Elfride's ingenious use of her voluminous underwear, which of course is a sign of her protected value in exchange as a woman.[11] When he is rescued they rush into one another's arms, 'moved by an impulse neither could resist'. But notice too that at this point Hardy switches the focalization from Knight to Elfride. She, not Knight, becomes the register of the second Darwinian law – that of sexual selection. Glimpsing on the horizon the boat on which Stephen is sailing home to her, she feels an overwhelming rush of exultation, a defiance of duty: 'Every nerve of her will was now in entire subjection to her feeling.' We have a powerful image here of the double perspective of Hardy's assimilation of Darwin. On the one hand, the evolutionary law in which atomic lives are swept up has no meaning, it grants no programme of action, no rationale of reality. On the other, however, the motive force of that law, the will to live and the will to reproduce, release an unfettered subjectivity through sexual attraction, which is life-saving. But Elfride alone fully experiences this. Knight does not 'take advantage' of the situation, and seeing her effectively naked – she is dressed only in a diaphanous outer garment – sees her 'as small as an infant'. It is clear that Knight will be unable to come to terms with Elfride's sexuality. As he discovers her previous relation with Stephen, the infant becomes for him corrupt, and ironically what damns her most is her impulsive flight from her father to him. She is right to see his view of her 'as that of a mere characterless toy, as to have no attraction in me apart from freshness' (32).

With this tension between natural and sexual selection the opening movement of the novel is no longer a romantic adventure fissured by the disruptive reality of class and sexual politics. On the contrary, the parental threat to development becomes the threat of male ambition in general to female sexuality. For if this *daughter* is an object in exchange,[12] she is his *fiancée* too. This involves a conspiracy to silence the women. Like Bathsheba, and to some extent Cytherea, Elfride sees her own predicament as one of language: 'Because I utter commonplace words,' she tells Knight, 'you must not suppose I think only commonplace thoughts. My poor stock of words are like a limited number of rough moulds I have to cast all my my materials in' (19). Knight, tellingly, regards this as 'an ingenious representation' but we have already seen her vitality transposed in her relationship with Stephen to whom, because of his inability to relate to her as an equal, she becomes *La belle dame sans merci* and by contrast she has to relate to Knight as the submissive *ingénue*. As she drifts into this submission she looks her duty to Stephen steadfastly in the face only by reading 'Wordsworth's astringent yet depressing ode to that Diety' – which, of course, begins 'Stern daughter of the voice of God' (20). Likewise, when Knight feels his 'love' for Elfride destroyed by his knowledge, it is through a Wordsworthian image of lost illusions: 'there had passed away a glory and a dream' (32). Love as it is defined in this novel is no way back from the solitude of despair, because it can relate neither to duty nor to innocence. It is what contests crass casualty on one level, but it is not available as a socializable motive. That is what breaks Hardy away from the possibilities of integration he might find in Tennyson, or in George Eliot, whose fullest expression of the problematic of the self in a structured society is beginning to appear precisely at the time of the composition of *A Pair of Blue Eyes* (begun 27 July 1872 although outlined in 1871; *Middlemarch* appeared 1871–2). It is not surprising that Knight has no defence to make against her irate father nor that he should return to his 'Eden', which Stephen earlier dubbed his 'heap of literature'. His attraction to Elfride descends from religion to temptation.

The end of this novel is sometimes taken as inadequately trite, but triteness here is only the grotesque comic punishment for the men who condemn Elfride to daughterhood. Meeting each other on the train, each fancying they can recuperate their lost love, Stephen and Knight find they are accompanying her coffin, and that she has married the local lord to look after his children. They are ridiculed for their failure to allow her to speak.

But if the novel explicitly cuts Elfride off by the love she offers from the modes of integration available, it cannot, any more than the males who condemn her, give her a way. She remains a pair of blue eyes, enigmatic and ultimately passive. It will take Hardy until *Tess of the d'Urbervilles* to find a heroine who can emerge from this narrative silencing of female sexuality, though this will be through a series of disruptive interjections. *A Pair of Blue Eyes* is instructive, because it encapsulates the double negation of crass casualty – the negation of insignificance, the negation of subversive desire – and places it within a social context structured by class oppression and sexual repression. But more than this, it shows why Hardy needs to find a narrative and fictional language which steps outside the categories of the individual and his story. The high moments of sexual encounter, other than the brief clasp on the cliff, are the games of chess Elfrida plays respectively with Stephen and with Knight, which show why in opposite ways they cannot relate to her sexuality: embarrassed by Stephen's ineptitude, patronized by Knight's skill, she is caught in a double situation of inequality which can only be declared in this oblique way. For once you take away the possibility of reintegration through duty, or self-preservation through innocence and the recall of the past, you have nowhere *in* society for the individual to go. What you have to do, on the contrary, is remake society so that it can accept individualism and experience without either distorting them or being destroyed by them. The game artificially encloses the conditions of equality necessary for this since theoretically it submits all players to the same rules. It becomes for Hardy a matter of finding the equivalent of the game where the voice of experience can be met, at least for an interval, by the voice of desire.

Elfride the novelist asks Knight the reviewer why he does not write novels. He says that one reason is that 'it requires a judicious omission of your real thoughts', to which she replies, 'I am sure you could learn to do that with practice' (17). Though with a resonance that will become increasingly obvious he replies that 'it is more distinguished to remain in obscurity', the novel here speaks out of itself towards the Hardy project – the playing off of public expectation against 'real thoughts'. Knight calls chess his favourite 'scientific game', which is how Hardy at this time supposedly came to see his novels. It is a game by which with practice you can learn to give pieces away in order to secure victory (as Knight does). Chess is also the coded form in this novel of the sexual politics which challenge the cosmic pessimism of natural selection.[13] With practice it might be the meeting ground of a man and a woman (as it is in *The Tempest*). *A Pair of Blue Eyes* tries to work these extra personal motifs into a conventional character-dominated narrative. It is clear that the shell of that narrative cannot accommodate those motifs.

Hardy has, however, already begun to answer this in terms of the formal break which his very entry into the writing trade inaugurates. The story is that, having tried to write directly about social injustice in *The Poor Man and the Lady* and finding no one to risk publishing it, Hardy took (or mistook) the advice of the novelist who above all was most conscious of the need to confront the values of the public for whom he wrote, George Meredith, and wrote a novel modelled on the work of the novelist whose immense public success and residual moral integrity most precisely resembled that of a brilliantly played game, Wilkie Collins. The sensational novel on which *Desperate Remedies* is modelled is already a subversive form, bringing the licensed margins of the gothic into daily life and, under cover of an adventure, exposing the oppressive values of a society which confuses identity with property and substitutes power disguised as respectability for virtue. The forces of right in a Collins novel are compelled to play the same devious game as the forces of evil. Property and power can actually change your identity such that you can only regain it through disguise and deception. Hardy's novel, however, transforms this instrument. Cytherea Gray's being is actually defined by the power relations she has to negotiate – it even transpires that she has the name of her employer and the insight that awaits her is not that she can win but that win or lose she will end up as a passing phrase in the memory of those who speak *of* her. On the other hand, the forces of evil in the novel turn out not to be motivated by greed and property, but by love, lesbian and bigamous respectively though they be. The wicked become not 'attractive' as they do in Collins, but sad and thwarted. Hardy is already in the process of transforming narrative from the war of good and evil (which, though a war of nerves, it is in Collins) into the history of sad gestures, the undermining of faith in our own endeavour.

Equally, however, he has already, by the time he writes *A Pair of Blue Eyes*, begun to find a way in which this narrative can be reaffirmed – not as the imitation of rewarded virtue, but as the trace of what 'reality' deletes. On the whole, it is difficult not to think of *Under the Greenwood Tree* as a slight tribute to William Barnes, though a close reading would reveal many of the themes we shall meet in later novels. But I restrict myself to one point with three aspects. The point is the most obvious, that this is a *self-consciously* pastoral text, a rural painting of the Dutch school (that is naturalistic but as distanced, as Gombrich says of Vermeer, as a still life).[14] Equally, it has a literary title. So we are invited to think of it all the time as a work of art, its characters 'different', 'dwellers in a wood', quaint, humorous, above all *not us*. Rural life is submitted to an urban gaze not with the unconscious complacency of some eighteenth-century poets, but at play with the gaze, which can easily become disrupted. Thus the quaintly and safely archaic church band at the end of Christmas day transforms itself into a Dionysiac revel in which the fiddlers 'kick back their chairs and saw madly at the strings with legs firmly spread and eyes closed, regardless of the visible world', and Dick and Fancy (you think their names are not puns?) dance so close together that 'they were practically one person'. The patronizing tone of a comedy of manners is shadowed by a pagan and erotic vitality which underwrites the idyll. So not only are the conditions of the text's socialization on display, but also they are sidestepped. Thirdly, however, the gaze is not only noted and eclipsed but *returned*. Reuben suddenly in a discussion of stories and coarseness teases the reader comfortably enjoying the aesthetic distance: 'I like a story with a bad moral. My sonnies all true stories have a coarse touch or a bad moral, depend upon't. If the storytellers could ha' got decency and good morals from true stories, who'd have troubled to invent parables?' (I. 8) Having had the benefit of Brecht, Bakhtin and Lévi-Strauss, we can see how, through alienation, heteroglossia and a structural account of mythmaking, even so limited a text as *Under the Greenwood Tree* can escape the social function (writing) to which it is committed. But though there is no reason why we shouldn't enjoy the manipulation of Hardy's Victorian reader, we should not expect to be spared in our turn.

I opened with a quotation from Lawrence's review of *Georgian Poetry 1911–1912*. It offers, I think, a much more accurate estimate of Hardy than the later book he wrote between *The Rainbow* and *Women in Love*.[15] In the early essay he regards Hardy exclusively as a nihilist and contrasts his demolition with Georgian 'joy'. In the later book, he is so busy turning Hardy into his ancestor that by a very transparent act of prestidigitation (Hardy's *prédilection d'artiste* – a concept as desperate as some new critical royalist readings of, say, Marvell's *Horatian Ode*) he turns a toy soldier and a rapist into phallic heroes and the most articulate woman in Hardy's fiction into a mere neurotic. Not surprisingly, however, his reading of *Under the Greenwood Tree* is completely accurate because what that text does is to subvert the moral prison of Victorian sentimentality by a trace of real earthiness. And this is what Lawrence, because he had to turn away from the offered political solutions, tried to make sufficiently effective. Lawrentian 'healthiness' worked and no one would now object to a bucolic painting in a Victorian drawing-room if it suddenly pulled up its skirts and farted. But this is not to demolish our faith in our own endeavour. Only in the very specific aesthetic condition of *Under the Greenwood Tree* and in specifically controlled recurrences of its terms of reference is Hardy the ancestor of the Lawrentian affirmation. I know that it is a part of Lawrence's final integrity that happiness is only available for the woman who rode away. But Hardy never lets go, even out of exhaustion, of the recognition that in a world structured on oppression, happiness is always at the cost of somebody else's pain; and there is certainly no question of his protagonists reaching an island of bliss except by embarking on a voyage to the unreal. For joy in Hardy's world we will have to make do with something very different from bourgeois dreams of personal bliss: 'If a way to the Better there be, it exacts a full look at the Worst.'[16] Only when he quotes it in a later preface does Hardy make this a statement of 'evolutionary meliorism'. In its original place it is the rational version of the feelings that 'delight is a delicate growth cramped by crookedness, custom, and fear'. The negations of delight are forms of mystification. Though Hardy was not explicitly revolutionary, he hopes that such a feeling 'disturbs the order here' – it has no place, that is, in accounts of Progress. And he was presumably even less of a Spinozan since knowledge for him is mainly pain. But the joy of Hardy is the joy of knowing, which is also the basis of a revolutionary ethic. Lawrence tried to bring love down to earth. Hardy demolishes love as he demolishes our faith in our own endeavour. His 'pessimism' is very important and not an in spite of. And especially, given the success and failure of certain times of liberation, it is what returns the gaze of the reader now. For, as we shall see, the game Hardy plays leads us ceaselessly back to the world in which, to quote again from 'In Tenebris', the 'Voice that is law' might say Cease, and only the writing makes space in which the voice cannot be silenced or displaced but given inverted commas, and a historical role. Already *Desperate Remedies* and *Under the Greenwood Tree* tell us that Hardy's fiction cannot *show* that historical role – for narrative does not discover, it makes gestures, and the image of the Better is locked within the terms of its construction. To say that it cannot show it, however, is simply to draw attention to the need to write it. In fact, quite as much as Dickens and Eliot, Hardy will be shown to have his influence, but that influence is, I try to argue, yet to come. In order to make that happen we need a particular strategy of reading which meets the strategy of writing, and that is a continuous dialectic in which meanings are always cancelled by opposing possibilities. Reading Hardy is always rereading. I do not think, with some other commentators with whom my analysis is broadly in sympathy, we need to propose an *unconscious* in order to account for this dialectic. For, as we have seen, it grows out of the nature of the activity itself and the specific conditions under which it is carried out. We only need to deconstruct the text because it deconstructs itself, and we need equally, by the same token, to go much further than deconstruction, to see the specific strategies which the text adopts.

The Gospel of the Body: *Far From the Madding Crowd*

Critics tend to treat *Far From the Madding Crowd* as though it were a first attempt, still full of an innocence which you can either cherish (Bayley praises its 'rich equanimity') or rebuke (Gregor, alert to its positives, nevertheless sees that its terms of reference will not accommodate the 'darker mood' of Hardy's total vision).[17] We have already seen, however, that it is the product both of a complex situation and the already knowing grasp of available strategies. Specifically, it constructs a definite ideological model which is indeed the affirmative base of all Hardy's fiction, but by the fictional realization of the model opens up the gap between that base and the historical actuality in which it seeks to intervene.

The affirmation is a structure of continuities, man and environment, man and man, man and woman, and the structure itself is fully manifest in chapter 22, 'The Great Barn and the Sheep Shearers'. The initial image is one of men working in continuity with nature: 'the quainter objects of the vegetable world' are comically personified ('like an apoplectic saint') or sensually assimilated to human physicality ('the toothwart approximating to human flesh'). The narrator moves like a naturalist from flora to fauna, but the fauna, of course, are men ('and of the animal, the metamorphosed figures of Jan Coggan . . . '). Moreover, they are more or less naked. It is a single composed picture – the work of the shearing is as much part of the landscape as the coming to fullness of the natural world.

This is related to a second level of continuity evident in the carefully orchestrated description of the Great Barn. First we are told that it resembles the church in form and vies with it in antiquity. Both the actual features ('vast porches', 'heavy pointed arches of stone', 'roof braced and tied in by huge collars, curves and diagonals') and more importantly, the evaluative vocabulary ('broadly and *boldly* cut', '*nobler* in design, because more *wealthy* in material') recall Ruskin's analysis of medieval architecture, as the work itself that takes place in it recalls the organicist promise of an ideal society, freed from the division of labour which is celebrated in the chapter of *The Stones of Venice* entitled 'The Nature of Gothic'.[18]

But Hardy goes on to affirm that through its *function*, the Barn links past and present, and in this is 'unlike and superior' to the other remnants of medievalism, church and castle: 'The eye regarded its present usage, the mind dwelt upon its past history, with a satisfied sense of continuity throughout ... For once medievalism and modernism had a common standpoint.' The text here might almost be a commentary on Ruskin, for whom medievalism and modernism are so much in contrast that the transition from one to the other is called 'The Fall'. Past and present are in antithesis, but it is important to discriminate this from the contrast involved in that phrase which is, of course, the title of Carlyle's gothic polemic. For Ruskin does not idealize the Middle Ages. He asserts rather that there were possibilities of the organic co-operation of the individual and the community which became lost under the double influence of capitalism and science. This is important for us, because Hardy is very specifically defining a continuity 'for once'. The 'for once' is in contrast with the other outmoded forms because of its basis in material reality: 'The defence and salvation of the body by daily bread is still a study, a religion, and a desire.' The church by contrast, which has to do with the salvation of the soul, is founded on a mistake, and the castle, which is about the defence of the body by force, gives rise to the reaction that batters it down. Ruskin made reverence and prowess in war central elements of his ideal world. Hardy uses a Ruskinian model to oppose Ruskin's conservative sociology. It is the world of the body that is a unifying human and natural reality, surviving in time and uniting men with one another. *Far From the Madding Crowd* is the gospel (good news) of the body 'without which we perish, so to speak it'.

Two further forms of continuity derive from this secular triad (man/nature; individual/community; past/present). First, there is continuity between work and the conditions of labour. In other words, although there is a social hierarchy it reflects function as well as possession. Thus Bathsheba is working as a supervisor, giving advice. She is the manager of her own farm. Secondly, the physical continuities accommodate sexual desire. Watching Gabriel shear a ewe, Bathsheba acknowledges its sexual intimacy: 'she blushes at the insult', and later in a simile whose context makes it less awkward than quotation makes it seem, we are told that the ewe rises 'like Aphrodite rising from the foam'. Production is itself the product of continuity and it is continuous with reproduction.

The secularization is polemical and progressive. The Barn is emphatically contrasted with the church and its '*worn out* religious creed' and the castle with its '*exploded* fortifying art'. In the shadow of Swinburne's and Pater's Hellenism the 'gospel of the body' is blasphemous and we note that Hardy has already stressed Gabriel's 'Laodicean neutrality ... between the Communion people and the drunken section' (the 'between' is ironic: it means that Gabriel goes neither to the altar nor the inn for his alcohol). The transformation of Ruskin's aesthetic indeed anticipates the transformation William Morris makes, appropriating 'nobleness', 'simplicity' and 'grandeur' to an entirely godless joy in labour which, though it privileges an ecologically benevolent nature, becomes the basis of his socialism in the eighties. For not only is the affirmation *secular*, but it refuses to look backwards. Its independence from the specific social order of feudalism is confirmed by the farmhouse, a building originally for pleasure of the early Classical Renaissance, retaining 'traces of the Gothic' extraction, and *reversed* by its entry into the world of work. With its abandoned façade and rich decoration it bears traces of the social order that is lost, like the church with its locked tower and unnoticed gargoyles. The actual working world of the body, located in another sequence of buildings, the shepherd's hut, the malthouse and the barn, is not conditional on a retention of the past. The past is present only insofar as within it certain continuing needs are fulfilled.

This is the gospel, the good news. It is obvious and, except for the emphasis on a polemical paganism, what everybody sees in the novel. However, Hardy's gospel has a lot of bad news as well, just as at the other end of his career as a novelist, his book of Job will turn out to be his most affirmative novel. But the bad news does not *displace* the good news. On the contrary it merely lifts it out of the comfortable level of charm, to raise it as a question. Or to put it another way, gospels are texts and cannot be univocal.

Here in chapter 22, the affirmative image is demolished almost as soon as it is set up. The chapter has opened with a complex paragraph about Gabriel's 'incurable loitering beside Bathsheba Everdene', which is temporarily set aside by the affirmed organic description of the sheep-shearing season which accommodates love as well as labour within an ecologically ordered totality ('every green was young, every pore was open'). This is a paragraph about the need for the right conjuncture of independence of thought and vigour of action on the one hand and 'opportunity' on the other. Appropriately then, 'heartless circumstance' intervenes to destroy Gabriel's momentary but 'entire' happiness. And it does this on two levels. Boldwood carries with him a 'social atmosphere of his own' and, being the nearest approach to aristocracy (i.e. not the squire, but only the farmer with the greatest wealth and power), he immediately reminds us of the *actual social relations of production* which underlie this apparently timeless image. Being away from his own farm, he can take Bathsheba away too. Their secret dialogue is not about the flock – Bathsheba 'demurely' regards a straw in a way that suggests 'less ovine criticism' than 'womanly embarrassment' (contrast this with the way she 'critically' watches Gabriel's skilful shears earlier). Finally she will go off with Boldwood, delegating Gabriel to take her place. It is the first moment that Bathsheba becomes a capitalist farmer appointing Gabriel effectively as manager (it is very important that Bathsheba has sacked her corrupt bailiff and refused to replace him). Significantly, her original work and personal relationship with Boldwood, although it has encompassed her emancipation, has been within the commercial context of the corn market.

The second level, as this suggests, is the level of desire. Not only does Boldwood confer on her modern relations of production but he also separates her sexuality from the physical labour which is taking place. She is helped over the spreading board by 'the courteous farmer', and later tossed by him into the saddle 'gently'. In this context such words designate romantic love as a matter which can be detached, like farming, from the actual physical process. It becomes part of a structure of social relations – the dependent woman and the chivalric man. This has consequences which reach back into the image of work. Watching Boldwood's manner, Gabriel, who has become 'constrained and sad', snips the sheep, this ovine Aphrodite, in the groin. The significance is obvious, the wounding is a sexual revenge to which Bathsheba appropriately responds. Just as work cannot exist without the conditions of labour which contain and reconstruct it, so love cannot be acted out without the social forms which allot it to the structures of power. The episode in the Barn is truly an organic image, drained of its conservative ideological medium, but it is violated by the historical actuality of the novel. That is why, for all its critical commitment to simplicity questioning the sophisticated world, critics who are wary of assigning this novel to the pastoral genre are right.[19]

At the same time, I think we must keep in mind a pastoral potential. For one way of reading the novel, given this original image, is to see it as a fable of the recuperation of the organic moment by the survival of the values of work and love through the self-destructive modes of capitalist farming and romantic love. Boldwood is, of course, only the first disruptive force, himself soon displaced by Troy. Troy has all the trappings of bourgeois romance – an aristocratic heredity, military training, sexual glamour, even a double life. Although prior to his marriage he may seem to be the very opposite of Boldwood, like Boldwood he is fundamentally dualistic: 'All romances end at marriage.' And to be sure, he quickly moves from being the romantic and adventurous soldier, defined by adventure, impulse and elopement, to becoming 'a farmer of a spirited and very modern school' – that is one who treats the farm merely as a fund-raising property and whose major interest is horse-racing. The central image, the obvious negative equivalent of the sheep-shearing supper, is the harvest supper, which is realized as a grotesque nightmare version of the appropriate celebrations of the shearing, reduced to stasis by the substitution of brandy for cider and consciously realized as an image of the grotesque:

> Many of the lights had quite gone out, others smoked and stank, grease dropping from them upon the floor. Here, under the table, and leaning against forms and chairs in every conceivable attitude except the perpendicular, were the wretched persons of all the work-folk, the hair of their heads at such low levels being suggestive of mops and brooms. (36)[20]

Not only is it an image of inversion and fixation but, of course, it is against nature in the sense that the warning signs of the oncoming storm are ignored as well, and it is in the solitary battle to save the work of the previous year that Bathsheba and Oak make contact as the equals they are to become at the end of the novel. This is the first sign of the possible renewal of the lost unities imaged in chapter 22 and worked out in detail in the story itself, specifically in the complex relationship of Gabriel and Bathsheba.

Both are realized initially as characters suspended between culturally constructed individualities. Hardy goes to a great deal of trouble in the opening chapters to establish Gabriel's uncertain formation, not as a kind of golden mean or moral neutrality, but rather as an emergent potential:

> He was at the brightest period of masculine growth, for his intellect and his emotions were clearly separated: he had passed the time during which the influence of youth indiscriminately mingles them in the character of impulse, and he had not yet arrived at the stage wherein they become united again in the character of prejudice by the influence of a wife and family. (1)

Suspended thus in growth between two forms of limiting unity of self (impulse and prejudice), and, as we have seen, ideologically between two extremes of intellectual closure, the Communion people and the drunken section, Gabriel is also uncontained by what might seem to be the rural projection of the title ('there is a way some men have, rural and urban alike').

This openness gives Gabriel an important privilege since it enables him to be alert to one of the major and recurrent perspectives in the novel. Just as the gospel of the body presents a secularized version of the organic vision of human culture, so the image of the unpeopled natural world presents a perspective which seems to demand, and in Ruskin does demand, a stoic awareness of the relative insignificance of the personal life. Again, however, we should be aware of the modifications Hardy makes. In the second chapter, Hardy gives a description of the midnight sky on Norcombe Hill which inaugurates, with deceptive casualness, a recurrent series of scenic descriptions which recur at moments of crisis, such as Boldwood's reception of the valentine in chapter 14, and Bathsheba's unconsciousness of 'the unresting world' when she has quarrelled with him (31). To persist with the Ruskinian model, such moments intensify the human feeling by a process, the very opposite of the pathetic fallacy, in which the external world continues its own drama apart from the individual mood. This is a way in which Hardy habitually uses natural settings, especially in the poetry. And in this novel it is made explicit in the storm when Gabriel and Bathsheba have to enact their interdependence in the face of a universe which reduces human passion to a triviality: 'but love, life, everything human, seemed small and trifling in such close juxtaposition with an infuriated universe', and again in the episode of the rain on Fanny Robin's grave which exposes the 'futility' of Troy's 'romantic doings'.

In this context, Gabriel seems to stand for the stoic who accepts his own relative insignificance. Indeed, we have been told that he has 'no great claim on the world's room' (1). He is therefore frequently taken to occupy a normative role in the novel – with a name which seems to couple the angelic with the resiliently vegetable, he is there as a resource to which Bathsheba can turn when she has exhausted the dramas of her romantic aspiration. Hardy clearly indicates that it is not as simple as this. In the first place, that phrase, given the hindsight of *Jude the Obscure*, should alert us to its sardonic tone (and if this should prove anachronistic, we have plenty of evidence from the early poems and novels that Hardy by no means accepts that kind of self-obliteration). Secondly, the sense of the universe registered on Norcombe Hill is not Gabriel's – on the contrary it is a disembodied spectator whose experience is contradictory. We are told that 'the instinctive act of humankind was to stand and listen', so that the implication is that the sense would impress itself on anybody, but at the same time we are told that anybody would first have to become very isolated from 'humankind' to enjoy the 'epic form' of this sensation, to have 'a sense of difference from the mass of civilized mankind, who are dreamwrapt and disregardful of all such proceedings at this time'. Much of the novel is stated in the form of this contradiction, which is, of course, central to pastoral: that the centrally human can only be experienced far from the madding crowd.

This is immediately related to a second form of the same contradiction. Stressing the vastness and sublimity of the perception of the universe, Hardy explicitly draws attention to the paradoxical nature of this perception: 'It is hard to get back to earth, and to believe that the consciousness of such majestic speeding is derived from a tiny human frame.' It is hard too, therefore, to accommodate the sublime within some sense of awe and submission, which is what it yields in romantic ideology from Wordsworth to Ruskin. Using 'nature' as a norm by which to measure social constraints, Hardy at the same time refuses the possibility of humbling the human subject in the face of that norm. Here already in the second chapter of this early text, the radical refusal to be positioned by awareness which is to motivate all the major novels is clearly stated.

But the passage goes further still. As soon as this awareness and its complexity is stated, it is questioned by the notes of Gabriel's flute which have 'a *clearness* which was to be found nowhere in the wind, and a *sequence* which was to be found nowhere in Nature' (my italics). The human *supplants* the natural with an affirmed rationality of its own, and this is what we associate with Gabriel. So far from being an angelic tree, he is in a very strict sense a farmer – his response to nature is alert but it is the very opposite of romantic submissiveness. When he emerges from the hut it is to make sure that the lambing goes without a hitch, and Hardy, paying tribute to his quiet energy, goes back to an eighteenth-century rationale, 'fitness being the basis of beauty', but assimilates it to *agriculture* which is the very opposite of naturalism because it seeks to use and forestall the randomness of the universe by work and knowledge and skill. Throughout the novel, Gabriel appears in this guise, rescuing the sheep from the effects of clover, anticipating the storm after the harvest supper. Important as the Ruskinian affirmation of organic unity is in the novel, it is not embodied in Gabriel. On the contrary, at his most assured Gabriel calls attention to its limits.

Two conclusions emerge from this. First, that Gabriel is not always assured, and that is crucial. And secondly, if we take note of this complex deployment of perspective, the relationship between rationality and the irrational world it confronts, we cannot read the novel in terms of a static fable. The fable itself questions and is questioned by the norms it invokes. More specifically, if Gabriel is a positive value insofar as he stands for endurance and work, he is also limited in the face of the realized possibility of human 'nature' (I use such terms with a full sense of their need of definition and placing). This clearly emerges in his relationship with Bathsheba. His response to that famous first appearance of Bathsheba when she secretly practises her smile in front of the mirror is certainly not intended to be endorsed by the reader (he is 'perhaps a little piqued by the comely traveller's indifference'). 'Vanity' neither accounts for the fascination that she exerts nor the complex of energies she embodies, merely for the confused response she calls forth from Gabriel.

The contrast between them is almost schematic. The contradiction in Gabriel is that his 'beauty', which has to do with the imposition of rationality on a random universe, is at loggerheads with his 'modesty', which comes from his sense that he has no great claim on the world's room. Bathsheba, on the other hand, alone has a manner 'by which she seemed to imply that the desirability of her existence could not be questioned' (3). At the same time, because she is a woman she has no clear mode of self-realization. Choices of action continually limit her to a specific role. This happens at the very beginning when she is riding the horse when, for completely practical reasons, she first of all lies back and then, sitting up, cocks her leg over 'in the manner demanded by the saddle though hardly expected of the woman'. Because, unknown to her, she is being watched, such gestures come to place her erotically. Again and again she is caught in the contradiction between wanting to be 'herself' and wanting to be a woman. Her double response to Gabriel's proposal makes this clear from the start: 'nobody has got me yet as a sweetheart . . . I *hate* to be thought men's property in that way' but also 'I want somebody to tame me; I am too independent; and you would never be able to I know' (4).

Gabriel's 'personal tragedy' defers this contradiction to the wise passiveness he seems to learn from it: 'There was left to him a dignified calm he had never before known, and that indifference to fate which, though it often makes a villain of a man is the basis of his sublimity when it does not' (VI). Though even this leaves him suspended between linked extremes as though reserved for an unfocused third term. Thus the schematic balance of his fall with Bathsheba's rise is loaded with an irony that not only looks back to their previous equality but forward to the working relationship that will restore it: 'Do you want a shepherd, *ma'am*?' (VII; my italics).

Moreover, the contradiction is merely refocused in the next phase of the novel, on Boldwood – appropriately, given her rise, since he is the 'nearest approach to aristocracy' and because in relation to him desire is embodied as challenge. Asserting herself as woman farmer, Bathsheba recognizes him as a 'species of Daniel in her kingdom' and 'a *marked* exception' (8 and 12; my italics) to the numerous evidences of her power to attract. The valentine is a double gesture against the static structure of relationships and, of course, simply turns a switch in the electrical circuit of Boldwood's dualistic personality: 'the perfect balance of enormous antagonistic forces, positives and negatives in fine adjustment' (18). Bathsheba can partly articulate the contradiction between not wanting to be someone's property and wanting to be tamed in respect of Gabriel, but Boldwood is both a social aspiration and a challenge to her desire to be recognized as a woman. It is a matter of 'interrupting the steady flow of this man's life'. The valentine is the sign that she exists as a woman, but it is a sign that is immediately sent out of the control of what it is intended to signify. Her awareness of that lack of control precipitates a wholly new sexual vocabulary in the novel. Her acceptance of Boldwood's love is a question of 'schooling herself to pay' (23) – the verbs of discipline and commerce exactly reproduce the context of religious guilt which the relationship establishes. She is 'struggling to make amends' illogically ('without thinking whether the sin quite deserved the penalty') and indeed getting out of it the emotional gratuity of Christian suppression, 'fearful joy' (23). For Boldwood is not held in check, like Gabriel, by cosmic modesty but is 'a man trained to

repression'. Christian dualism within an established social hierarchy can spring the trap that in the face of Laodicean stoicism
Bathsheba has eluded.

At this point the narrative is structured, in a highly coded form,
by the aesthetic project of Swinburne's *Poems and Ballads* in which,
as the programmatic poem 'Laus Veneris' announces, the
repression of the erotic by Christian dualism provokes its own
infernal revenge as the goddess of love trapped under the hill in
turn destroys the male values which contain and sublimate her.
The sheep shearing itself is a pristine communal high point of
celebration which is the very opposite of the Last Supper: 'The
shearers reclined against each other as at suppers in the early ages
of the world and so silent and absorbed were they that their
breathing could almost he heard between the bars' (23). This has
its own sexual politics, as the high moment of the feast is
Bathsheba's song in which *both* Gabriel and Boldwood, as flute
player and bass, participate, forming a 'rich, unexplored shadow
which threw her tones into relief'. Shadows are subordinate, and
maybe, for the preservation of this rich and fragile polyandrous
moment of peace, had better remain unexplored – which is
precisely what cannot happen. For the actual social relations and
the dominant sexual values will ensure that the woman is left alone
with the prevailing man, the erotic is privatized into the couple and
male desire becomes the 'responsibility' of the repressed woman.

We have to follow what happens next very carefully. Having
schooled herself, Bathsheba recovers some of her social freedom
walking alone in the fir plantation to check the farm – 'with the
coolness of a metropolitan policeman'. Within this solitary space,
there is a strange revival of the physicality of the shearing in the
sound of the cows munching which recalls 'pink white nostrils
shaped as caverns, and very clammy and humid on their surfaces'
(24). Recovering her independence in performing a routine duty,
Bathsheba makes contact with the female sexuality that the men in
her life so far have only recognized in song. Walking back through
the fir plantation (which has obvious genital associations) she gets
entangled with Troy. The whole episode, like 'The Hollow amid
the Ferns', later reminds us of the hidden female sexuality which
has just been sacrificed, and its metaphoric precision gives
meaning to Bathsheba's confused response to Boldwood. Once she
has experienced her own 'electricity' in the sword exercise, she
comes to realize the inadequacy of the available codes of love:
'Loving is misery for women always. I shall never forgive God for
making me a woman' (30).

Not surprisingly, confronted with her own 'unfeminine' sexuality, Bathsheba finds Liddy's comment that she is 'so tall as a lion' alarming: '"I hope I am not a bold sort of a maid – mannish." "Oh no, not mannish; but so almighty womannish that tis getting on that way sometimes."' (31) To be almighty womannish is to have no way of negotiating a relationship which does not commit her to becoming a man's property (this is precise – we are six years before the Married Women's Property Act) and feeling the need to be tamed. Her development must be measured by her recognition that the contradiction is focused in language: 'It is difficult for a woman to define her feelings in language which is chiefly made by men to express theirs' (51). The valentine is a message whose coded form 'Marry Me' is the language of a patriarchal monogamy and, were it not for the accidental entanglement with Troy in the residual act of independence, *her* meaning would be schooled to privatize and contain Boldwood's escaped desire. Bathsheba's articulation of her plight here is central to the sexual politics of Hardy's fiction. The problematic of woman and language is irretrievably bound up with the writer's scientific game. Her coding is as necessary and as limiting as his.

Lawrence saw Troy, like Vronski, as the personification of phallic consciousness betrayed by the moral cowardice of the novel, and it is not difficult to show that, committed as he is to an extended Ruskinian ideology that Hardy has already decentred, he cannot see how Bathsheba's sexuality actually exposes the pretence of Troy's and with it any organicist subordination of the female. The sword exercise in particular is taken either as a pre-Lawrentian erotic drama, or more realistically as the exposure of the theatricality of male domination. But the link of woman and writer defined above insists that we take both of these readings dialectically to produce a third.

The landscape is, even more than the fir plantation, so obviously reminiscent of female genitalia that it is impossible to read the episode as anything other than symbolic of Bathsheba's sexual 'experience'. It takes place in a hollow amid ferns whose soft feathery arms absorb her. She sees a dim spot of artificial red moving around the shoulder of the rise (emulating the bristling ball of gold in the West which still sweeps the tips of the ferns with its long, luxuriant rays). At the bottom of the pit, Troy looks up at her. Here the fern *abruptly* stops, and is replaced by a yielding 'thick mossy carpet'. The sword gleams 'like a living thing' and seems to pass through her body, emerging 'free from blood' held vertically in Troy's hand. Later she is enclosed in a firmament of light, and of sharp hisses resembling a sky full of meteors close at hand. At the end, after a mere kiss, and the theft of a lock of hair (which has clear echoes) the blood comes beating into her face:

> set her stinging as if aflame to the very hollows of her feet,
> and *enlarged* emotion to a compass which quite *swamped*
> thought. It had brought upon her a stroke resulting as it did
> Moses in Horeb, in a *liquid stream* – here a stream of tears.
> She felt like one who has sinned a great sin. (28; my italics)

In Horeb, Moses received the commandments on tablets of stone.
The revelation is quickly turned to a sense of sin but not before it
has introduced a foreign element, 'folly', like a lymph on the dart of
Eros which will now colour her whole constitution. Between the
encounter of the fir plantation and the demonstration of sexual
mastery in the hollow, Bathsheba has become enclosed from
Boldwood as Boldwood has enclosed her from Gabriel, in a
structure by which the chivalric oppression of women is revenged,
romance.

But romance is not the same as fulfilled desire. What Troy gains
from Bathsheba in the face of her contradiction of Gabriel and
Boldwood is not true for him. That dim spot is an artificial red; the
demonstration is a sword exercise. In two senses it is distanced
from the sexuality it calls forth. First, it is about warfare – 'you are
my antagonist' – and he has already demonstrated the diabolical
infantry cuts which are 'rather deathy'. His response to
Bathsheba's enchantment is 'Bravely borne . . . wonderful in a
woman.' The test is of her pluck, the skill she needs is to be still as
a statue. The sublimation of emasculated male domination in
warfare is a motif of many reactionary texts from *Maud* to *The
Crown of Wild Olive*, and Tannhäuser, the hero of 'Laus Veneris' is
a Christian knight. But if Troy echoes the defunct feudal defence
system associated with the castle (as Boldwood may be linked with
the church), he is consciously offering warfare with 'this difference
. . . that I shall miss you every time by one hair's breadth'. It is not
warfare but its theatrical display: 'quicker than lightning, and as
promiscuously – with just enough rule to *regulate instinct* and yet *not
to fetter it*' (my italics). When Bathsheba comments that it is
'magic', he replies, 'O no, dexterity.' Troy is not an image of male
sexuality in response to Bathsheba's female desire. The phallus is
turned into a sword, and the sword into a theatrical prop. Like
Vronski in fact, Troy's masculinity is only operative in the social
role which calls it into being. He is a man of gestures for whom
timing and display are everything. Fanny Robin loses him because
she does not appear in the right scenario at the right moment, and

Troy feels exposed to his audience. Once he is married to Bathsheba, he feels no need to play the romantic role (all romances, as he says, end at marriage). His new role as gentleman farmer, betting and preserving a romantic sentiment for Fanny, who suffers as much from it as Bathsheba, confirms the accommodation of male sexuality by an oppressive sexual structure. Although he is a hypocrite, pretending to enter the church by the tower, Christianity none the less provides the final expression of his duality – the elaborate sentimental attention to Fanny's grave, which seems to be the only genuine moment of passion he reveals. Whereas Bathsheba's sexuality is highlighted by the pristine sheep-shearing supper, his arrival at the farm is imaged in a hideous parody of the Last Supper, with Gabriel even as a parodic Judas. Not surprisingly, the denouement of the novel is brought about by Troy's second reappearance, 'disguised' as Dick Turpin. I put disguised in inverted commas because disguise is, of course, what is most real about Troy.

The equal validity of these two ways of reading the sword exercise takes us to the heart of the novel's devious strategy. For if Bathsheba's sexuality is called into being as folly by the emulation of warfare (the redoubled phallocentrism of destruction and cheat), *it is the only way in which it can be called into being*. Because he displaces two lovers, not one, Troy cannot be dismissed as appearance rather than reality. On the other hand, he can no more be regarded as the ironic blow to the novel's affirmations. On the contrary, as I shall now try to show, the devious strategy his role privileges strengthens the gospel which the novel is.

At the end of the novel, Bathsheba is not only to grow up but to form what, in terms of nineteenth-century ideology, is a revolutionary relationship with Gabriel:

> the romance growing up in the interstices of a mass of hard prosaic reality. This good fellowship – camaraderie – usually occurring through similarity of pursuits, is unfortunately seldom superadded to love between the sexes, because men and women associate, not in their labours, but in their pleasures merely. Where, however, happy circumstance permits its development the compounded feeling proves itself to be the only love which is strong as death. (56)

Passion is not marginalized within an order – on the contrary the romance (Troy's word) grows up (which aptly means both develops and becomes more adult) in the interstices (which is a rationalist more than it is an organicist word), and yields camaraderie, a word linked rather with labour than with pleasure. It participates in a discourse of sexual partnership which has a young enough history in 1874 but which through Mill, Morris and Schreiner will form one possible element of a new politics of gender.

But Oak is too suspended for this possibility. In fact the immediate effect of Troy's arrival is to bring Oak into emotional alliance with Boldwood. Having been displaced by the capitalist farmer and 'promoted' (that is, marginalized) to management, Gabriel reappears in a position of supremacy once more in the storm scene (it is a reminder that it took a fire to bring him back into Bathsheba's life at all). The conditions of this reinstatement are specific, though not simple. First, he is right because he reads the weather correctly – a candle beside gas he may be but by that very token he is more sensitive to the weather, so that the first condition is his advantage as a worker. But when he goes to the ricks, something other than this organicist superiority appears in the text.

The stacked ricks embody, of course, the accumulated labour of the farming year, and the means of the community's sustenance. In other words, they can be seen ahistorically as what the human community creates and needs – in its most concrete form they represent work, and Gregor and Williams have both correctly pointed to the central significance of work in the novel.[21] Only that is not how Gabriel's mind works:

Their value to Bathsheba, and indeed to anybody, Oak mentally estimated by the following simple calculations:-

$$5 \times 30 = 150 \text{ quarters} = 500l$$
$$3 \times 40 = 120 \text{ quarters} = \underline{250l}$$
$$\text{Total} = \overline{750l}$$

Seven hundred and fifty pounds in the divinest form that money can wear.

What he sees immediately are commodities whose use value ('necessary food for man and beast') is merely the clothing (even if the divinest form – we are still in the gospel of the body for all the transformations) of its exchange values. Hardy seems to stress the process of transformation by the typographical intervention (of which he will make many more). The actual wealth (that is the wheat and barley) is converted into its money equivalent as though it represented money and not the other way round. We are actually watching the fetishism of commodities take place in the textualization of Gabriel's experience. Given this sudden entry into the madding crowd of the middle-class readership of the novel, it is not surprising that Gabriel blames the likely waste not on the dishonesty of Troy or the corruptibility of the farm workers but on the 'instability of a woman', nor that we should eventually see this Laodicean saying his prayers as though doubt had never crossed his mind.

Hardy spells out the inference of this bourgeois and patriarchal ·alliance. In the following chapter, Gabriel and the unstable woman work steadily together in the face of the wheeling universe. They touch and, looking into the barn with her, he even feels her breath, as she had felt the breath of the cows in the fir plantation. Almost immediately, however, this turns into another version of Bathsheba's contrition: she has married Troy only because circumstance has made it seem that she has spent the night with him. More importantly the episode serves as much to bring Oak to Boldwood as Gabriel to Bathsheba. Even before the storm, Oak 'for a minute rose above his own grief in noticing Boldwood's' (35) and after it has brought 'the two together' (Oak and Bathsheba) we have a chapter entitled 'One Solitary Meets Another' which confirms a deeper sympathy, as Boldwood reveals that he has not protected his ricks:

> It is difficult to describe the intense dramatic effect that announcement had on Oak at such a moment. All night he had been feeling that the neglect he was labouring to repair [note that Bathsheba's support is now forgotten] was abnormal and isolated – the only instance of the kind within the circuit of the country. Yet at this very time, within the same parish, a greater waste has been going on uncomplained of and disregarded. (38)

It will not be long before this alliance is consolidated as a social relationship. Gabriel's effective transfer to Bathsheba's bailiff is made official as the result of her 'general apathy', and this is rapidly followed by his appointment to the management of Boldwood's lower farm. Now we see Oak mounted on a strong cob, daily trotting the length and breadth of 2,000 acres in a cheerful spirit of *surveillance*. Later, we find out that he has shares in the Boldwood estate. It is much better than any prospect held out to the independent Farmer Oak. His selflessness is rewarding – we are reading a bourgeois fantasy.

At least it would be were it not for two radical limitations. The first is that the conditions of Oak's rise are both visible and ambiguous. This is partly just that it takes place as the overall mood of the novel comes to be dominated by Fanny's death and the despair of Bathsheba and Boldwood, so that we are less conscious of the rise in his fortunes than of the rapid deterioration of everybody else's. But more than that, the action makes it clear that Oak needs Troy just as much as Bathsheba, and needs him to be the theatrical character he is; for without the melodrama he initiates, Oak's real value remains as silenced by Boldwood's prosperity as Bathsheba's sexuality. (I have already made it clear that Oak's real value includes his sexuality, which is silenced not by his gender but by his false class position.) This gives us a different story. Forced by circumstance – not, that is, nature's vicissitudes but the lack of sufficient insurance caused by his lack of adequate capital, Farmer Oak is forced into many disguises – bailiff, dairyman, shepherd and finally entertainer – before the contingent dramas of the fire and the storm respectively give him an opportunity to play roles that advance his social position. But it is the more flamboyant actor Troy who makes possible the dislocation of Bathsheba's desire from the structure of power embodied in the resolutely undramatic Boldwood. Thus if the gospel of the body is made once more available at the end, it is only by the melodramatic deaths of Troy and the revelation of Boldwood's insanity. And that means that there is a marked price to pay for its recovery – and on two levels. First, we are conscious that it only comes about by the desperate overplotting of the denouement, by which Troy has to appear drowned, return as Dick Turpin and provoke Boldwood into an insane act which leaves the stage clear of everybody except the principal boy and girl, and the chorus of rustics. At the same time, it is purchased at the cost of marginalizing all the human emotions in the novel (and if you can moralize Troy's and Boldwood's and Bathsheba's away as 'passion', you can't do that to Fanny's). The text seems conscious of this price: 'Then Oak laughed, and Bathsheba smiled (for she never laughed readily now)' (67). If we try to justify this as moral realism, it becomes hard to take the overt stylization at the end. We normally exchange incredulity for an excess of good feeling or vice versa. This story shortchanges us either way.

But there is another story. The last section is dominated by Fanny Robin's death, and its effects on Bathsheba and Troy. It is neither melodramatic nor incidental, as some critics have claimed. It follows a chapter in which the marriage is emblematized by the smart cut of Troy's whip on Poppy's flank, the mare representing the disturbance caused by Bathsheba's questions and Fanny's cry. The death itself is an angry and perceptive piece of writing. Fanny's effort to help herself to the workhouse with crutches is commented on with a Swiftian emulation of abstract rationality: 'Mechanism only transfers labour being powerless to supersede it', and this is placed against the overwhelming sense of pain and obstacle in Fanny's mind, having to lie to herself to get her body to respond to encouragement, and finally confronting the last half mile, 'like a stolid Juggernaut. It was an impassive king of her world' (machinery, patriarchy, rule). The workhouse is described with Dickensian savagery and the final detail of the dog who is stoned away clinches the episode. Fanny like the dog is marginal, merely an unwanted experience. Nobody learns from it. The chapter entitled 'Fanny is Sent For' is angrily ironic. She is not even buried with dignity. Her coffin is delayed by drunkenness (Poorgrass's preference for the living over the dead is not the gospel of the body so much as an act of macabre fanaticism or, in terms of another discourse, natural selection is re-edited as the survival of the fittest). Her corpse becomes the focus of jealousy; her grave, the creation anyway of maudlin regret, is broken up by a lethal alliance of masculine carelessness, religious mockery (the gargoyle) and nature's indifference. It is not surprising that it was Fanny that worried Hardy's editor. In no way is her story right for the middle-class reader of the *Cornhill Magazine*. It tells us that the awkward conjunction of narrative fantasy and moral realism is not the product of incompetence, but the sign that the scientific game is played reluctantly.

Apart from Troy, who merely deceives and bullies her, the only character in the novel who speaks to her is Gabriel. He gives her a shilling, which is all he has when he is on the road, and by this touches her wrist, recognizing her frailness and the 'tragic intensity' which throbs in it. Leaving her behind, he descends into the village to begin his story: 'He fancied that he felt himself in the penumbra of a very deep sadness when touching that slight and fragile creature. But *wisdom lies in moderating mere impressions* and Gabriel endeavoured to think little of this' (7; my italics). Fanny is not incidental – she is made incidental, but the price we pay for that exclusion is the recalcitrant horror that dogs (precisely) the denouement. For she is the victim of an oppressive world who cannot be included in the world Gabriel is about to negotiate. The recovery of unity is at the cost of leaving this impression behind, of moderating it (which means both actively changing it and making it more moderate). The wisdom is the condition on which the text exists in order to call into being the fiction for which it is designed. The gospel of the body is radical, but the terms of its realization are fraught with irony and exclusion. It is far from the madding crowd in a sense other than that of its rusticity. To be a good hand at a serial means not writing *The Poor Man and the Lady*, and even less writing the story of Fanny Robin. The text itself is flute and valentine.

But as Gabriel is not flute player and Bathsheba is not a flirt, so Hardy is already not a family novelist. Performing within strongly felt parameters, the authorial voice of the novel is awkward and self-conscious. It tries too hard not to be patronizing to the rustics, who are treated in a tone of arch if endorsing mockery. And the protagonists, especially at the beginning of the novel, are treated with a pseudo-psychologistic behaviourism which especially manifests itself as a strangely incongruous authorial sexism ('woman's prescriptive infirmity'). Obviously it would be perverse to argue that the awkwardness is deliberate, but I do think it is the result of a sense Hardy already has of having to deform the drive of his text towards a radical denunciation of the Ruskinian ideology it tries to reform, and which licences it as a literary discourse. We are already, with this novel, in a position to analyse the precise terms of this discourse.

Reading Hardy is unsettling. To hold the text in a fixed focus, as we must to see it at all, is only to watch it become clasped in the mists of authorial deviousness. As soon as we frame it one way, it insists on another perspective. Here, the title and its context implies a programmatic pastoral simplification. Gray has been lamenting the 'obscure destiny' of the hamlet's dead, but is already consoling himself that if they fail to achieve fame at least, and more importantly, they have avoided infamy. Hardy's narrative, however, far from ignoring ignoble strife, is the story of wishes and their consequences which are neither sober nor noiseless. Moreover, their vale of life, if it is sequestered, is cold rather than cool, since nature mocks man's sentiments and the majestic sky of Norcombe Hill fails to awaken Gabriel, the frozen dawn fails to echo Boldwood's newly fired passion, and the rain fails to commiserate with Troy but breaks up Fanny's grave instead. The organicist image of human unity is produced only metaphorically and imagistically through a set piece, linked with a specific architectural style on condition that it does not move beyond the controlled rhythms of the season and its task. As soon as the narrative activates the tableau, that unity is replaced by the division of labour and the separation of love and comradeship, only to be recovered by the theatrical threat of the third man, and the melodramatic manipulation of the author wrenching the spatial metaphor from a metonymy which exposes its fragility to one which brings it whirling back on stage amidst the destruction of that which took it over. The title thus stands less for the polemical privileging of the rural over the urban than a self-conscious artifice by which the 'human' is preserved from its history – humankind rescued from the madding crowd (i.e. itself). In Gray's poem, the hamlet is idealized by being kept in a very distant prospect whose linguistic equivalent is precisely the hypnotic verse which can yield such evocative and imprecise descriptions as this title. Hardy's novel, like Gray's hamlet, is only pastoral if we do not look too closely at it. Or rather, since this is not a question of restraint, if we *moderate* the impression left by Fanny's throbbing wrist and Bathsheba's laughless smile.

This is not the same as saying that the text moves (ineptly or redeemingly) from pastoral to realism, for if pastoral poses a version of the human residing in the lost simplicity of an abandoned past, realism poses one by which it can be negotiated within the actual. It would require us to show that the novel's scepticism could be a matter of adjustment, that the resilient values of the human community reside in work and love as opposed to riot and romance. This does not emerge: Gabriel survives only by the pure luck of other's destruction (that is, the contrived contingencies of authorial allocation). Work and love and their interdependence are the novel's central affirmation. This is what gives it its unfactitious warmth and makes it the affirmative key to all the subsequent novels which explore the absence of that triad; but we have to be clear about the mode of its incorporation.

Work is a cohesive human force and the barn which stands for it glows through the mists of time because it locates the satisfaction of the physical needs of the community which is the basis of human interaction – the gospel of the body. But it is only an appearance whose actuality is the specific conditions of labour evident in the appearance of the capitalist Boldwood, Bathsheba's delegation of surveillance, and her accommodation within the chivalric sexual politics he brings. Two other images of work frame this privileged moment. The first is the fruitless care Gabriel gives his ewes – fruitless because his lack of capital is enough to deprive him of the means of labour. The second is Fanny's 'labour saving device' the crutches with which she tries to struggle to the workhouse. Both remind us that work is not a natural activity, but the product of specific social relations which set potentially crippling limits to the negotiability of the real world. Equally love which embodies the human accommodation of reproduction is realized only in the specific conditions of the theatrical end as an integrated partnership. It is otherwise throughout either a destructive romantic passion or a silent victimization, because love, too, is the product of specific social relationships (as Gabriel's voyeurism and

Bathsheba's valentine make clear).

If work and love cannot be located in a given society or negotiated in an enclave of the actual, what gives them their status? In this novel it is the intervention of the work of art itself. The author produces the conditions of that unity in scene and narrative by the self-conscious deployment of literary resources. For this is far from being a novel in which a provincial writer lovingly recreates his experience. If there are elements which can be related to Hardy's own life in the novel, they are fully reworked as available metaphors and conventions. Bakhtin has argued that Idyll, whose major characteristics are unity of place (blurring temporal boundaries), the sublimation of basic realities, and the linking of human life with nature, especially in the combined form of the love idyll and the labour idyll, privileges its themes in a way which questions social convention through a sense of time which is both collective and tensed towards the future. He adds, however, that it is equally prone to 'historic inversion', by which the future is transposed onto the past as golden age, or as a hidden present (far from the madding crowd) or as eschatology.[22] He argues that this is not intrinsic to idyll but emerges as it establishes itself as myth on the one hand (the pastoral projection of a golden age) or realism on the other, which is the break-up of idyll in the infinite distancing of collective life. The great classical text of the labour idyll is Virgil's *Georgics*, which also assimilates work and love through the image of creation and the story of Eurydice respectively. But it does not offer nature as a norm, rather as a battlefield which man must master by savage labour and cunning. Hardy's novel is in my view much closer to Virgil than it is to either modern transformation of idyll into pastoral or the realistic break-up that the nineteenth-century realist novel claims to be. Hardy is not able to be as visible as Virgil for he enters our homes, in the family magazine charged with the task of supplying an illusion. But the closer we look at the illusion the more we see that it is of a world that has to be made, which the writer makes in advance of the history whose agent, like us all, he is.

Cancelled Words

Thus by 1874, Hardy has already met the conditions of his situation as a writer and found a mode by which they can be exploited. Yet another twelve years will pass before he publishes a text, *The Mayor of Casterbridge*, which is a satisfactory advance on *Far From the Madding Crowd*. The difficulty and the precise nature of that advance will be the subject of the next chapter, but there is an astonishing glimpse of the problem in the novel which follows *Far From the Madding Crowd*, *The Hand of Ethelberta*. Linking the theatrical function of Troy with the questioning voice of woman and the class relations focused in the predicament of Gabriel Oak, Hardy creates a protagonist who is at once the most active and articulate woman before Sue Bridehead, and a 'good hand at contrivances',[23] making her way from the downstairs environment of her family into 'high civilization'. He tries to make out of her career a *comedy*, the story of integration through knowledge. It relies on a sustained ironic view of that civilization whose 'hallmark' is a 'complete divorce between thinking and saying' and Ethelberta's talent for exploiting that gap – first through a narrative art which convinces this world that she has a wealth of knowledge and experience she has merely imagined, and then, after reaching the limits of her effort and touching the exhaustion of creativity, turning to a precisely calculated marriage game. What is astonishing is how Hardy balances the pressure on Ethelberta against the price of success. The epigraph from Lucretius, 'men conceal the back scenes of their lives' is both a fact and an opportunity. Life, says Ethelberta, is a battle, but only in the sense that a game of chess is a battle (17). The comedy proves her point. The novel, however, makes it clear that life is not a comedy, that in the last resort, the only loser is Ethelberta herself, condemned to 'the psychological difficulty of striving for what in her soul she did not desire' (18).

Battle and game are thus dramatized as a complex dialectic mirroring and yet limiting each other. The game not only provides Ethelberta with a career but also establishes a scenario which brings together a range of issues which add up to nothing less than the state of English society, the sexual and class power relations of its institutions, the effect of increasing urbanization, the state of the arts and the role of the estranged consciousness in the individual's negotiation of the social world. The novel takes on too much too soon. It is a set of scenes and insights whose plot is too conventional and slight to do justice to any of its motifs. The implications of its project are, however, clear; it spells out the unacceptable conditions of success in a class-based society.

This emerges in the intractable confrontation of comedy, the art of contrivance, with psychology, the insistent voice of desire, and on two levels. First, on the level of Ethelberta's integration in high civilization, it becomes increasingly clear that the price of success is that outside the strict rules of the game which can be played, the conditions which set up the game are not negotiable. At the height

of her success as an entertainer, when she is accepted as a star at a
social gathering at Knollsea, we are told:

> It will be seen that Ethelberta was the sort of woman that
> well rooted local people might like to look on at such a free
> and friendly occasion as an archaeological meeting, where, to
> gratify a pleasant whim, the picturesque form of acquaint-
> ance is for the novice preferred to the useful, the spirits being
> so brisk as to swerve from strict attention to the select and
> sequent effects of heaven, blood and acres, to consider for an
> idle moment the subversive Mephistopholean endowment
> brains. (31)

'The sort of woman' deletes Ethelberta's self-made success. She is
part of the ritual. If her brains are subversive, they are only so in
the sense that Mephistopheles is allowed an interval of picturesque
success in a world governed by heavenly graces, that is ancestry
and law. It is not as herself she is accepted, but only as the disguise
she is allowed to make. For all the satire of high society made
possible by Ethelberta's career, it is high society which finally
governs her. She ends up owing a duty to the aristocratic family
she has contrived to marry into. Two early episodes foreshadow
this. Her earlier target, Neigh, turns out to be as *arriviste* as herself,
and there is a nightmarish episode when she goes to survey the
Neigh family estate and discovers that it is a knacker's yard.
Secondly, her control is parodied by the urban servant Menlove
('we are all independent here') whose own ironic vision is manifest
in a macabre parody of a high-society waltz. The servants may
mock the masks but the mockery is also mere emulation. The
episode at Knollsea brings her the opportunity of entering the
upper classes through marriage to the decadent and voyeuristic
Viscount Mountclere. By the end of the chapter, she is in a
position of real artistic power as opposed to the limited conditions
of the entertainer: 'A landscape was to be altered to suit her whim.'
But again the price is paid in a macabre image which surely
foreshadows the world of *Jude the Obscure*, 'the viscount busying
himself round and round her person like the head scraper at a pig
killing'.

It is that last uncompromising novel too which is foreshadowed
in the other dimension of Ethelberta's social mobility, her
relationship with her family. She never escapes the contradiction
that by serving her family by self-emancipation, she inevitably
walls herself off from them. But more specifically, she confronts in
her brother Sol a more articulate version of the division of classes.

Sol is, significantly, like Jude, a stonemason whose urbanization leads him into radical politics. One of the ironic twists of the plot is that Sol allies with a younger Mountclere to prevent the marriage and it is within the comic convention that travelling together Sol refuses to transfer the perceived social difference in servility. One of the few positive moments of the novel is when Mountclere is forced to fry his own bacon. This limited triumph, however, is set against the poignant dialogues between Ethelberta and her brother at the end of the novel when he simply accuses her of being 'a deserter of your own lot'. This is not merely a matter of lost organicism. Sol is not saying that she should remain one of her own kind but advocating a different way of overcoming class oppression: I don't care for history. Prophecy is the only king can do poor men any good' (46). Later he says: 'You have joined 'em and 'rayed yourself against us.' Sol brings into the novel at the end a politics which the comedy is designed to exclude. Ethelberta rejects it explicitly, but we are left with a sense of her heroic efforts being both a debasement and a self-defeat. Making it does not end her struggle. 'She must,' her father says of the early days of her marriage, 'have had a will of iron.' Now she has achieved her insertion, she lives, we are told, 'mostly in the library' ('Sequel').

Politics is not an issue that ever enters Hardy's fiction so directly again. *The Hand of Ethelberta* shows us both how it lies close to the perimeter of Hardy's concerns and how if it were allowed to enter it would have done so. It also shows us what occupies its absence. As she turns from entertainment to marriage, Ethelberta represses 'a desire for obscurity' (36). (She herself sees the possibility of realizing that desire in a career which looks forward to *The Return of the Native* and *Jude the Obscure* as 'going back to give the rudiments of education to remote hamleteers'.) The opposite to obscurity is secrecy, and it is not incidental that she supplies the intellectual rationalization of this from an old treatise on Casuistry, the '*disciplini arcani*, or the doctrine of reserve'. In fact she is forced to choose between two forms of obscurity; neither through return nor performance will she come into the light. Life is reduced to a choice of *roles*, and the one that she chooses is a form of self-textualization, turning 'another page' of her history. It is significant that, in the sequel, she is a reported case. The articulation of herself in the available codes is closely identified with the way Hardy saw himself as a writer. But she has also written a 'sincere' poem which she calls 'Cancelled Words' declaring her love for the man she finally offers to her sister (the novel is relevant to *Tess of the d'Urbervilles*).

The writing age, cancelled words. If I had to choose a succinct way of describing Hardy's posture as a writer towards his virtual public it would be in the conjuncture of these two phrases: a specific opportunity with specific denials through which to make his way.[24] But because it cancels too much, and because what it cancels cannot be silenced (the desire for release from the game), comedy is not a mode Hardy can develop or explore. He has to find, not a less theatrical form necessarily, but one which will allow the other perception Ethelberta feels at the beginning of her crisis of choice, as she looks at the historical remnants of Coomb Castle, that the social fight is matched against 'the attenuating effects of time'. If gesture and return posit an ontological predicament by the very sameness of their obscurity, the transformed monument, embodying not continuity but the tragic finality of wasted passion, demands a form which will not be enclosed in the unharmed gaze of the socially safe, as the grave of Milton is contained in Cripplegate. In order to achieve that form, a break has to be made with the ideology of submission. That break begins to be made by *The Return of the Native* but *The Hand of Ethelberta* takes us to the edge: 'But don't you go believing in Sayings, Picotee: they are all made by men, for their own advantages' (20).

The sage sets in order many proverbs. Hardy is no longer a sage, and yet he has to be more than an entertainer. The cancelled words of the good news will leave their trace on Hardy's fiction as the metaphor of barn transformed to monument and the interacting metonymies of gesture and return by which men and women mark the structures which rule them out.[25]

2 Defects of the Natural Law: 1878–1886

Tragical Possibilities: *The Return of the Native*

'Mother, what is doing well?' (III. 2). 'All the beauty and pulsing that is going on in the great arteries of the world. That was the shape of my youthful dream, but I did not get it' (IV. 6). Clym at the onset and Eustacia at the denouement voice the themes of *The Return of the Native* with these large abstract statements. Yet they are both made within specific performative contexts which are in different ways seeking authorization – the mother, the world at large (since Eustacia does not speak of life, but 'what is called life'). Hardy continually revised his novels as though he needed to renegotiate the terms on which he meets the reader. But no novel is reworked as much or with such drastic effect as this and this tells us two things about it. First, that it is a novel about which he felt very uncertain, because there are intractable problems in the realization of its project. But second, it means that it is a centrally important text that Hardy goes on needing to get right. It is both necessary and impossible because it poses questions which ought to be answerable in their own abstract terms, by a system of ethics or an ontological discourse, but they are posed in terms which require detailed contextual answers.

Indeed the novel is generally rebuked for falling into the gap. Hardy does not seem able to decide about the attitude he wants us to take to his protagonists – is Eustacia, for example, a romantic rebel or a silly provincial little girl whose idea of life is a shopping trip to Budmouth?[1] Nor does he mediate the individual experience with the sense of community we find in *Far From the Madding Crowd*: it seems to be a novel nakedly confronting 'the march of mind'.[2] Which would be all right were it not for the fact that privileging the human consciousness merely leads him, as it had led Arnold, to marginalize human experience.[3]

Hardy was capable of rehearsing the mid-Victorian sagacity promoted above all by Ruskin and Arnold (the stirrings of intellect wearing down the flesh, seeing life steadily and seeing it whole[4]) which found the highest form of awareness to be submission to the inscrutable. Clym's question clearly echoes the axiom on which Arnold's most important book, *Literature and Dogma*, rests, that conduct is three fourths of life. The whole of Ruskin's ideological project is dominated by the lessons of landscape, which is the most obvious concern of *The Return of the Native*, and there are many local details in which this novel echoes both writers. Certainly Diggory Venn is concealed from his proper station yet performs its duties by ensuring as far as possible that the acquiescent are preserved and the rebellious thwarted, thus making possible the adaptational myth frequently excavated from the text. But how in the local texture of storytelling can you embody the lofty closures of the Victorian sage?

It is the most thematically ambitious novel he has yet attempted by a very long way, and yet it seems to lead nowhere. No amount of rereading can make the three novels which follow it anything but bad novels which we would not read if Hardy had not written them. At precisely the point when you would expect Hardy, having reached his mid-forties and achieved a certain reputation, to be at the height of his career, he goes through an eight-year period during which his best work is a few powerful scenes, some brilliant ideas and a handful of short stories. And yet, to perplex us even more, at the end of it appears *The Mayor of Casterbridge* which inaugurates the series of late novels which make him the first great modern novelist.

This complex situation arises because *The Return of the Native* inscribes the ideological alienation which lies around the formal strategies and in the margins of the earlier texts. As *Far From the Madding Crowd* effects a formal break in the productive relations of the novelist, *The Return of the Native* initiates an ideological break which it cannot complete, but which is never again repaired and which makes Hardy's late novels the radical challenge they continue to be. The criticisms challenge the organizing concepts of the novel – experience, conduct, culture, but the novel only organizes these terms in order to expose them, to *see* them as negations. Aesthetic organization does not reproduce the organic function of ideology but displaces it, makes it visible.

Had Eustacia's dream been less trivialized by her ladylike

education and rustic perspective, it would still have been denied. Its importance is thus unaffected by its provincialism. Whatever its form, it is a dream of integration, by which I mean the realization of desire in the actual world. 'Arteries', whether one thinks of roads or blood, implies significant communication with the centres of 'what is called life'. At this moment she is merely demanding what is affirmed in *Far From the Madding Crowd*, in which the youthful dream of what is called life can be realized because Hardy creates a framework of communal activity which enhances not merely human need but human desire, recuperated, it is true, as we have seen, not from a historically specific moment but from the literary models it self-consciously enlists and parodies. But we have also seen that this distancing takes place not because the affirmation is an illusion but because it is *still to be made* and therefore has no history. Eustacia's dream is, on the contrary, mocked by the history into which it is locked – the *double cross* of the heath and her hero's *return*, which both say no. But that hero's return, like the mother's hostility to it and to his marriage to Eustacia, are also versions of the same youthful dream – to find what makes life meaningful, to get in touch or back in touch with the sources of good living.

The title to be sure predicates the return as the repressive function of inter-individual relationship,[5] gained from its juxtaposition with 'native'. Its significance is primarily to subordinate the aspiring self to the desire for regression, the recovery of the place of birth (which is both the birthplace and the mother), that is to privilege atavism, marginalize self-fulfilment, subordinate the personal life not to the communal centre which exists only as an absence but to an abstract will-lessness.

This project is inaugurated, however, by an opening which structurally displaces the reader by an extreme retardation of the narrative. Although the first Book offers as its title a 'human' interest ('The Three Women') its actual material, as is often observed, is effectively the small region in which they live out their lives. If we recall the opening of *Far From the Madding Crowd* we can see to what extent Hardy is deliberately teasing the reader. In the earlier text the main character is sketched, his opposite brought in, they confront one another and the story henceforward only diverts itself to multiply the triangles which finally cancel one another out and rectify the original separation of the opening pair. Here, the native is held back until the second Book and not brought directly in front of the reader until the third.

This deferral is made more puzzling by the tortuous movement of the narrative. The first chapter offers a human precision on its opening moment – 'a Saturday afternoon in November was approaching the time of twilight' – the imperfect tense and the actual naming of a day prepare us for a tale which does not follow, for the momentum is repressed by a long descriptive essay on an empty landscape. It gets back to the road by the end of the chapter and in the next places an old man on it, but he turns out to be very marginal to the story and his only function here is to perceive a van and enable the reddleman to insinuate, rather than explain ('there is no reason why I should tell you abut that') what has happened to the unnamed Tamsin. This in any case will not be the focus of the story but only a functional incident in it. The old man drops out, and we are not then taken into the van and to further explanation as we might expect, but make a further perception through the reddleman's eyes of a solitary figure who is immediately displaced by characters who are less interesting but who nevertheless now occupy the greater part of the next chapter. They give us a little background information about the first theme, but spend most of the time discussing festive occasions and sexual debility. A solitary figure intrudes on the scene at the end of the chapter but it is not the shape who has appeared on the heath but a third woman apart from the group, Mrs Yeobright, who specifically cannot stop to talk but *goes off* with one of them to find the niece whom we know to be the girl in the van. The story now at last begins to unfold (or rather, tie together), and during the next two chapters we are have the episode of the discovery that Tamsin and Wildeve are not married and the consequent embarrassment of the redundant visitation. Even this is pushed to one side at the end as Wildeve goes off to seek Eustacia, who turns out to be the figure on the barrow and who will eventually be the heroine of the main story which is not to start until the next Book. Shklovski says that 'the crooked road, the road on which the foot senses the stones, the road which turns back on itself – this is the road of art';[6] but the opening of this novel has so many ruts and hairpin bends that the reader is almost forbidden to progress. It is a device familiar in comic texts such as *Tristram Shandy* and in texts designed to maximize suspense such as the novels of Wilkie Collins, but deliberate as it seems to be here, its purpose is entirely ideological – it is to push the narratives, the lives of the individuals, to the side of a context which is as a whole immovable, levelling or, to use a word which is used at key moments of the text and which will be central to Hardy's greatest novel, *obscuring*. It is to push them, however, against the resistance of the narrative-demanding reader who is established and thwarted at once. The novel is its own Promethean resistance to its metaphoric sublation.

Yet once the story is inaugurated it proceeds with amazing singlemindedness, and the heath becomes more and more a mere backdrop to the complex sequence of changing relationships and strategies of the central drama between Eustacia, Clym and Mrs Yeobright. The obscuring perspective re-enters rather as a sequence of parenthetical closures on the crises of the narrative. Thus at the height of his romantic involvement with Eustacia, immediately after they have decided on the wedding day and Clym has watched her walk away, he is overpowered by the 'dead flat of the scenery': 'There was something in its oppressive horizontality which too much reminded him of the arena of life; it gave him a sense of bare equality with, and no superiority to, a single living thing under the sun' (III. 5).

It overshadows his discovery of Eustacia's 'responsibility' for his mother's death, and when, in a very deliberate allusion, 'his mouth had passed into the phase more or less imaginatively rendered in studies of Oedipus', as he goes to confront his wife with his passion and her guilt: 'Instead of there being before him the pale face of Eustacia, and a masculine shape unknown, there was only the imperturbable countenance of the heath, which, having defied the cataclysmal onsets of centuries, reduced to insignificance by its seamed and antique features the wildest turmoil of a single man' (V. 2). The allusion to Greek tragedy (which is one of several) together with the general shape of the novel (its five-act structure, its one-year time span, its relative unity of space and action) is sometimes taken to mean that Hardy is trying to write the modern equivalent of classical tragedy. But equally the 'oppressive horizontality' and its reduction of man's emotional dramas to 'insignificance' is taken to indicate that the deterministic ideology of the novel precludes the 'dignity' of tragedy.

Hardy makes it clear, however, that to invoke the model of tragedy is both relevant and inappropriate. This is explicit at the beginning of Book III during a digressive paragraph on the displacement of the Hellenic view of life: 'What the Greeks only suspected we know well; what *their Aeschylus* imagined our nursery children feel' (III. 1; my italics). Not Aeschylus, but their Aeschylus, not Oedipus, but studies of Oedipus. The heath has a lonely face suggesting 'tragical possibilities' (I. 1) not tragedy. Clym is thought of on the heath as a man with a choice of futures: 'if he were making a fortune and a name, so much the better for him; if he were making a tragical figure in the world, so much the better for a narrative' (V. 1; my italics). Each of these allusions distance or make optional the literary form. It is a possible trajectory but has to be set against a less individuating totality.

The individual life is marginalized not against the community but against whatever the setting means. And Clym's vision is not less shared than Eustacia's aspiration. The thwarted need to be in touch and the insistent separation of the struggle for existence, the flaw in a universe in which desire and circumstance are at war, are obviously potential material for tragedy; but it is the project of the novel to suggest that it is not, that this is not a universal but a *common* fate, not the substance of a drama, but a fundamental condition of existence, reducing tragic aspiration to mere wilfulness. Clym himself describes Promethean rebelliousness as a phase he has grown out of.

The aesthetic privileging of solitude in these terms comes to seem like a romantic illusion which has to be undermined. Our view of Eustacia on the barrow is disappointed by its replacement by the collective bonfire, but what we have to learn is that the romantic rebellion of the solitary is no more valid than the grotesque rebellion of the community. That does not mean, however, that the possibility of tragedy is not there: it enters the novel as a negated model, an abandoned coherence. In case we miss the point, Mrs Yeobright's death is depicted in a chapter entitled 'The Tragic Meeting of Two Old Friends', but the two old friends turn out not to be her and her son (who wrongly thinks that they have recovered a continuity with 'that friendly past that had been their experience before the division' not yet knowing that his mother has denounced him) but her and the adder which may have bitten her and which is to be sacrificed for her homeopathic treatment. 'Mrs Yeobright saw the creature, and the creature saw her' – like Henry Knight's eyeball to eyeball encounter with the fossil on the cliff, it reduces the human drama to an incident of natural history, and makes the title of the chapter grimly sardonic.

Why Hardy should want both to invoke and deny 'tragical possibilities' depends on how we read the 'heath', the object of the return (for Clym is 'inwoven with the heath' in his boyhood and 'native' is an appropriate word in more than one sense). The opening gives us a developed version of the paradox of Norwood Hill in *Far From the Madding Crowd*, that is of the overwhelming dimensions of the natural world – here in time as well as space – and of the tiny frame which is necessary to perceive that vastness. Egdon is not, however, the universe. Importantly it is seen as separate from the overarching sky (which recurs at Mrs Yeobright's death, and is invoked at least by the mallard who gazes on Diggory Venn bearing within him a communication from 'regions unknown to man') and the sea which Captain Vye scans with his telescope. It is rather a specific domain of experience which tells the individual one thing rather than another. This is stressed at the opening when the clearly marked horizon presents the imaginary furze cutter with a choice whether to continue his work or finish for the day. As the description develops we are aware that the heath functions as a meaningful vision rather than an impersonal image, evocative of human moods, *saddening* noon, anticipating the *frowning* of storms, and intensifying the opacity of a moonless midnight to a cause of *shaking and dread*. The frame, indeed, is what gives the heath its existence. In the following paragraph we are told that it is at the transitional point of its nightly roll into darkness that the 'great and particular glory' of the heath can best be understood – 'then and then only did it *tell its true tale*' (my italics).

Again and again the vocabulary stresses the heath as an object of *appreciation*. It is not the universe but specifically the earth, and it is not earth but specifically a landscape. Nature does not make landscapes – they are artefacts constructed to take possession of an area within a specific perspective. But just as Hardy does not implicitly invoke the model of tragedy but rather intentionally inserts it into the way he tells the story, so he does not 'naturally' subjectivize Egdon Heath – the production of it as landscape is deliberate and emphatic: 'Here at least were intelligible facts regarding landscape – far reaching proofs productive of genuine satisfaction.'

Indeed, of course, what he next goes on to do is to relativize the landscape historically. Egdon, for all its sense of old age and obscurity, is offered as the landscape most likely to appeal to the modern mind for whom orthodox beauty is too smiling and therefore a mockery. Its modernity *includes* its regressive, unmoving taciturnity. 'To many,' we are later told, 'this Egdon was a place which had slipped out of its century generations ago, to intrude as an uncouth object into this' (III. 2). It stands against the simple joy of the Hellenic, the vale of Tempe, and the context of chapter 1 clearly links it with the revival of interest in Nordic art and mythology which we find in Ruskin, Arnold and Morris. It offers *a way back to the obsolete*, the titanic which has been overthrown, the Ishmaelitish for whom civilization is the enemy. It is the landscape of the excluded, the 'barbarous' – that which the Hellenic and post-Hellenic worlds ignore. The heath rather than any of the humans on it offers an image of man – 'slighted and enduring, and withal singularly colossal in its swarthy monotony' – as though what this novel wishes to recover is a sense of human nature not expressible in cultures and communities. But at the same time this sense is offered solely as a constructed view, as a landscape for appreciation.

Thus landscape adds to the paradoxical treatment of tragical possibilities a further paradox – those possibilities are thwarted not by deterministic nature undermining their significance, but by a specifically modern 'view' of nature that privileges the archaic. The questions posed by the lives of the main characters are not really about their place in reality but about the specifically historical construction of their subjectivities. The novel is about man's place in nature but this is not the universal question it seems since it was put in 1863 by T. H. Huxley. This is sharply focused when Clym invites Eustacia to help him bring 'high class teaching' to the community of Egdon:

> 'I have not much love for my fellow creatures. Sometimes I quite hate them.'
> 'Still I think that if you were to hear my scheme you might take an interest in it. There is no use in hating people – if you hate anything you should hate what produced them.'
> Do you mean Nature? I hate her already.' (III. 3)

People are produced not by their history but by Nature. Clym does not contradict this for he has not returned to establish the power of the heathen to bring about change but only 'how to breast the misery they were born to' (III. 2). This gives a proper context to Gregor's observation that the novel lacks a communal basis for labour and love. Hardy has not decided to become a metaphysician; rather the historical construction of the subjectivities he wishes to portray – the modern – precisely decentres social history in order to privilege man's place in nature with its concomitant exclusions.[7]

As tragedy is a mode to be recalled by its very absence, however, community is voiced by its very decentring. The digressive tactics of the opening drive a wedge between what is seen to be common to humanity and the actual human group. The heath is perfectly accordant with man's nature but has a lonely face. It is titanic but also the communal bonfire is Promethean, like the most revolutionary Titan, although less enduring than that of the outsider Eustacia. Communal values are not absent, they are positively ineffective. Thus the specific community that underwrites the individual confrontation of the world in the idyllic earlier text is here reduced to an abstraction, 'one's fellow creatures'. Clym picks up the tone of both Ruskin and Arnold when he says that nature remains a great teacher, and one whose message is to submit, and Hardy explicitly ironizes his Arnoldian aims:

A man who advocates aesthetic effort and deprecates social effort is only likely to be understood by a class to which social effort has become a stale matter. To argue upon the possibility of culture before luxury to the bucolic world may be to argue truly, but it is an attempt to disturb a sequence to which humanity has been long accustomed. (III. 2)

Thus we have the negation of continuity both in time and in space: the possibility of meaning being given to 'experience' by its insertion into history on the one hand or social action on the other is repressed not silently but by calling up structures (more accurately, sutures) to expose their silencing. The novel liberates itself from the historical specificity of a social order only to commit itself with equal specificity to a sense of the historical development of ideology. By making the heath a landscape, a view, it also makes the question of man's place in nature appear, as it did in the post-Darwinian epoch, a product of a view of life, a dominant ideology which demands signs of intelligence beyond social action constructed within man's history (whether to naturalize or overlook the social order). This is true not only of the ideological project that emerges from Darwin (initially in *The Descent of Man*) but in a discourse opposing it such as Ruskin's. Ruskin more than anybody else privileges landscape not merely where it is appropriate as in *Modern Painters* but also in the remarkable polemical texts of the sixties and early seventies – *The Ethics of the Dust*, *The Queen of the Air* and *The Eagle's Nest* – which provide many of the concepts and images reworked in Hardy's novel.[8]

In *Far From the Madding Crowd* the community is already precarious; it takes a self-made outsider to protect the vulnerable though affirmative gospel of Poorgrass in a manner that can also give a home to Bathsheba's sexuality, and this is made possible only by the deft authorial disposition of literary conventions. The community has become farcical and shabby in *The Return of the Native*. The blushing Poorgrass reappears as the impotent Christian Cantle (whose name implies the emasculation of healthy paganism by Christianity) and the preservation of memory, so crucial to the Malthouse, is reduced to the silly evocations of Granfer's soldiery. Incapacity and excess proclaim a gospel that is lost, voiced only in the vestigial rites and performances which at best mean the mechanical and incompetent survivals of bonfires and mumming and at worst lead to the kind of reprisals practised by Susan Nonsuch. Agriculture is reduced to furze cutting, which is collecting rather than farming. It is a mode of minimal and marginal survival: 'there has been no obliteration because there had been no tending' (I. 3). Oak's role is parodied by Venn, who is not self-made but a fully fledged bourgeois farmer in disguise, who does not participate but intervenes with moralizing theatrical machinations. The sexuality of the woman is specifically excluded by the disguise which Eustacia has to put on to satisfy its curiosity. The barn is replaced by the barrow which does not make a relationship between past and present. The context for labour and love is there as a failed vestige. The novel liberates itself from the specificity of the social order only to make visible the price of that liberation.

I have already suggested that the barrow serves a similar function to the barn in *Far From the Madding Crowd*, that is it stands for collective and historic human endeavour. But, of course, it is radically different from the barn because it does not fulfil any meaningful function in the present. Its very survival is seen as an irony:

> He frequently walked the heath alone, when the past seized upon him with its shadowy hand, and held him there to listen to its tale. His imagination would then people the spot with its ancient inhabitants: forgotten Celtic tribes trod their tracks about him and he could almost live among them, look in their faces, and see them standing beside the barrows which swelled around, untouched and perfect as at the time of their erection. Those of the dyed barbarians who had chosen the cultivable tracts were, in comparison with those who had left their marks here, as writers on paper beside writers on parchment. Their records had perished long ago by the plough, while the works of these remained. Yet they all had lived and died unconscious of the different fates awaiting their relics. It reminded him that unforeseen factors operate in the evolution of immortality. (VI. 1)

Relative sophistication is more effectively obliterated by its own efficiency ('perished long ago by the plough'); the future is 'unconscious' and the only sense of time to come is the sense of the unforeseen which seems to mock forethought. This inverts the qualified affirmation of work in *Far From the Madding Crowd*, and it is the last line that completes the frame which has from the beginning singled out the Rainbarrow and the road as the only signs of 'pickaxe, plough, or spade' on the heath but which has seen them 'crystallized to natural products by long continuance'. Projects are, of course, continually ironized – from Wildeve's patch, to Clym's plans, to Mrs Yeobright's 'dozen hasty schemes for preserving him and Eustacia from this mode of life' (IV. 5). This perspective is at its most lugubrious when after Wildeve has asked Eustacia to run away with him to America, their separating figures are seen against the dark sky above the heath as 'two horns which the sluggish heath had put forth from its crown, like a mollusc, and had now again drawn in' (I. 9). Later, Clym himself is seen by Mrs Yeobright 'as a mere parasite of the heath, fretting its surface in his daily labour as a moth frets a garment' (IV. 5) At its most positive, it dissolves the individual into the heath as part of the landscape's pigmentation, so that Tamsin, for example, appears as a 'pale blue spot in a vast field of neutral brown' (II. 8); 'field' is, of course, a technical term from painting. And it is surely at its most bizarre in the appearance of Diggory Venn as a heap of turves listening to Eustacia and Wildeve.

Adaptation is not a real mode of survival in this vision. The nearest to a programme of action is Venn's grotesque opportunism, spying, tricking, desperately relying on the vicissitudes of chance (to recover Mrs Yeobright's guineas, for example). So that whereas the barn is a reminder of the continuity of work and the meaning of circumspection, the barrow only reminds us that man, like the mollusc, is subject to the most meaningless, but most peremptory, processes of natural selection. Thus the kind of historic sense which is invoked in *Far From the Madding Crowd* is not strictly speaking ignored by the novel; it is placed there as a positive absence, the most enduring human construct asking and denying an answer to the central moral question, What is doing well?, when it is put in the context of 'man's place in nature'. The barrow is actually there to say that in this landscape nothing shows human history rather than natural change, but, of course *it does say it*, so we have it there as a negated possibility like tragedy.

Moreover, the irony of this passage is questioned by the fact that Clym can in imagination reach back to the Celts, who have been so obliterated by all but this silent and naturalized monument. We are reminded of the first appearance of the Rainbarrow. The traveller's eye, we are told, finally settles on one 'noteworthy' object, which at first seems as a mere mole on the Atlantean brow of the heath, and then as its most prominent feature, even, the passage continues, the *pole and axis* of the heath. The unnamed Eustacia appears on this like 'one of the Celts who built the barrow, so far had all of modern date withdrawn from the scene'. In the mind's eye, therefore, the heath, the barrow and the silhouette of Eustacia form an architectural whole: 'it seemed to be the only obvious justification of their outline' (I. 2). On the one hand, of course, this is an illusion – Eustacia will turn out to be trying to escape from the heath, not complete it, and she is immediately displaced by the communal bonfire which is the custom of the country, in a country which is Ishmaelitish and has civilization, vestigially at least represented by the yokels, as its enemy. But the very anthropomorphism with which the heath and the barrow are presented makes it difficult to dismiss the illusion, especially in a novel which, I have shown, is carefully limited to the terminology of vision and landscape, and makes no claims for the accurate representation of the 'real world'.

The allusions to Titans (such as Atlas) and Prometheus (who is the son of a Titan) clarify the tension in this double perspective of the heath which mocks human aspiration and yet represents some human resistance to the obliterating forces of time. The Titans are at once an older race of gods, but of course, especially in romantic versions of the myth of their overthrow, they are involved in the seizure of power by the human race from the oppressive structures of the Olympians. A little before the passage quoted from the closing part of the novel, Hardy explains why ultimately Clym accepts his fate with a wry resignation: 'Human beings, in their generous endeavour to construct a hypothesis that shall not degrade a First Cause, have always hesitated to conceive a dominant power of lower moral quality than their own' (VI. 1). The other trail of allusions, which are to Virgil's Tartarus and Dante's limbo, have the same ambiguity. Both poets end by making us more aware of their compassion for human pain and their admiration for human rebellion than of the inexorability of the justice at work in their construction. The Divine is as morally disreputable in this as in any other Hardy text, but the double context of modern science and classical literature ensures that the condemnation is within the terms offered by the dominant ideology of the traditional intellectual and not merely that of the village atheist. It is absolutely central to the project of this novel that if the meaningfulness of human life is called in question by the problem of man's place in nature, the problem of man's place in nature has to be defined solely in terms of the significance rational man can give it.

That is why the apparent opposition of Clym and Eustacia is overtaken by a continuity in the sense of an absent human history to which they both finally have to be referred. But this is further extended in the following chapter in which Eustacia is displaced by the rustics who light their bonfire. For again a separation is made more meaningful by the repressed continuities it indicates. The bonfire itself is 'the instinctive and resistant act of man ... a spontaneous Promethean rebelliousness against the fiat that this recurrent season shall bring foul times . . . Black chaos comes and the fettered gods of earth say "Let there be light"' (I. 3). This reinvokes the Titans and the slighted and enduring face of man, but here neither as landscape nor romantic solitary but as Dionysiac group whose dance defies the order of nature ('all was unstable . . . for all was in extremity' – the bonfires too are 'Maenades'). and thus foreshadows Eustacia's wild dance with Wildeve at the gypsying. For the couple too 'the dance had come like an irresistible attack on whatever sense of social order there was in their minds, to drive them back in the old paths' (IV. 3). It is a revival of paganism.

But the links go further than this. The bonfire is for Guy Fawkes night and has no awareness of its anthropological origins, and yet the ashes created by it are linked with the undisturbed ashes of 'the original British pyre which blazed from that summit' which lie 'beneath their tread'. The rustics displace Eustacia but continue her protest against fettering and winter. They are cut off from any historical continuity with the past and yet through a similar process of rebellion they make another bonfire as removed in time as it is in space from the other points of light throughout the heath, and yet all tending towards the same protest. Thus the very pattern of contrasts – the solitary and the group, the past and the present, the submissive and the rebellious – is seen as produced by a 'human' attempt to compensate for the lack of meaning in the vision of man's place in the natural world. I think that this makes sense of the otherwise tedious dialogue of this chapter which focuses on whether significantly human events such as marriage or Christmas should be celebrated, whether they are going to go to church and whether the one among them named Christian is in fact a real man at all. This may seem very disruptive of the main story but I think it serves to establish a level of sardonic atheism in the novel which privileges the notion of protest at the same time as it exposes its futility. It emerges again in the mumming episode, which is a merely vestigial rite, almost losing its sense of representativeness (the ribbons) and reducing the struggle between good and evil to a 'fossilised survival' in language. Lighting of fires, the dramatization of the forces of good and evil, the very act of coming together constitute our first image of the civilization which is the enemy of the heath (for there is no sense of the heathens sharing Clym's nostalgia or Eustacia's reluctant belonging): 'Tis well to call the neighbours together and to hae a good racket once now and then; and it may as well be when there is a wedding as at tide-times. I don't care for close ways' (I. 3). This is part of a pattern whose other extreme is Parisian jewellery (we have seen that luxury is defined as a necessary precondition of Clym's culture, and ironically what lies beyond Parisian jewellery is Parisian renunciation of progress – nothing is more sophisticated about Clym than his rejection of sophistication). The dance obliterates the permanent moral expression of each face, but that only means that it obliterates the process of isolated individuation that the heath privileges: first Eustacia; then Mrs Yeobright, who has 'something of an estranged mien: the solitude exhaled from the heath was concentrated in this face that had risen from it' (I. 3); and finally Clym himself, whose typically modern face is like the modern face of the heath itself. Far from standing for any objective reality, therefore, the heath endorses the alienated solitude of the ache of modernism – the most accommodated man on the heath is paradoxically but appropriately the most estranged character, Diggory Venn. It is not our civilization that Egdon opposes but the civilizing process itself, and that is seen dialectically as *a product of the civilizing process*. Finally producing the subject man, man has to launch himself, like Empedocles on Etna, Arnold's only successful myth of modernity, back to the earth from which he has emerged.

Thus the novel enacts a specific and dialectical moment in the history of ideology, the moment at which man's place in nature seems to be a question of being placed by nature, so that the fundamental irony defining each of the protagonists is a doomed but necessary struggle between aspiration and survival. We are told that, in the case of Eustacia, 'Egdon was her Hades' but at the same time she completes the heath and her sigh is linked to the winds of the heath. It is as though in her very discontent she vindicates a transition in 'an emotional listener' from fetishism to the sense of a transcendent unity of being ('the spirit moved them' – the discourse here is surely Comtist). Caught up in the furze she surrenders unconsciously to its tenacity because she 'imbibed much of what was dark in its tone'.

This relates to an articulately worked out larger dilemma of which she herself is finally to become conscious. It can be summed up in the mumming episode. She wishes to meet Clym because Clym promises her the pulsings of the world – 'all things were possible to the speaker of that good night' – but she can only contrive to meet him by adopting a role in a traditional and vestigially meaningful play, thus accepting a place in the society from which she wishes to escape, a place for which she has to sell her sexuality at least symbolically, and literally disguise it. (It may seem trivial that she obtains the part in exchange for holding Charley's hand but it is to have important consequences later, in that Charley lights the fire which is to summon Wildeve to the fatal elopement and it reflects the whole basis of her relationship with Wildeve.) She can only reach the agent of her liberation through a self-imprisonment in another identity and, of course, this merely foreshadows the larger perspective of her marriage: seeking to be free of the constricting world of her grandfather and the heath forces her to adopt the role of Clym's wife. Beyond that it allows her to envisage liberation only in terms of an inaccessible other conformity – the fashionable world of Budmouth and Paris rather than 'the lawless state of the world without'.

Mrs Yeobright too is trapped in the same way. Outside the rustic community and with her loyalties far away from it, she does not aim at any form of self that is not completely conventional, and all her actions are dependent on the heath and her need to work within its limits.

On the other hand it is precisely because Clym's major motivation is the escape from chafing social necessities that of all the protagonists he is most able to be accommodated on the heath. He is initially drawn to Eustacia by his horror of barbarity and his revulsion from the attack on her witchcraft (itself a sign of her not belonging). They recognize one another as he tries to draw water from the civilized well (it is specifically not essential that she has water from the well but the fact that she gets her hands torn in the process foreshadows what she will suffer from her 'helical' entanglement with Clym's sophistication). As I have said, Clym's final position is not a rejection of his Parisian sophistication but a logical consequence and selective application. The educator is educated by his own experience; this confirms the education but it also exacts a great price. The blindness defeats philanthropic fantasies, but leaves untouched the illusion of objectivity. The simple dualism of Clym's ordeal is summed up in the passage about the fir plantation which follows his rupture with his mother: 'the wet young beeches were undergoing amputations ... from which the wasting sap would bleed for many a day to come, and which would leave scars visible to the day of their burning' (III. 6). Scars visible are part of the growing process. The vestigial community identifies its humanity by its refusal to accept the mere conditions of its existence. Clym becomes a furze cutter but he does not become one of them.

This rejection of privileged subjectivity by its alienation from the historical process is ideologically located by a passage from Arnold's essay on Heine which Hardy copied in his note-book:

Modern times find themselves with an immense system of institutions, established facts, accredited dogmas, customs, rules, which have come to them from times not modern. In this system their life has to be carried forward; yet they have a sense that this system is not of their own creation, that it by no means corresponds exactly with the wants of their actual life, that, for them, it is customary, not rational. The awakening of this sense is the awakening of the modern spirit.[9]

The modern spirit awakens to the absolute opposition of reason and system. There is no question of making the system reasonable – the task of Arnoldian culture is to find an unvexed relationship to this awareness. It shares the sense of absolute opposition with Ruskinian submission and Social Darwinian adaptation – ideological positions very different from it. Wisdom is the ideological project of *The Return of the Native* and wisdom is the recovery of poise in the aftermath of this awakening. But as I have already indicated, this historical specificity is manifest not merely as theme but as the specific task of creating an aesthetic equivalent of that wisdom, of realizing it as tragedy, as landscape, and ultimately that to which they are both subordinate, language itself. The realization of this project (which is not unconscious but marked) will forestall its closure and move Hardy into an ideological position that corresponds to the formal fissure which the cancelled words of *The Hand of Ethelberta* reveals as the total effect of *Far From the Madding Crowd*.

If Hardy had been looking for models of tragedy in his comtemporaries, the most obvious would have been those of Arnold and Swinburne, who have a common starting point in readings of Greek tragedy but elaborate mutually exclusive positions from it. In *The Greek Poets*, a book which Hardy extracted at some length, J. A. Symonds modifies Schlegel's description of Greek tragedy as a protest against fate by saying that it is also an offence against justice. He argues that the development from Aeschylus to Sophocles and finally Euripedes shows the absolute religious acceptance of that justice giving way to the moral possibilities of dignity in the face of it, and finally the confrontation of it as mere spectacle.[10] Neither Arnold nor Swinburne submit human reason to the acceptance of justice and in this sense are 'beyond' even Euripedes (in spite of Arnold's nostalgic allegiance to Sophocles and Swinburne's dependent contempt of Euripedes). The difference is that whereas for Swinburne tragic possibility is in human defiance of the gods ('the supreme evil, God'), Arnold seeks the possibility of repose, 'the sublime acquiescence in the course of fate, and the dispensations of human life'.[11] Eustacia and Clym reproduce this contradiction in their reactions to his blindness. 'Yeobright,' we are told, 'was an absolute stoic in the face of his mishaps' (IV. 2). Eustacia cries, 'if I were a man in such a position I would curse rather than sing'. Yeobright is dehumanized by his work, becoming 'a brown spot in the midst of an olive green, gorse and nothing more'. Empedocles reaches his destiny by merging into the elements of which he is composed. On the other hand, Yeobright sings Parisian songs and boasts to his 'inexperienced girl' that he is capable of rebelling 'in high Promethean fashion, against the gods as well as you'.

It is absurd to look either to Clym or to Eustacia for the novel's 'truth'. If Clym is more knowing, he is by the same token more dehumanized and the singing of French songs is a mere taunt to her desires, which are certainly not invalidated by their marginaliz- ation. At the end, she recovers a 'pride of life' and in a phrase that anticipates Yeats declares that she 'will be bitterly merry and ironically gay' (IV. 3).[12] In her death, it is as though 'a sense of dignity had just compelled her to leave off speaking' (IV. 9) whereas Clym is condemned to wander the heath preaching. Her rebellion and his submission are equally destructive and are equally responses to the privileged landscape of the heath. He has the face of the future which in its lack of physical beauty corresponds to the appeal of the heath. But she too completes the barrow and is inwound with the vegetation. If the heath reflects the grimness of the general human situation so also it is Ishmaelitish, invoking a figure of high rebellion against God the father whose most obvious contemporary occurrence is in Arnold's most important cultural intervention, *Literature and Dogma*, where it is linked with the modern cult of nature and with the ideal of Bohemian Paris. Ishmael is clearly the personification of rebellious selfhood, and so the heath offers no norm of conduct – it is merely slighted and enduring (in this respect, Hardy's novel is closely linked with the general issues of Arnold's text which defines religion as righteousness, what is doing well, and righteousness with our sense of what is 'not ourselves'). The tragic possibilities of Eustacia and Clym are the negated closures of Hardy's double metonymy – gesture and return neither enhance nor overwhelm one another but are locked in stalemate. As tragedy has no recourse to justice, it can only divide into opposite dead ends – a death which is meaningless, a life which is futile.

This dilemma is fully worked out by the fourth Book. Clym is no more than a brown spot. Eustacia is split between frustration and ecstasy: 'a clear line of difference divided like a tangible fence her experience within this maze of motions from her experience without it' (III. 3). The only resolution that the plot has initiated affects them only indirectly and in terms of a mere theatricality which unlike Troy's is no agent of liberation but a game played on the forgotten margins of the plot on behalf of the social order (such as it is) – I mean Diggory Venn's jiggery pokery. But no one is consoled by the marrying off of Tamsin and Venn, as Hardy, in a remarkable footnote which lays bare the ideological constraints he felt himself under, instructs us. What saves the novel from the paralysis at the end of the fascination is not Venn's defence of Tamsin, but Mrs Yeobright's death. Suddenly in two chapters the discrepancies and indecisions of the novel are articulated into a single fiction. 'The philosophy of her nature and its limitation by circumstances,' we are told earlier, 'was almost *written* in her movements' (III. 3). The first phrase is amplified as 'her natural pride of life' which links her to Eustacia, whose 'pride of life' is released in the pagan dance, but equally that pride has been 'hindered in its blooming by her necessities'. Thus she is both motivated and aware, locked neither into a dream of passion nor into a daze of cosmic alertness. Pushing her to the fore of the narrative, Hardy breaks totally with his previous fictional practice and resolves the formal dilemma of the novel. For, because she is a parent, Mrs Yeobright cannot make the entirely contrived choice between action and acceptance. Her recognition of the furze cutter as Clym is to take cognizance of 'a strange reality' which hitherto has been authorial: compare 'the silent being who thus occupied himself seemed to be of no more account in life than an insect' with the authorial 'he was a brown spot in the midst of an expanse of olive-green gorse, and nothing more'). Her response, however, is to plan 'a dozen hasty schemes' to save him. The inveterate hostility of the setting, the 'metallic violet' of the solsticial zenith and the mad carousal of the natural life have a psychological as well as a descriptive value. The only previous moment in the novel when the external has had this value is significantly when Clym breaks with his mother and watches the wet young beeches undergoing amputations. Mrs Yeobright contemplates the storm-beaten trees outside Clym's house but the difference is that this is not pathetic fallacy – they do not reflect her consciousness even implicitly but call her out of herself, and she is called out of herself again in the hour of her death.

The penultimate paragraph of Book IV, chapter 7 encapsulates many of the dualisms of the novel. Mrs Yeobright sits down in front of a colony of ants, and looks upward at a heron flying with his face to the sun: the corporate and the solitary lives, life and death, history and art (the ants, she recalls, have been in the spot for years, while the heron has come dripping wet from some pool in the valleys, and the zenith where he flies seems a 'free and happy place'). Momentarily she wishes she could 'arise uncrushed' from the earth's surface, but 'being a mother it was inevitable' that she should cease to ruminate on her condition. Thus awareness on the one hand provokes action and on the other ends self-involvement. She establishes a third tragic possibility by which tragedy is not undermined by its lack of status and its inherent ordinariness but decentred. It is a tragic sense *on behalf* of the children.

The use of the parent as the focus of tragic awareness is a major breakthrough for Hardy. All the major protagonists from now on – Henchard, Tess, Sue and Jude – are parents (not always biological, of course). It is significant that both Arnold and Swinburne focus on the mother in *Merope*, *Atalanta in Calydon* and *Erectheus*. Through parental awareness they begin to escape the simplistic dualism of rebellion and submission. For even *Merope* does not bear out the promise of its Preface: the mother is left questioning the value of the tragic action which has brought revenge on the usurping stepfather and it ends on a note of baffled anxiety. In *Erectheus*, the mother becomes the voice of Mazzinian patriotism which accepts individual sacrifice for the good of the community. The two plays contradict one another in ways opposite from those of *Empedocles* and *Atalanta*. The absence of justice means that even submission can only be spoken in a tone of reproach.

But the dialectic of Mrs Yeobright's experience is 'almost written' in her face. As she is dying, Johnny Nonsuch gazes into the face like 'one examining some strange old manuscript the key to whose character is undiscoverable'. Mrs Yeobright's experience of the heath during her journey is complex and inclusive, a text in which a wide though determinate range of attitudes is inscribed. Under the inveterately hostile metallic *silence* of the sky, she has found the mad *carousal* of independent worlds of ephemerons, watched the 'maggoty shapes of innumerable obscure creatures . . . heaving and wallowing with enjoyment'. She has heard the perpetual moan of the blasted trees and the intermittent husky notes of the male grasshoppers, and learnt that the fulness of life goes on amid the prostration of the larger animal species. And finally she looks down at the business of the ants and up at the detachment of the heron before her mind drifts back to Clym. Even in her death, she has time to return the look of the accusing adder who has caused her death and is being melted to save her. It is a

Darwinian world she sees, the tangled bank which is the climactic image of *The Origin of Species* which shows that life is generated out of the endless 'war of nature'.[13] But this does not ask what nature is like. Rather, it questions the meaning of what she sees, her experience and its legibility.

Of course, what she sees is not 'reality' but a landscape, and there are no landscapes in nature. Landscape becomes a metaphor for language.[14] Not only is the face of a life a readable manuscript but the human environment, as it is defined in this modern view of the ancient domain of man, is the site of man's determinative linguistic history. The first major sign that Hardy is thinking of philology as much as he is of physical morphology (though there are earlier indications, such as the use of the lexicographical term 'obsolete' in the opening chapter) is in the first image of Eustacia, when the multiplicity of winds is described as 'the linguistic peculiarity of the heath' (I. 6). He goes on to extend the analogy, describing them as 'the ruins of human song' and 'a worn whisper dry and papery'. Later these voices are blended in a single person of something else speaking through each at once, and this 'wild rhetoric of night' is added to by Eustacia's sigh, 'but as another phrase of the same discourse as theirs'. Johnny Nonsuch is unabashed by the 'shrivelled voice of the heath' but disconcerted by thorn bushes that 'whistled gloomily' (I. 8). When Venn sees Eustacia and Wildeve emerging from the dark of the heath like the twin horns of a mollusc, the breeze blows round his mouth carrying off the accents of a commination (I. 9). The mallard who comes from regions unknown to men brings through his Northern knowledge a wonderful 'catalogue of commonplaces. (I. 10). Clym's voice surprises Eustacia by remarking on the friendliness and geniality 'written in the faces of the hills' and it is significant that what she cannot understand is defined as a linguistic puzzle, a riddle (II. 3). Clym's mind is later imaged as 'a tablet whereon to trace its idiosyncrasies as they developed themselves'. The landscape and the people in it are pervasively described in terms of kinds of speech, traces of writing, forms of language.

It has a double effect, parallel to the emergence of Mrs Yeobright. First, the linguistic analogies break down the barriers between the 'real' and the phenomenal. If the mind is naturalized, nature is given a mind, or more precisely nature exists as the mental picture of it embodied in the forms of language by which it is experienced. But equally it breaks down these barriers by a process of decentring, for it is not controlled articulate language that emerges from the heath but the ruins of language, the traces of the experience it registers. In 1871 Max Müller re-issued his

Lectures on the Science of Language with a new preface refuting the naturalistic account of language in *The Descent of Man*. Müller saw philology as a 'physical research' which proceeded by definite laws (phonetic decay and dialectic regeneration) to investigate the petrified strata of language preserved not in literary texts, but in the living varieties of language in which those laws can be traced. Dialect, he argued, citing as one authority Hardy's mentor and friend William Barnes, was not a deviation from a linguistic norm but a parallel stream and feeder of official language. To speak therefore of the history of language was to presuppose a degree of rational control not evident in the development of linguistic forms, which therefore must be treated in terms of growth, not organic and regular, but like the inorganic changes of the earth's crust. Language, in other words, is a landscape whose origin we can explain but not reproduce.[15]

Language and landscape in Hardy's novel thus become the embodiments of the trace of human desire and need, not recoverable as continuity through the myth of work, say, as in *Far From the Madding Crowd* but evident in the perpetual moan, the waste tablet, the vestigial survivals of human statement. As, in the metonymy, Mrs Yeobright encapsulates gesture and return and their impasse in a single journey which is neither stopped by awareness nor driven into solipsism by dream, so, in metaphor, the move into the landscape becomes not a transcendence of mere human awareness, but the decentred, broken collectivization of it. Clym and Eustacia have to yield to the mother, and the heath to the barrow. Of course, I speak always of the aesthetic project. No one would suggest that Mrs Yeobright has a solution to life's problems, any more than the barrow is more truly representative of human endeavour. Both simply embody more accurately the forward thrust of the modern.

The barrow is a deformed barn. Its function is not work but the opposition to oblivion and its meaning is not recoverable in the continuous life of the community. At the very end of the novel, turning his back on the *words* of solace, Clym walks on the heath alone, to be seized by the shadowy hand of the past which holds him while it tells its tale. It is not the recent past but rather the forgotten Celtic tribes who built the barrow and whose work ironically remains when the work of the cultivating people's has gone under the plough. The barrow has had no future: 'all had lived and died unconscious of the different fates awaiting their relics'. Arnold had written of the value of philology in carrying us towards affinity with the lost Celtic tribes, but Clym clearly is not about to uncover a consoling organicism from the Celtic element in literature, with which Arnold repairs the gaps philology leaves exposed.[16]

The available tragic possibilities, despite the palpable absence of justice, imply the closure of a defiant or submissive response. Neither of Mrs Yeobright's moments of revelation permit such a closure. She recognizes that the heron would resolve her plight but as a mother she must return to earth. The exchange of looks with the adder, whose sacrifice, like hers, is pointless, makes her quiver throughout and avert her eyes. When Clym asks the Doctor what it means, his first response is silence. It is all over, but the struggle for existence goes on. Eustacia's death leaves the question of meaning open – it is as if a sense of dignity had compelled her to leave off speaking. It is not the silence of completed statement but the ruin of human song. Clym's vision of the Celtic tribes is a vision of ignorance, not of wisdom. The moments have repose, but it is not the repose of submission, but rather exhaustion and bafflement. Nor is Clym ennobled by his discovery – he is only left with the raw confrontation with his fault. Once the question of his marriage to Tamsin is out of the way, he retreats to the memory of his mother, but it is not a memory that enables him to come to terms with what has happened: 'he should have heeded her for Eustacia's sake even more than his own' (VI. 4). This memory too has to co-exist with 'his tenderness for Eustacia'. The pain is unending and cannot be distanced through judgement.

But this leads to a very important affirmation, a positive if severely limited commitment which keeps open the question of tragedy. At the end, he is no longer the silent being who submits his very humanity to cosmic wisdom. After a sharp break, we see 'a motionless figure standing on the top of the tumulus'. It is as though the story is to begin again – an unnamed figure on a barrow brought into focus as the emaciated thirty-three-year-old is about to preach what is in effect his first sermon on the mount. It is an epiphany more than it is a closing image, a sudden illumination which concentrates withut resolving all the themes of the novel. For Clym's eminence, in spite of the allusions to Jesus, is distanced by the crowd which listens 'while they abstractedly pulled heather, stripped ferns, or tossed pebbles down the slope'. Nor is the Rainbarrow any longer unique – there will be other sermons from other eminences. Above all, he has no special message, 'finding enough . . . to occupy his tongue in the opinions and actions common to all men'. His words are dealt with critically by the crowd, 'but everywhere he was kindly received, for the story of his life had become generally known'. It is an astonishingly downbeat last sentence, but it is full of what the novel has explored. It picks up the slighted and enduring image of man and places it in the context of speech, but not the contents of speech – rather *the human story the act of speaking carries.*

It is not the voice of tragic knowledge but the utterance of tragic bafflement, not 'experience' congealed into a single state of mind but a self-conscious echo of what has previously been said and done, the actions and opinions *common* to all men. 'Whereso'er men are,' the Chorus tells Merope, 'there is grief / In a thousand countries, a thousand homes, e'en now there is wail / Mothers lamenting their sons.'[17] For Arnold such recognition threatens the tragic possibility of the protagonist. But Hardy is already almost through to a form that is not cowed by this recognition. For in his utterance or rather the performative context of that utterance (captured only, of course, in the written record of it as event) Clym remains the spokesman for both Eustacia and his mother, for the recognition that tragedy does not exist because there is no justice ('And all this by the will of the Gods' – the Chorus of *Merope* ends on this note of incredulous amazement), and thus there is nothing to privilege individual experience. In the many broken voices, the obliterated but obtrusive stories, the obscure lives, Hardy finds not tragedy, but tragic possibility, the equivalent at least for a sense of repose. The novel itself is the community the landscape forgets. Its refusal to complete the sentence is its coherence. It is a self-reflexive text, but this is true of many texts, including those of 'realism'. What is important is that its self-commentary, its mirror on mirror that is all its show, produces, from the unacceptable presence of closed forms, a form deforming of forms. It stands on the edge of an ideological break which becomes the centre of the Hardy project.

The Failure of Things

Jameson usefully defines ideology as a set of strategies of containment,[18] but though this is clearly its primary effect, it is also to see it negatively from the outside, from the privileged critical position of the 'traditional' as opposed to the organic intellectual.[19] Most of us are unable to think in a vacuum – we need terms of reference which will enable us to get on with contributing to and benefiting from the social structure within which we live. The least negotiable issue is the relationship between structure and agency, our sense that the world is a given reality but that we have to operate within that given as though there were choices that we can, indeed must, make. Ideology attempts to overcome this opposition by establishing co-ordinates on which all the cultural relations within a group can be inscribed as a coherent curve. It is not therefore a description of a set of beliefs or a world picture, it must include widely diverging attitudes, incorporate continuities from the past and allow for changes to come. It is not an illusion nor is it optional. We cannot talk of emancipating ourselves from it as though it were a coat to cast off or a closet to come out of. It is an instrument of social activity without which no development of the relations of production and therefore no production could happen. In a sense it is the language by which life gets done – it enables us to speak in sentences.

The version of this articulation which prevails during the formation of industrial capitalism in Britain is in the double allegiance of Empiricism to the subject as defined by 'experience' and the properly ordered universe as the state of nature.[20] Nature and experience co-ordinate structure and agency. They do not represent beliefs or even values, since it is possible to see either in widely differing ways. Nature, for example, may be humane or imponderable, gradual or metamorphic – what is important is that in the last instance it is the reference for the true or the good (or rather the true and the good seen as a single term). Likewise experience does not demand a consensus about individuality. On the contrary the nature of identity, its formation, its correlation with social groups, are the subject of much analysis. But experience is the criterion of the many different versions of the self that can be produced. Just as 'natural' and 'unnatural' are inexorably favourable and unfavourable respectively, so 'experience' is primary (even for Blake, though so severely modified that it is not surprising that it took Rossetti and Swinburne, who both work on the fringe of the ideological break I am about to define, to see his importance).[21] Myself, my personality, my desire can be denied or repressed but nothing can deny my experience.

Although we should not make too facile a connection between uneven developments, it is not difficult to see why nature and experience are such useful concepts for capitalist relations of production. In capitalist production, the theory of economic activity suppresses the labour process as much as possible in order to show the surplus value produced by labour but appropriated by capital as profit.[22] Commodities are use values in translation as exchange values, and the basic commodity, money which has no use value, is presented as though it grows. Growth is natural. Experience is unquestionable because the precondition of primitive accumulation is 'free labour'. Experience will not tell me who I am but it demands that the question be freely put. Capitalism appropriates labour not as persons (e.g. serfs or slaves) but as hands and minds, and makes the assumption that there is an unaccommodated private space for the labour equivalent of the accumulating privacy of the owner of the means of production (we have already seen how clearly Hardy sees this to be a specific historical process in *A Pair of Blue Eyes*). I may not know what John Goode is really like or why he is like it, but I do know that he is that and that his role in the relations of production does not affect who he is. Labourer or capitalist, it is the 'same' John Goode defined by his experience of being that person.

The co-ordination of nature and experience constitutes the ideological effect, but it neither simply reflects nor results from industrial capitalism. On the contrary the most articulate literary text of this calculus is *The Prelude*, which is far from being the product of a capitalist functionary. If it were merely the illusion generated by the economic base it would be optional – we could simply measure intellectual activity by its relative indifference to such absolutes – whereas, on the contrary, the co-ordination of nature and experience appears precisely as the opportunity to create a space which appears to be 'outside' ideology.

Therefore when I speak of an ideological break I do not mean a break with ideology but a break in it, and I use the term break because at certain points in cultural history there occur multi-dimensional shifts in the terms of reference of discourses. These progressively dismantle a specific articulation of structure and agency reflecting and emulsifying in an uneven and dialectical way changes in the mode of production. Constants are overthrown both because they are no longer satisfactory as explanatory or referential concepts *and* contradictorily because the changing role of production demands different ways of seeing things. Such a break occurs in the latter half of the nineteenth century, and Hardy's precise place in it is the source of his current significance.

The break occurs in two opposing ways. First it is clear that in the 1860s the experience/nature co-ordinate becomes less appropriate to the need of capitalist development.[23] One of the crucial issues, perhaps the crucial issue overshadowing the many different forms which the ideological crisis took, is the debate leading to the Second Reform Act, which precisely raised the question of membership of the *pays légal*.[24] It asked who could be incorporated within the political domain defined by this calculus without putting society at risk. It even became necessary to designate, as Bright did, the mass of the working class as a 'residuum'.[25] On the level of the history of ideas we can see this inconvenience operating most specifically in the work of J. S. Mill, whose *On Liberty* (which

Hardy claims to have known by heart), merely takes the category of experience to its inconveniently logical conclusion, however politically embarrassing. He sees that liberty in our culture is ultimately confined to the concept of free trade and that beyond it constraint is replaced not by freedom but by convention. Thus, for example, it does not apply to certain non-hegemonic groups. At the other end of the decade, his *The Subjection of Women* is specifically bound up with giving women a voice/vote. Some kinds of experience thus become too disruptive and it is notorious that in popular ideology such as that of Samuel Smiles, self-help gives way increasingly to the notion of co-operation, and in this context, of course, Arnold's abhorrence of doing as one likes is coherent with the need to find corporate accounts of the self.[26]

The self becomes decentred by history, by evolution, by the need to negotiate the complex demands of a social network which is alien but undeniable. By the mid-seventies the idea that the self can be defined in terms of experience is effectively demolished. The texts which most powerfully indicate this are F. H. Bradley's *Ethical Studies* (1874) and Eliot's *Daniel Deronda* (1876).[27] Different as they are from one another, both confront the self with an overwhelming (I mean this precisely) demand for the sacrifice of its consciousness to the wider movement of an impersonal force. Darwin and Hegel form a powerful if incongruous alliance against the nature and experience calculus. I won't ever know what is going on and in any case it is an illusion or a sign of moral underdevelopment to suppose that it matters that I won't.

Nature too becomes potentially disruptive, though the full effect of its normative inconvenience lags behind that of experience (see chapter 5) because what is more important is the recognition of its inadequacy as a concept of truth/goodness. The only condition on which it is still admitted is that of its inscrutability and its demands for submission, to which the whole work of Ruskin is devoted. Mill, ever the thorn in the flesh of his own allegiances, ditched nature altogether in 1854, though it is interesting that the essay in which he did it was not published until he was dead.[28] Darwin finally, of course, demolished the possibility of 'natural' as an unproblematic normative term, but he equally opened up the determinative power of natural processes so that accepting Darwin means that you can't reject the natural world any more than you can find it acceptable.

This break is both a critical response to the ideology of romanticism *and* a reflex of the political demands of a new phase of capitalism which requires the reaffirmation of a non-rational tradition in order to seek darker frontiers and build more complex organizations. It needs as well to silence the inconvenient self (of workers and women to begin with), so that the break is radical but also the basis of conservation. Obviously the most radical product of the Darwin/Hegel axis is *Capital* (even if it separates itself from both). And even in England, where Marx was almost completely unknown, the influence of Positivism, which was receptive to Marx, at least opened up the possibility of a committed historical and scientific analysis of social relationships. Hardy's notebooks show him trying to assimilate Comte, especially in 1876, as for example in Note 717, where he tries to relate ideological and social trends in a manner that gives us a purchase on much of his future practice: 'the two interdependent problems bequeathed by the Middle Age – the incorporation of the proletariat into modern society, the replacement of supernatural creeds by a demonstrable faith'.[29]

But secondly, the dialectical origins of this break mean that the terms of its foreclosure are within it – specifically in the emergence of many levels of irrationalism by which late capitalism re-forms its ideology around the empire and the corporation.[30] Two in particular are relevant to Hardy and his place in literary history and they can be related to a certain development of Darwinism on the one hand and Hegelian idealism on the other. The 'natural' is reincorporated as a 'subversive' force on the one hand and on the other tradition as a realm of the ideal community. They account for the impersonal projections that we see in Lawrence (via Haeckel) and T. S. Eliot (partly via Bradley) respectively. Thus the maintenance of Mill's individualism and, for example, Huxley's rationalism is by no means simply the preservation of a fossilized ideology, and the resilient allegiance to these affirmations in the face of the coming irrationalism makes Meredith at least until the mid-eighties a very radical novelist (*The Egoist* is published in 1879) and transforms Morris from an aesthete into a Marxist. These resistant strands are in Hardy as well and mean that he does not anticipate Lawrence ideologically any more than he does formally, and they explain why to the corporatism of Eliot and Leavis he appears as nothing more than an intellectual peasant. Hardy's ideological formation is to be located at an exact point before the radical disenfranchisement of the empirical calculus capitulates to the symbolic order in the name of the Other. In the mid-eighties, it is true, Hardy will use von Hartmann's totalizing concept of the Unconscious as well as the metaphysical pessimism of Schopenhauer, but neither offer him a refuge: the break, for Hardy, is never repaired.

This does not mean that we can allow a non-ideological utopia in by the back door begging for our charity in the guise of anarchic pluralism. He does not go on, however, like Morris, to make a new ideological position (though as we shall see there are more connections to be made with Morris than meet the eye). But the first point to make is that the fracture of the nature/experience syntax nearly silences him. For each of the three novels which follow *The Return of the Native* try to uncover a transindividual project which effectively ends the story before it begins. Hardy attempts to reconstruct a continuity between human relationships and a larger wisdom – history in *The Trumpet Major*, 'the march of mind' in *A Laodicean*, the cosmos itself in *Two on a Tower*. The project itself ends the story before it begins; at best it yields a powerful metaphor which the narrative can only fuss around. Nevertheless, as we move through the novels, we move nearer to the possibility of a new ideological project which does not seek wisdom, but seeks to represent instead the opposition of structure and agency, the project of the ideological break itself.

At various times during the seventies, Hardy planned to write a literary account of Napoleon which finally came to fruition a quarter of a century later as *The Dynasts*. The upstart who nearly ruled Europe clearly fascinated the *ariviste* who conquered by writing the culture which did not know him. It is not surprising that the first coherent response to this ambivalent hero is to repress him, to represent him, indeed, as an absence (this is explicit in 'A Tradition of 1804'). Thus *The Trumpet Major* represents the 'unwritten history' of ordinary people whose individuality lies buried behind the spectacle of great events. The novel's central affirmation is in the twelfth chapter, when the group whose lives the text rescues from obscurity watch a parade of soldiers at a royal visit. Contrasting their interest with the mass of spectators who 'had no personal interest in the soldiery', the narrator asks, 'Who thought of every point in the line as an isolated man, each dwelling all to himself in the hermitage of his own mind?' The double vision – the hermitage mind in the line of troops – exposes the inability of the novel to mediate between experience and history; individuality is only brought into focus to be lost immediately in the historical distance which is invoked (the use of 'point' has a precise geometric despair; it has location without dimension).

This is explicit in the next chapter as Anne watches the military: 'Anne now felt herself close to and looking into the stream of recorded history, within whose banks the littlest things are great, and outside which she and the general bulk of the human race were content to live on as an unreckoned, unheeded superfluity' (13). Scott's novels articulate the way in which recorded history incorporates the unreckoned lives of the general bulk of the human race. For Hardy, however, history is subjected to a double impasse. On the one hand it is trivialized by its exclusion of the bulk of the human race, and on the other that exclusion reduces the lives of the people in the novel to a superfluity, of which, since this is Anne's feeling, they are potentially aware. The historical dimension thus becomes embarrassing. There seems no reason why the lightweight romantic intrigue should be set at a particular time. At best history is only local colour – at worst it imparts a coy tone of quaintness. And yet the end of the novel suddenly catches the intrigue up in the stream without conferring meaning on either. John, the worthy rejected lover, says goodbye: 'and in another moment he had plunged into the darkness, the ring of his smart step dying away upon the bridge as he gained his companions in arms, and went off to blow his trumpet till silenced forever upon one of the bloody battlefields of Spain.' 'One of' closes the particular life with an ironic anonymity which places the reader in the position of recorded history itself. So 'history' is not a perspective but a blindfold. It has nothing to do with the people of the novel yet it sweeps them up into its anonymity. The story becomes superfluous – Anne's choice in the light of history does not matter. History is absurd.

Neither *A Laodicean* nor *Two on a Tower* resolve this impasse but they show Hardy coming to terms with it. Restoring the locus of human desire to a balance with cosmic wisdom, they seek stories which will break the stalemate between Clym and Eustacia. Both, however, embody the contradiction in a metaphoric structure (centred on a building) which overwhelms narrative potential as recorded history does in *The Trumpet Major*. *A Laodicean* is explicitly about modernity but this is posed as a paralysing self-consciousness. The starting point of the novel is a bitter denunciation of experience:

It is an old story, and perhaps only deserves the light tone in which the soaring of a young man into the empyrean, and his descent again, is always narrated. But as has often been said, the light and the truth may be on the side of the dreamer: a far wider view than the wise ones have may be his at that recalcitrant time, and his reduction to common measure be nothing less than a tragic event. The operation called lunging, in which a haltered colt is made to trot round and round a horsebreaker who holds the rope, till the beholder grows dizzy in looking at them, is a very unhappy one for the animal concerned. During its progress the colt springs upwards, across the circle, stops, flies over the turf with the velocity of a bird, and indulges in all sorts of graceful antics; but he always ends in one way – thanks to the knotted whipcord – in a level trot round the lunger with the regularity of a horizontal wheel, and in the loss for ever to his character of the bold contours which the fine hand of Nature gave it. Yet the process is considered to be the making of him. (I. 1)

The action of the inevitable lunge which has already happened leaves Somerset nowhere to go, and he merely 'suffers the modern malady of unlimited appreciativeness', becoming a mere spectator of events he can do little to influence. An equivalent indecisiveness characterizes Paula, product, as Somerset puts it, of the march of mind, but, as she replies, the *daughter* of its representative who can only enact passively the desire to return to the medievalism her father had absorbed. The story is a highly contrived, even silly device to stall their drearily appropriate marriage by a pantomime pair of aristocratic schemers of whom the father is an ineffective voyeur and the son a *naive* baddy whose attempts to utilize modern technology do not mitigate his obviousness.

But the passage quoted not only indicates that the premature foreclosure of the narrative by the tragic event has already happened, but by its argument also presages the ideology of the later project. For it shows that Hardy cannot resort to the comforts of the absurd. *The Trumpet Major* tries to resolve the impasse of modern knowingness by recourse to history but the modern finally enters the novel to destroy its patronizing air of warmth. Here modernity is confronted in a specific way. The image of the lunge retains, obviously, a residual protest against it. The fine hand of Nature is not ironic but the word 'inevitable' in the following paragraph keeps it pessimistically in place. But most importantly, the protest is by this directed against the reader, first by questioning whether by being an old story it is any more acceptable, and then by questioning the truth of the inevitable (a far wider view than the wise ones have). The image clarifies this paradox: the inevitable is a form of oppression. The 'making' of a character is his unmaking. The novel is refusing to be that inevitable lunge. Unfortunately all Paula and Somerset can do with their unacceptable disillusion is to restore 'the fossil of feudalism', de Stancy Castle, as a tribute to a not-self which actively appears only as the oppression of the stagey villain. In spite of the hopeful sign of the new technology at the beginning (telegraphy), in the end the castle, its contents destroyed by the arson of the man who at the end seems to control technology (in the form of photography), remains an uninhabitable 'mouldy pile', like the barrow, an inert metaphor of human history. With an irony which seems to embody Hardy's own exasperation with the text, the denouement leaves the lovers free to build a new house, 'a perfect representative of the modern spirit' (VI. 5) which means eclectic and in sight of the ruin, 'representing neither the senses and understanding, nor the heart and imagination; but what a finished writer calls "the imaginative reason"'. Why 'finished'? Because Arnold's phrase only encapsulates the contradictions in a polished phrase and the phrase leaves open its anomalies. Arnold provides an ideology of modernism which does nothing to redress the lunge, and if it weren't so trivial, the last note of the novel would be as disconsolate and perplexing as that of *The Trumpet Major*: 'I wish my castle wasn't burnt; and I wish you were a de Stancy.' It is commonly regarded as Hardy's worst novel, written at the time of a prolonged illness only not to renege on his contract (which tells us more about the scientific game). But it could not have succeeded, in spite of the startling images of modernity which impose fragments of a disconnected world on a fossilized past, and like the lunge image itself turn the history of aristocratic oppression into the problem of inevitability. For it is not life that lunges us but our masters. But the images foreclose on this: human endeavour is diminished as 'an old story'.

Two on a Tower resides in the same impasse and even more clearly declares this by its privileged monumental metaphor. The eighteenth-century tower is erected on a man-made, Roman or British or Saxon hill. Like the barrow and the castle it is another powerful image of the hermitage of man's mind, memorializing the forgotten: 'and yet the whole aspect of the memorial betokened forgetfulness' (1). It is inaccessible, assimilated into the indifferent natural environment. The heroine only visits it to escape her ennui and the hero to gaze at the stars and thus be raised above 'such emphemeral trivialities as human tragedy' (5). The accumulated human history is in all these ways made obscure and benighted. It forecloses the narrative, which only raises the question of whether Viviette will scale down the philosopher St Cleeve to 'inamorato'. There is no middle distance between absolute detachment and cliché. On the one hand together they contemplate the indifference of the universe to their tiny human magnitudes as nightmare; on the other they are forced to act out their relationship in terms of conventionally oppressed romance. On the one hand there is a detailed discussion of the implications of astronomy; on the other a thin intrigue to maintain their relationship in the face of conventional disapproval. Much of the narrative idles over colourful characters or suspenseful actions, and the story itself, which turns on the truth or falsity of the report of Viviette's husband's death, locks the protagonists' awareness away from the details of the situation.

Suddenly this changes. When, out of a 'maternal' concern for his scientific passion, Viviette decides to let Swithin go, she becomes caught up in a Positivist version of human evolution from egoism to altruism (35). It is a disastrous development. The inevitable lunge for the woman is self-sacrifice but in this novel it only leads her to a situation which is unacceptable to the conventions which privilege that denial of self-formation of character. For, finding herself pregnant when she has already let Swithin go to Africa, she contrives to marry a bishop – which hardly makes matters any better. But Viviette is never judged by the novel, which thus breaks the rules of the scientific game. It is as though Fanny Robin or Tamsin were to take charge of their own destinies with the coolness of Bathsheba or, more precisely, Ethelberta. But her strategy is explained in terms which radically challenge Positivism as a whole and the whole ideological project of George Eliot in particular: 'in her terror she said she had sown the wind to reap the whirlwind. Then the instinct of self preservation flamed up in her like a fire. Her altruism in subjecting her self love to benevolence, and letting Swithin go away from her, was demolished by the new necessity, as if it had been a gossamer web' (37). Her allusion to the Book of Job places her in a line which will conclude with·Jude himself. But what is important here is that altruism and benevolence disappear under necessity like a gossamer web. (Is Hardy thinking of the 'particular' web of *Middlemarch*, where it is an image of what binds lives together?) The narrative that follows and above all the responses it calls forth take us, in the last part of the text, beyond the conventions of the Victorian novel and into Hardy's major phase.

First, however, I need to discuss the wider implications of the imagery in this passage. Verbally through 'necessity' and 'web', though not logically, the passage recalls a famous passage in Pater's essay on Winckelmann which Gregor has rightly seen as central to the project of Hardy's fiction:

For us, necessity is not, as of old, a sort of mythological personage, with whom we can do warfare. It is rather a magic web woven through and through us, like that magnetic system of which modern science speaks, penetrating us with a network, subtler than our subtlest nerves, yet bearing in it the central forces of the world.[31]

Obviously there could be no clearer example of the penetration of necessity than the pregnant woman, especially given the special privileging of the parental experience that we have noted already and will need to return to. It is of course an image available to Hardy from 1867 onward and he has clearly alluded to it before as, for example, in the image of Eustacia inwoven with the heath. Pater's text is not merely concerned with 'the chief factor in the thoughts of the modern mind concerning itself' but the basis of a practical question – how can literary production *deal* with modern life? How can it *reflect* and *affect* modern life so as to satisfy the spirit when what the spirit needs is a sense of freedom the lack of which precisely constitutes the main feature of the modern mind concerning itself? Two postures are by this rejected: the first explicitly is warfare with the external, while the other, implicit in the whole texture of the essay, is the wise passiveness of acceptance. Although modern poetry, reflecting life as the modern mind regards it, confers 'blitheness and repose', this is clearly different from Arnoldian detachment which rises above the *Zeitgeist* altogether. Blitheness and repose offer no ideological repair of the basic situation, only a strategy to adopt in the face of it. In Goethe and Hugo, for example, 'this entanglement, this network of law, becomes the tragic situation, in which certain groups of noble men and women work out *for themselves* a supreme denouement' (my italics). There is no question of accommodation, or transcendence, and above all it is something made not found, a *praxis*. It responds to a reworking of the original question: 'Can art represent man and women in these bewildering toils so as to give the spirit at least an equivalent of the sense of freedom?' That question is carefully phrased – 'represent so as' situates the practice of art in a dialectical encounter between mimesis and fiction and 'equivalent of the sense' leaves intact the opposition of agency and structure. The work of art is not naturalized. Its privilege is the privilege of work. Because it does not offer a perception of the reconciliation of agency and structure but a model of bringing them together to make a product, I call this a break in ideology, not simply a breakdown leaving open the way to different totalities such as we see in Bradley and Spencer, but a break in which there is work to be done, to use Sartre's distinction, a totalization rather than a totality.[32]

The text now becomes an intervention, not, as in the scientific game, through the disguise of the socially constructed aesthetic forms but, on the contrary, as the explicit vehicle of the new. In the Conclusion to his *Studies in the History of the Renaissance*, Pater reconstructs experience not as the subject of the natural predicate but as an end in itself giving no access to totality. Art which reflects experience has, like speculative philosophy, to startle the human spirit into eager observation, to prevent the formation of habit.

Let us now return to the startling end of *Two on a Tower*, which displaces the question of conduct and the possibility of wisdom. Swithin's response to Viviette's marriage is to confront life with amazement: 'He was as one who suddenly finds the world a stranger place than he thought; but is excluded by age, temperament and situation from being much more than an astonished spectator of its tragedy' (40). Tragedy, however, does not take him towards any kind of repose. For the second break for Swithin is with the scientific detachment that had brought ambiguity into his relationship with Viviette. In the southern hemisphere, the paradox of Norcombe Hill, by which a totality is maintained in the articulation of the tiny human magnitude in the face of the vastness of the cosmos, lies in ruins. Space here, 'being less the historic haunt of human thought seemed to be pervaded with a more lonely loneliness'. But precisely because of this, because there is no historic wisdom to bring together subject and predicate, it leaves him a divided being, and leaves untouched 'the sympathetic instincts which create the changes in a life'. We have already moved a long way from the forms of totality offered even in the wake of the breakdown of the experience/nature co-ordinate. The cosmos is too large even to overwhelmed. Man has instincts which reach out of himself (sympathetic) but which make not for continuity, for organic repair, for tradition, but for change. The initial change is a change in the way of seeing: 'that which is the foreground and measuring base of one perspective draught may be the vanishing point of another perspective draught while yet they are both draughts of the same thing'. Perspective is a way of seeing by which we possess the object of our sight. It is no accident that the supreme representative of possessive individualism, the land-scape park, of which the tower is a part, should be designed to give the maximized perspective, though not, of course, the infinite perspective which Swithin uses it for.[33]

Swithin can no longer see Viviette within a single perspective. The possessive love of the lover dies away because she is no longer 'attractive' and is displaced by 'loving kindness' which is to be a key term in the re-ordering of human relations that Hardy's novels make possible. Here it is a tribute to what she has been through, to her *experience* not as an absolute but something to be known, to be brought into relation with. She dies of joy and he is literally left holding the baby, having to accept responsibility, though it does not socially belong to him. Romantic love is displaced by a concept of parenthood, which we have already seen in Mrs Yeobright, decentring experience. The acceptance of the child constitutes a denouement in Pater's sense because Swithin is not called to it by his experience of the actual. His 'natural response' to Viviette is to her loss of 'beauty', and his logical response to her dismissal is to turn away. But he makes a choice *against nature*, recognizing necessity yet not relying on it for his being. Swithin becomes in these few pages the first truly Hardyan protagonist because he no longer seeks answers by which to motivate his life but takes decisions (of course he acts only in a mode already worked out by Viviette). Neither Bathsheba nor Ethelberta do more than veer between gesture and negotiation, though they, as well as Mrs Yeobright, are the obvious forebears. There is a curious insistent way in which Pater deliberately does not talk about Man or men but men and women, which I feel sure is deliberate and would make sense given the writers he most admires in his own time, for example William Morris.

Loving kindness is a concept we shall meet again and again in Hardy until it is invoked climactically at the end of *The Dynasts*. On the face of it it seems like a tame echo of the Positivist law of development but, in view of the gossamer-like substance of altruism in the face of necessity, it is clearly very different in its outcome. It occurs again in an important story of these years called 'A Tryst at an Ancient Earthworks' which is about another privileged monument bearing the debatable trace of human history. The narrator imagines the harps of the past celebrating daring, strength, cruelty, *worship*, superstition, *love*, birth and death – 'simple loving kindness perhaps, never'. It is the obscure, unmemorialized emotion that is not inscribed in the monument. It becomes the Hardy equivalent of a sense of freedom, an agency that does not try to defeat or succumb to the inexorable law.

This is clarified in a passage in the *Life* dated May 1881 at the end of the long illness during which he completed *A Laodicean* and during the composition of *Two on a Tower*:

> General Principles. Law has produced in man a child who cannot but constantly reproach its parent for doing much and yet not all, and constantly say to such parent that it would have been better never to have begun doing than to have *overdone* so indecisively; that is than to have created so far beyond all apparent first intention (on the emotional side), without mending matters by a second intent and execution, to eliminate the evils of the blunder of overdoing. The

emotions have no place in a world of defect, and it is a cruel injustice that they should have developed in it.[34]

This comes after 'infinite trying to reconcile a scientific view of life with the emotional and spiritual so that they may not be interdestructive'. On the one hand it is an intensified assertion of 'crass casualty' because there is nothing, not even the triumph of structure, to reconcile structure and agency. It is the law both that man should have emotions and that he should be punished for them. On the other hand it opens up a positive ideological programme, 'cannot but reproach'. To the compelling injustice of things is added the equally compelling voice against it which by definition asserts the possible other case, that which is not available but ought to be. Novels which claim to be realistic implicitly call upon the reader to submit to the real, but Hardy's novel will reflect the impossibility of that submission, and act out in its own existence as a text the sense of injustice that this contradiction incites. 'If the Law itself had consciousness,' he goes on, 'how the aspect of its creatures would terrify it, fill it with remorse.' 'Terrify', 'remorse' are the Aristotelian constituents of tragedy, terror and pity, drained of cathartic consolation. The Law is an unconscious parent, the reader is made conscious by the novel and has to take the reproach of the child created by the writer. It is not the calm of the tragic denouement that is offered but the terrified question of a shared loving kindness. Necessity, in Hardy, is always held against the justice it denies – awareness and desire are hostile to one another but the presentation of that hostility, as many critics who have found Hardy philosophically inconsistent have found, is only the starting point of his novels and not their point of rest.

There are three consequences of this ideological break for Hardy's later fiction. First it transforms the scientific game. Up till now, Hardy, the product of the writing age, has written fictions which co-operate with acceptable forms and ideological perspectives while, by exploiting the gap between the text and its possible readings, he precisely subverts these orientations. The end of *Two on a Tower* puts an end to that accommodation. In July, 1883, he writes: 'In future I am not going to praise things because the accumulated wisdom of ages say they are great and good, if those accumulated remarks are not based on observation. And I am not going to condemn things because a pile of accepted views raked together from tradition, and acquired by instillation, say antecedently that they are bad.'[35] Note how 'raked from tradition' decisively and consciously rejects the critical project dedicated to the best that is thought and done which dominates a certain phase of literary studies. It is not surprising that Eliot and Leavis needed to be patronizing about Hardy. More importantly this inaugurates the long battle with conventional morality with which the novels of the next twelve years are involved. In a story written in the previous year, he writes of 'the narrative smile' of his storyteller,[36] but by the time he writes *The Mayor of Casterbridge* the smile has gone. Although there are many remarks about the pleasure of fiction in subsequent years, most of them have to do with strangeness.

In addition, it decisively affects the subject matter. In August, 188?, he has the following unattached note: 'an ample theme: the interest passions and strategy that throb through the commonest lives'.[37] This may look as though he is trying to recover the social domain he had abandoned in *A Laodicean* and *Two on a Tower* but the stories of these years show that he has moved a long way from *Far From the Madding Crowd* and *The Return of the Native* in directions to be taken by the later novels.

First, as Millgate notes, there is an intensified regionalism.[38] Four especially, 'The Distracted Preacher', 'Fellow Townsmen', 'Three Strangers' and 'Interlopers at the Knap' have a specific localized social interest. This is different from the earlier use of 'Wessex' which is predominantly a literary metaphor, whether as reworked convention, as in *Far From the Madding Crowd*, or, as in *The Return of the Native*, as a landscape for working out the strange disease of modern life. But the interest in smuggling on the Dorset coast, or the development of Port Bredy, or the nature of beekeeping at the Knap (which can be contrasted with the stylized episode in *Under the Greenwood Tree*) – these have a detailed documentary base.

Secondly, the first three of these stories are properly historical. In contrast with *The Trumpet Major*, where the past is a device of aesthetic distance, history is presented as a process of change which impinges on the daily lives of the people. 'The Distracted Preacher', for example, shows the decline of the livelihood of the smuggling community brought about by the increasing violence of the state. 'Fellow Townsmen' is about the changing status of the middle class. This means that values are relativized not by the *Zeitgeist*, as they are in *The Return of the Native*, but by the interaction of consciousness and circumstance. The heroine of 'The Distracted Preacher', for example, justifies smuggling in terms of the community's needs and refuses to give it up even for love because it is part of her social life (note too the way in which the added footnote insists on the gap between history and permitted fiction, and the values it embodies).

And thirdly, as this implies (and this is evident as well in 'An Honourable Laura', 'The Romantic Adventures of a Milkmaid' and 'A Mere Interlude'), Hardy's already radical treatment of women is taken further. For now the interest does not focus on women who are exceptionally allotted male roles, like Bathsheba or Ethelberta, or exceptionally caught between the demand for such a role and its limitations, as with Eustacia. Nevertheless, all these stories turn on the refusal of women to accept the roles allotted to them by the conventions either of society or of romantic narrative. Even the smuggling widow of 'The Distracted Preacher', who wears her husband's clothes as a disguise, leads the conventional life of a landlady and feels the need of love and security (but refuses to make a romantic choice out of that). And the romantic milkmaid has very predictable and entirely endorsed desires. The difference now is that repression does not give rise to waywardness but provides the chance of an entirely vindicated resistance to simple accommodation. Having minds of their own is not a tragic or comic flaw. So that when Hardy writes of 'interests, passions and strategy' he is defining a precise break with his earlier practice, made possible by the recognition that there is no reconciliation between a scientific and an imaginative view of life, and therefore no judgement of the many different kinds of negotiation made by those forced to live within that contradiction and yet defined precisely by their stand against it. Not only has he jettisoned tradition, but he has ruled out the chance of writing moral fables. Each of these stories is a challenge to the reader not to foreclose on the action ideologically.

This leads to the final consequence, which is a question of form. In a long note, vaguely dated (but apparently made about the time he finished *The Mayor of Casterbridge*), Hardy writes: 'it becomes impossible to estimate the intrinsic value of ideas, acts, material things: we are forced to appraise them by the curves of their career'.[39] Experience in the novel is a way of finding out who you are – character is what you are.[40] Hardy's earlier novels proceed from strong character delineations (think of the opening description of Gabriel, the Queen of the Night and the face of the future), which are then thwarted, disguised or revealed by events. Character in this sense is not a constituent category of his later fiction – it is rather the life, the curve of a career. That is the real meaning of 'character is destiny' – neither Henchard, nor Tess nor Jude are themselves until they have lived their lives through. The form of the earlier novels subordinates the chain of events to the organizing metaphor, the barn and the barrow, for example. The lives of the characters (what they are) define themselves in relation to it. The two stories that most privilege the monumental metaphor in this period, 'What the Shepherd Saw' and 'A Tryst at an Ancient Earthworks', precisely overturn this priority. What the monument embodies is less important than the drama it makes possible. The second of these, effectively a prose poem about Maiden Castle, is a calling up of the narratives that lie buried there both on the level of the narrator's imagination and on that of the fanatical archaeologist's criminal excavation to show that it was a Roman fort. The lost voices need to be recovered. The determinative motifs of the stories are all gesture and return. The ideological break imparts a new need for narrative.

In his essay on Heine, Arnold quotes from his subject:

> The Englishman loves liberty like his lawful wife, the Frenchman loves her like his mistress, the German loves her like his old grandmother. And yet after all, no one can ever tell how things may turn out. The grumpy Englishman, in an ill temper with his wife, is capable of some day putting a rope round her neck, and taking her to be sold at Smithfield.[41]

This 'sell-out' of liberty is precisely what Mill had already protested against, but Heine's ironic comparison to the lawful wife makes it also an act of truth since one's property is also a kind of liability. *The Mayor of Casterbridge* begins with a real wife-selling, appalling and yet enabling. It is as though Hardy is going to act out Arnold's flirtation with the modern. Above all it enables the curve of a career. On Easter Sunday before the completion of his new novel Hardy wrote a note in praise of the biblical narrative.[42] His recovery of the chain of events in such a dramatic manner as this opening is an exchange of the rights of metaphor for the commitment not just to the trace of human endeavour but to the history it both re-presents and demands, an aesthetic of what Virginia Woolf, clearly echoing Hardy, will come to call 'obscure lives'.

3   The Profitable Reading of Fiction

A Changed Man: *The Mayor of Casterbridge*

We know immediately that *The Mayor of Casterbridge* is different. Its powerful narrative enchainment (by which I mean not only its excellent story but its intense sequential drive) is firmly located in a literal, historically precise, unaestheticized social world. We feel free to read it innocently, as history or even epic, a text whose meaning is articulated by its bearing on the real world. But if it is unlike anything we have yet encountered in Hardy, it is also unlike those texts of Balzac and Stendhal, Dickens and Eliot with which under the impact of the immediate response we may be tempted to compare it. For in these writers, once we have recognized the specific conditions under which they address the reader (no great realist text mystifies its illusion as a transparency), selectivity is at the behest of the typical and the function of detail is to mediate that typification with actual historical conditions. Hardy is concerned with actual historical conditions as well, but in a specifically mediated form which constantly re-presents authorial activity (as opposed to stance) as the motivation of the text.[1]

In the first place it is brought to us within an overt ideological frame, initiated in the first instance by Susan at the beginning and echoed by Elizabeth Jane at the end. Susan: 'When she plodded on in the shade of the hedge silently thinking, she had the hard, half apathetic expression of one who deems anything possible at the hands of Time and Chance except, perhaps, fair play.' Although this 'phase' of her expression is 'probably' the work of civilization and there is another, 'even handsome', that is the work of Nature, both the uncertainty of the adverb and the consequential register of the noun (which foreshadows, of course, the determinist psychology which structures the project of *Tess of the d'Urbervilles*) ensure its predominance. Compare this with the summary of Elizabeth Jane's experience at the end of the novel:

> Her position was, indeed, to a marked degree one that, *in the common phrase*, afforded much to be thankful for. That she was not demonstrably thankful *was no fault of hers*. Her experience had been of a kind to teach her, rightly or wrongly, that the doubtful honour of a brief transit through a sorry world hardly called for effusiveness, even when the path was suddenly irradiated at some half-way point by daybeams rich as hers. But her strong sense that neither *she nor any human being deserved less than was given*, did not blind her to the fact that there were others receiving less who deserved much more. And in *being forced* to class herself among the more fortunate, she did not cease to wonder at the persistence of the unforeseen, when the one to whom such unbroken tranquillity had been accorded in the adult stage was she whose youth had seemed to teach that happiness was but the occasional episode in the general drama of pain. [my italics]

Beginning and end, penury to prosperity, a new generation, but the child's vision suggests absolutely no advance on the parent's. 'In the common phrase' sardonically places the subdued but negotiated ending that so many novels which trace lost illusions offer to ideological assimilation. Her unthankfulness mirrors the hard apathy of Susan's recognition of the predominance of the unforeseen. Moreover, that the only affirmation is that of the unforeseen seems to preclude meaningful narrative, since meaning cannot be taken from pure contingency. Thus it is really a frame. It does not enter the novel but encloses it. To be sure there are mnemonic echoes in the course of events but they tend to lie outside the story – I think of Mother Cuxom's comment on Susan's death, and even Elizabeth Jane's vigil and its 'chaos of consciousness'.

The only hint of causality is in Susan's 'except fair play' and its more clearly pessimistic reshaping in Elizabeth Jane's 'she nor any other human being deserved less than was given'. They both echo the reproach of 'General Principles', and help to mark off Hardy's pessimism from any comforting ideology of passiveness. Their bearing on the story is problematic since Henchard is not self-evidently more deserving than as his fate treats him. But Henchard never learns to articulate this pessimism – his only confrontation with it is 'sullen misery' – 'I am to suffer, I perceive' (19). It is the women, including Lucetta, who voice this wisdom which does not make any sense of one's life. 'Daybeams' invites itself to be read as 'daydreams' not merely in the sense of illusion but also in the sense that the women of the stories which we have seen anticipating this novel enact a 'nevertheless' which is the equivalent at least for a sense of freedom. Narrative is not, as it aspires to be in *The Return of the Native*, a product of the Law. It is rather a protest against it. This is confirmed by the withdrawal of judgement. The inertia of the reading of the real and the sense of injustice is the frame around the space in which narrative can be released. These conditions are universalized by the feminine wisdom around the text.[2] They do not give us the right to colonize the interior of the text either as realism (that is how it is) or as moral fable (that would have been the finer way to act).

Nevertheless the *effect* of this engendering is to constitute the narrative as *performance*. Miller, who like Gregor wants to legitimate the novel's epic appearance, says too casually that it begins *in medias res*.[2] Henchard emerges from and returns to nowhere. His life has no explicit continuity with the real historical process. He only *is* as through violent gesture he makes himself. The haytrusser of the second paragraph is not a man of character but an anthropological object, predominantly a costume making a stage entry. All Henchard's decisive acts are theatrical and the story is constructed around them – the auction, the oath, the banquet, the meeting with Susan in the arena, the embrace of Farfrae, the visit to the soothsayer, the greeting for the royal personage, the reading out of Lucetta's letters, his meeting with her in the arena, the fight with Farfrae, the last exit. The self-begotten, arranged significant and egocentric gesture is the dominant unifying force of the narrative. Susan and Elizabeth Jane enter Casterbridge as though it were a theatre: 'the lamplights now glimmered through the engirdling trees . . . rendering . . . the unlighted country without strangely solitary and vacant in aspect' (4). There is even a band to welcome them and their first glimpse of Henchard is in tableau, performing a role.

This theatricality does not enter and transform the novel: it is the very condition of its existence. This is confirmed by the lacuna between the prelude and the banquet. We have no indication of the details of Henchard's rise from journeyman to Mayor and are surely not intended to think that being teetotal is a guarantee of such success. The only explanation Hardy ever offers is the admittedly very significant 'the one talent of energy'.[3] We are given only a gesture and a quality. It is not within the terms of the novel that the life story should have general significance (as for example the almost contemporary *Rise of Silas Lapham* by William

Dean Howells). What we shall see, however, is that this is a positive absence. The enclosure within the theatre is there to be seen and placed against what lies outside it. Thus the rightly praised qualities of narrative power (Hardy's significant word is 'momentum') and localization do not enhance one another as they do in the earlier writers I have mentioned. Rather they inhibit one another – the curve of the career is retarded by the opacity of the environment as the typicality of the novel's world is left inert by the trajectory of the protagonist.

I must make a further discrimination. One of the perceptible developments in the European novel in the late nineteenth century is exactly this shift from interaction of character and environment to strict opposition.[4] Desire and its context become mutually exclusive in their demands. The obvious and pioneering example is *Madame Bovary* but we may think as well of the proleptic duck/pond image in the Prelude of *Middlemarch*. Different as Flaubert and Eliot are from one another, they precisely build a 'reality' out of that opposition. In *Madame Bovary*, this is an ironic reality by which the 'world' Emma finds herself in parodies her own romantic clichés by its own linguistic trivia. In *Middlemarch*, the opposition itself becomes the given so that, without submitting to the world, the protagonist can negotiate a viable treaty by submitting to her recognition of its inexorability. In *The Mayor of Casterbridge*, Hardy does not present this opposition to the protagonist, but to the reader. The 'world' of the novel is a retardation which threatens to demolish the narrative altogether. This happens in two ways: first, the presentation of Casterbridge itself, and second by the development of a different and exclusive narrative mode which is not the story of a man of character but the education of Elizabeth Jane.

As they turn into the High Street the theatrical formality that had greeted Susan and Elizabeth Jane disappears, giving way to a miscellany of houses and a detailed list of the objects in the shop windows:

> Scythes, reap-hooks, sheep-shears, bill-hooks, spades, mat-tocks, and hoes at the ironmonger's; bee-hives, butter-firkins, churns, milking stools and pails, hay-rakes, field-flagons, and seed lips at the cooper's; cart-ropes and plough-harness at the saddler's; carts, wheelbarrows, and mill gear at the wheel-wright's and machinist's; horse-embrocations at the chem-ist's; at the glover's and leather-cutter's, hedging gloves, thatchers' knee-caps, ploughmen's leggings, villagers' pattens and clogs. (4)

The list is clearly longer than its obvious function, the establish-
ment of the rural character of the town's trade, demands. The list
itself seems to take over, and it is not the only example – compare
the list of side shows at Weydon Priors (1), the interior of the
Three Mariners (7) or the catalogue of flowers when Elizabeth
Jane glimpses the rear gardens of the houses in the High Street (9);
and at the end of the novel (39) Grower becomes aware of the
skimmity ride via a list of eight ancient instruments. Such lists are
not synechdochic (to use Jakobsen's term about Tolstoi)[5] – they do
not indicate a whole world by indicative detail. They hold the text
up, clutter it. The stage is now a kind of back lot reminding us that
actual theatres are very untheatrical. The clutter of objects is
followed by the miscellaneous cacophony of church bells displacing
the town band. In this disorder Susan meets a woman with her
gown sleeves rolled up so high that the edge of her underlinen is
visible, with her skirt tucked up through her pocket hole, and
learns about the bread and the fault of the factor. With this
underside in our minds we recover the town band and the
theatrical window of the King's Arms. Our new view of Henchard
has been held up by an intrusive world of objects and actualities.
This happens throughout the novel. At every turn, Henchard's
sequence of gestures is undermined or opposed by the reluctant
other of the contingent world. It never is as simple as scripture
history.

The first effect of this is to establish an archaeology of modern
Casterbridge which is linked with the survival of Roman objects
and which in turn confirms the negating function of the ideological
frame. Henchard chooses the Roman amphitheatre as the arena of
his reconciliation with Susan seeking privacy but for us establishing another theatrical scene carefully prepared. The survival of
ancient skeletons makes more for a gap than meaningful continuity: 'they had lived so long ago, their time was so unlike the
present, their hopes and motives were so widely removed from
ours, that between them and the living there seemed to stretch a
gulf too wide for even a spirit to pass' (11). Memory is active only
as a deterrent for the meeting of happy lovers, and its 'dismal
privacy' discourages the cricket matches started there. The story of
unjust cruelty to the eighteenth-century murderess hangs over it
and the knowledgeable spectator can fleetingly imagine the
cruelties and crimes which have taken place, but without that
offering any perspective on the present except as warning of its
coming obliteration. The physical comparison is to the spittoon of
the Jotuns, which links it to the squalid social underclothing of the
Three Mariners. The object world and the social reality which

emerges from it resist the significance Henchard's gestures confer on his life. It is there as the inert other.

Two further points emerge from these moments of entrance and encounter. The first is about Casterbridge society. Just as we have no details of Henchard's rise, so in the opening movement (which ends at chapter 19) we have little of Henchard's own milieu. The most specific image of social life is the town's lower end, as though it were dominated by the tosspots of the Three Mariners and the dregs of Mixen Lane. We have little sense of the class to which Henchard has risen. Thus social life, like the world of objects, operates as a separate and disruptive underworld above which Henchard acts out his life, and which both threatens him and provides a residual domain into which he will fall. It will, of ourse, operate its own satiric theatre through the skimmity ride, and it is at this level that the past, Susan, or the furmity woman or Newsom (who literally crosses a plank into Durnover), reasserts itself as a third form of resistance in addition to objects and social relations, another kind of theatre. This reminds us of the servants' parody of high life in *The Hand of Ethelberta* but it is taken much further: 'We be bruckle folk here – the best o' us is hardly honest sometimes what with the hard winters, and so many mouths to fill' (8). It is characteristically ironic that Henchard's career should be brought to an end by a drunken old woman pissing against a church wall. Society does not work here as 'men and morals in 1830' works in Stendhal's *Le Rouge et le Noir* to limit and educate. It is only a resident contingency.

Finally, the scene in the Ring ends with a dialogue which points to yet another level of limitation, arguably the most important:

> 'But just one word. Do you forgive me, Susan?'
> She murmured something; but seemed to find it difficult to frame her answer.
> 'Never mind – all in good time,' said he. 'Judge me by my future works. Good bye.'

As always he is trying to make it as simple as scripture history (with a ready-made biblical reference) seeking for a *word* of forgiveness, asking to be judged by what *he makes happen*. But the response he evokes is inaudible, and just as Susan has already upstaged him once at the wife auction (at which she finally takes the initiative) so now, as we shall learn, she holds him by an ironic knowledge that he will only learn when he speaks what he thinks is the truth to Elizabeth Jane. Just as the furmity woman 'presides' over the prelude, Susan presides, by her stratagem, over the first movement of the actual drama (as opposed to the theatre). There is a whole dimension which is the preserve of the silenced woman that undermines the self creating will of the man of character.[6]

These points merely ironize the plot, though it is important to remember that they can have two different statuses. We can either see them as dramatic ironies, by which Henchard's one talent is seen to be lacking (sweetness and light, presumably, to complete the Arnoldian implication of 'energy'). Or, as the radical level at which they operate seems to make more likely (though at present it is difficult to see the purpose), an irony against the reader's propensity to be caught up in the narrative as though it were anything but an illusion. The illusion would be comparable to theatre, and confirmed by the implication of the frame that the drama of human life is insignificant in the play of time. The story thus seems to be on the premise of the 'nevertheless' enacted in the short stories that precede it. But this is contradicted by the fact that the other voice which provides the static ironic questions is not the voice of a higher power (an overview that we might expect from the tragic vision, as in formal terms it is in *The Dynasts*), but precisely the edict of the disprivileged, the very agents of that 'nevertheless' we have found to be the decisive motif of the stories, who act only in response to the power imposed on them by Henchard. It would be gratifying at this point to produce a Brechtian novel out of a Lacanian hat, revolutionary theatre from irrepressible other. Alas, revolutions do not happen in bed, even when all they aspire to be is literary texts.

Instead, Hardy develops the static ironies within the domain of an alternative mode of narration which positively embodies the exclusions of Henchard's story. Elizabeth Jane enters the novel preoccupied with respectability, trying to stop her mother from speaking to the furmity woman, undertaking the waitressing in order to secure respectable accommodation, finding Farfrae attractive because he is so 'respectable and educated' (8). Her desire, we are told, is to become 'a woman of wider knowledge, higher repute – "better" as she termed it' (4). The vocabulary indicates a mode of social aspiration different from Henchard's. It is not to do with conquest but with acceptance and its mode of belonging is not self-creation but awareness. As waitress she is 'a spectator of all that went on without herself being particularly seen' (8). Later, she is 'that silent observing woman' (8). At the same time, she is 'occupied with an inner chamber of ideas and has 'slight need for visible objects' (15). But this does not contradict her need for acceptance: at the lowest point of her fortunes, when her mother has died, Henchard rejected her and Farfrae seems unavailable, she is 'construed by not a single contiguous being' (20). The inner chamber of ideas, like the pursuit of respectability and self-improvement, is a function of her awareness which at every point contrasts her with Henchard. She is, as many critics have noted, a centre of consciousness.[7] She comes out of that history of the novel which privileges education, the encounter with the world not as adventure but as a real to find oneself in.

This means that everything I have said about the existence of Henchard's character has to be reversed. First, she does appear *in medias res* – she already has a history, a formative past which gives her an identity (Hardy stresses how much she resembles her mother's youth). Her attraction to Farfrae is based on her *experience*: 'He seemed to feel exactly as she felt about life and its surroundings – that they were a tragical rather than a comical thing' (8) and her story is about finding a place. The excluded middle of Henchard's rise is compensated by our detailed knowledge of her emergence and development. More importantly, she becomes the agent of a middle Casterbridge.

The novel's first movement is completed by Susan's death. The first seventeen chapters are preoccupied with Henchard's subjective momentum – the oath, the remarriage, the adoption of and quarrel with Farfrae. By the end of chapter 17, Henchard is faced with Farfrae's business rivalry. Hardy now reminds us that Casterbridge is not merely the tosspots of Durnover, but 'the large farmers, corn merchants, millers, auctioneers and others' (this threatens to become another list) who dominate the town. Henchard is now seen as one amongst many. Moreover, names taken from earlier texts, Everdene, Shiner, Darton, give Casterbridge an explicit and historical continuity with a 'real' world (a Balzacian trick to endorse his claim that he was merely the secretary of society). We also become aware that there are other mayors – Farfrae is as eponymous as Henchard. Here too Henchard is compared to Bellerophon, a heroic figure systematically punished for the privileges he received from the gods, and the rider of Pegasus, thrown because he rode too close to the sun. Hardy is only now asking us to see the theatre of Henchard's story as a complex world. It is only as simple as scripture history as long as Henchard has space to make it so (Hardy's note on the biblical narratives comments on their apparent naturalness and their actual artificiality). But theatrical space is constituted by the complex world it sets itself apart from.

The next chapter opens with a comment about Elizabeth Jane: 'There came a shock which had been foreseen . . . by Elizabeth, as the box passenger foresees the approaching jerk.' The spectator whose role has been established from the beginning is moved by this into a position of privileged centrality. The chapter which follows is about the death of Susan, though it begins with the letter from Lucetta which Henchard looks at 'as at a picture, a vision, a vista of past enactments'. Characteristically it leads him to *resolve* to marry Lucetta if Susan dies. At the same time, Elizabeth Jane watches her mother die, and we have a complex paragraph in which 'the subtle souled girl' asks herself why she was born, why things are as they are and what, above all, in a Paterian image, 'that chaos called consciousness, which spun in her at this moment like a top, tended to'. The contrast is explicit – vista and chaos, resolution and subtlety. Elizabeth Jane is on a different level. The contrast is pursued systematically: Henchard feels dissevered and has to seek 'some human object for pouring out his heart upon'. Her loneliness is that she is unconstrued, depressed by her own 'superfluity'. She learns to take the universe seriously, but misery '*taught* him nothing more than defiant endurance of it' (my italics). Her chaos of consciousness is contrasted with what, in Paterian terms, is a more primitive sense of 'the scheme of some sinister intelligence'. Elizabeth Jane is modern and her modernity completes the marginalizing process which is inherent in the structure.

For us, that is, because it is not a development in her character. She has foreseen this shock, she already feels life to be tragical. It is rather that she is offered to the reader as a point of view at this turn in the novel. Between chapters 19 and 20, she turns the novel inside out. In chapter 19 Henchard's realization of Elizabeth Jane's true paternity leads him to seek a landscape of his misery – he is still trying to impose his subjectivity on the inert exterior (though Hardy's comment that 'it impressed Henchard more than he expected' is proleptic). The chapter ends firmly within his experience and its primitive, scriptural parameters: 'the fruition of the whole scheme was such dust and ashes as this'.

Now look at the next sentence which opens chapter 20. 'Of all the enigmas which ever confronted a girl there can have been seldom one like that which followed Henchard's announcement of himself to Elizabeth as her father.' It is not just a shift in point of view. The shift reconstructs the (to us) known subjectivity of Henchard as enigma, the riddle. In becoming the father, Henchard has become the Law which speaks only darkly and has to be interpreted. Acknowledging her father, Elizabeth locates a mystery whose source we know but which is none the less present to us through Elizabeth, who takes over the narrative. I am not overreading a simple plot device – the fact that the mystery is brought about by Henchard finding that he is not the biological father only serves to remind us that Hardy is as aware as Engels of the cultural protection necessary to biological fatherhood.[8] Acquiring a father, she no longer understands. Life becomes ordeal as soon as she enters the family and it is significant that the ordeal focuses on Henchard's criticism of her language and on the *the improper masculinity of her handwriting*. Henchard now retreats into his own history. The dinner at the King's Arms is his Austerlitz. The Napoleonic reference clasps him into a legendary status (though this is only the first stage of his marginalization).

Both are released from the nullity caused by Susan's death by the arrival of Lucetta, but this link only highlights the contrast between them. For Henchard, Lucetta will be another human object around which his sentiments will gather 'by an almost mechanical transfer' (that is, by momentum, narrative). For Elizabeth Jane, Lucetta is an extension of vision in two crucial ways. First, by installing herself at High Hall, Elizabeth shares with Lucetta a voyeuristic privilege watching the dramas of the market place, which Lucetta justifies in exactly the terms of Elizabeth Jane's sense of superfluity: 'I look as at a picture merely . . . But it is amusing to look for somebody one knows in a crowd, even if one does not want him. It takes off the oppressiveness of being surrounded by a throng, and having no point of junction with it through a single individual' (23). She too is unconstrued, and she constructs herself through knowledge and sentiment.

But secondly, Elizabeth Jane watches Lucetta, and the rivalry of Henchard and Farfrae. She now becomes the 'discerning silent witch' (24) who can metonymically complete the growing romance of Lucetta and Farfrae, and finally, at the tea table where Henchard and Farfrae do battle over a piece of bread and butter, the 'evangelist' at the darkening table like some Tuscan painting of the two disciples supping at Emmaeus (which is surely, as Eliot is to exploit in *The Waste Land*, the least simple bit of scripture history). The contrast between her knowing and Henchard's energy is explicit: 'to Elizabeth Jane it was plain as the town pump that Donald and Lucetta were incipient lovers . . . But Henchard was constructed on too large a scale to discern such minutiae as these by any evening light which to him were as the notes of an insect that lie above the compass of the human ear.' (26) The discerning, silent witch/evangelist is needed because what now asserts itself against the momentum of Henchard's character is the social comedy of the middle range. Neither Mixen Lane nor a sinister intelligence will overthrow Henchard but the controlled adaptive capacity of Farfrae, of the middle world which keeps emotion in its proper place (in songs and in sentimental but practical arrangements) and which goes for modest but reliable success, sincere but tepid affections. Farfrae survives because he is a divided character, and it is this division that brings him into contact with the role-playing Lucetta, and destines him ultimately for the Minerva-like Elizabeth Jane. Significantly Hardy feels it necessary to change the whole narrative structure so that we witness the 'fall' of Henchard as a transformation of the novel's epistemology which progressively marginalizes and diminishes him, so that he goes from 'character' to enigma (legend) and finally to bull. Clearly this is his own image but also an image for Elizabeth Jane's scrutiny: 'she paused to look at the bull, now rather to be pitied with his bleeding nose, having perhaps rather intended a practical joke than a murder' (29). Insofar as he enters the novel at all in this section, it is as a superstitious rustic whose magisterial role, for example, is compared to that of Justice Shallow. The function of Elizabeth Jane's narrative is not to enable us to see Henchard more clearly, but to see what he cannot see, that at the centre of Casterbridge is the 'human', historical world of romantic love, practical marriage and improving machinery. Life is 'tragical' in such a world only in so far as it is lonely, unconstrued by a contiguous being. Together we can be as a bee and a butterfly in league for life. Marriage is the bourgeois articulation of work and beauty.

The obvious ironies of the Lucetta/Farfrae relationship should not blind us to the serious task of Elizabeth Jane's narrative. There is a level at which we must take Lucetta seriously as well. When she asks Elizabeth Jane how long she has before she loses her charm, the younger woman answers with devastating unsentimentality, 'five years . . . Or with a quiet life as many as ten. With no love you might calculate on ten.' (24). Elizabeth Jane's privilege offers a global feminization of the text by which the apparent mediocrities of even the flighty show an access to time which Henchard's momentum lacks. Howe has written shrewdly of the insidious attraction to male fantasy of the wife-selling. Henchard's story is an adventure, but it is one that depends on silencing and opposing the experience of time and love with which the oppressed women question it. But this is problematic, for without that exclusion of awareness, without the 'fetishism' which appropriates the external world as the object of desire, there can be no Henchard. The two modes of narrative do not contrast, they exclude one another.

The immediate effect of Elizabeth Jane's narrative domination is to provide an ambience in which Farfrae can supersede Henchard.

Henchard deals with Farfrae as a less manly character and the irony of this becomes evident just before the turnover when, in chapter 26, Henchard starts to laugh at the Scotsman's dancing and then realizes that however effeminate it might seem it makes him attractive to women, 'every girl being in a *coming on disposition* towards one who understood the poetry of motion as well as he' (my italics). Although we are never asked to view Farfrae sympathetically we are made to recognize that he takes account of femininity and that this is crucial to his success. (I haven't defined 'femininity' deliberately, because I am not trying to indicate a concept that has any status outside the text. By 'femininity' here I simply mean that set of attributes which is explicitly associated with the sensibilities of the female characters in the novel.)

It is at precisely this point in the narrative, as Farfrae becomes a narrative challenge and Elizabeth Jane becomes the narrative authority, that the novel raises the question of the subtitle. Commenting on Farfrae's success in Casterbridge, Hardy writes:

> but most probably luck had little to do with it. Character is fate, said Novalis, and Farfrae's character was just the reverse of Henchard's who might not inaptly be described as Faust has been described. As a vehement gloomy being who had quitted the ways of vulgar men, without light to guide him on a better way. (17)

The word has acquired a second meaning from the implication of the subtitle. 'A man of character' implies a quality. At no point do we sympathize with Henchard either and, of course, Hardy makes no attempt to enter his point of view after chapter 2, but 'character' is certainly evaluative. Henchard is heroic because he has character (though this too is ambiguous, as the most intelligent reviewer of the novel, R. H. Hutton realized; to have character and to be 'a character' are both evaluative but without the same values). By the time it is re-used in chapter 17, it is a purely descriptive term – your fate is decided by whatever character you have. It raises the question 'Who is the Mayor of Casterbridge?' It is, of course, Henchard, except that for the final part of the novel it is Farfrae. It is Henchard because Henchard is the character in the novel and Farfrae, the divided man, has no character all. But in terms of the social history that the novel portrays, the Mayor is whoever reaches the top of the tree, and in this sense Farfrae supersedes Henchard. And it is his character which accounts for it.

There is certainly an ideological aporia implicit in this semantic shift. But it can be subjected to two readings. On the one hand, it is a degeneration myth in which the unitary being of character is overtaken by the delegated and compartmentalized personality working through machine and system, thus displacing desire by awareness as the motivating factor of development. As such the novel would take its place in a long series of texts throughout the nineteenth century, such as Tennyson's *The Morte d'Arthur*, Carlyle's 'The Hero as God' and Arnold's 'Balder Dead', the most recent and radical example of which would have been Morris's *Sigurd the Volsung*,[9] and thus look forward to the kind of celebration of unity of being or character as opposed to personality that we find in Yeats or Lawrence.[10] Equally, however, the vocabulary makes the story available as a positivist fable, by which the fetishist whose only talent is energy is overtaken by monotheistic intelligence. Of course, the novel might hesitate between these two which are really opposite evaluations of an identical process. Thus, for example, to cite an earlier model, Mrs Gaskell's *Sylvia's Lovers* presents such a shift as a dialectical drama. Hardy's novel, however, poses the choice as one of narrative method. How you see Henchard depends on whether life is to be presented as simple as scripture history or as the awareness of a discerning silent witch. Neither mode prevails. And Elizabeth Jane's reality only prevails for a while, long enough to show us that it is by no means as simple as scripture history, but not long enough to avert the intrusive theatre of the skimmity ride. Or to put it the other way round, the aware narrative of Elizabeth Jane does not preclude the diminution of scale of which it is aware. Elizabeth Jane knows that what she sees is too small for Henchard. The two narrative procedures, on the contrary, offer *us* two different readings of the novel and thus may be thought of as precisely being about the ambiguous nature of character.

The whole issue is clarified in the climactic episode of the novel in which, after the visit of the Royal Personage, Henchard momentarily confronts Farfrae in the barn, one arm tied behind his back, 'face to face – man and man' (38). Farfrae's initial response is in terms of awareness, 'what does it all mean', and his resource is reflection, 'wait till you cool; and you will see things the same way as I do'. Henchard's grim joke in response to this meets awareness with energy since for him to cool down means to be a corpse. The turn, however, derives from something quite different. In response to Farfrae's imputation of Henchard's desire to take his life, Henchard is defeated by the recall of his love. Confronted with memory, Henchard ceases to be a man. Once again his heroic stature is undermined by the femininity of narrative but this time from within: 'so thoroughly subdued was he that he remained on the sacks in a crouching attitude, unusual for a man, and for such a man. Its womanliness sat tragically on the figure of so stern a piece of virility.' 'Tragically' implies downfall, of course, but the downfall entails the gain of something else; 'womanliness' is not merely emasculation – it is also bound up with an excluded knowledge. When Farfrae has left him, Henchard remains behind 'till the thin shades thickened to opaque obscurity'.

Thus *The Mayor of Casterbridge* is not the reproduction of an impasse but the representation of conflicting modes of narrative totalization. It is an intervention in the current debate about the art of fiction far more effective than the inadequate essays Hardy wrote during the eighties in response to editorial demand. R. L. Stevenson, in the first flush of success of *Treasure Island* which James criticized because it lay outside the realm of experience, drew distinctions between the novel of character and the dramatic novel which concentrated great passions.[11] The Henchard reading of the novel places it somewhere between the novel of adventure and the dramatic novel, but outside the Jamesian novel of character. Stevenson's novel is important in the social history of fiction publishing because it owed some of its success to the fact that a new publisher, Cassell, was prepared to break the rigid publishing process by which novels appeared first in a three-volume format which made them too expensive for the private buyer. *The Mayor of Casterbridge* was published in two volumes, generally thought of as the worst format commercially, and it sold badly. It is as though it was hesitating between adventure and analysis. Moreover, the transition from theatrical to analytic modes recalls Stephen's distinction between Fielding and Richardson as the masculine and feminine modes of narration.[12]

In ideological terms it seems to propose a choice between emasculation discourse which leads to one strand of modernism – the phallocentric pastoralism of Yeats, Eliot and Lawrence – and the feminization of narrative which leads to James and Woolf, who deploy the obscure life as a strategic escape from possession. On the other hand, Hardy's novel seems to ironize both, since, as we have seen, neither assimilate the ideological frame, and both depend on limiting modes of awareness – fetishism and respectability. But the essential achievement of *The Mayor of Casterbridge* is that in presenting these two readings as at once mutually exclusive and equally valid it is forced to produce a third concept of character which is in fact inaugurated in chapter 31 and which is indicated programmatically in the barn episode in the image of the man crouching like a woman in the opaque obscurity of the thickening shadows. The marriage has taken place, and Elizabeth Jane withdrawn to do her netting. We momentarily return to the theatrical mode of the first movement, as Henchard is described as passing 'the ridge of his prosperity'. Note first that it is not his act that causes his downfall but the sudden appearance of the act out of the past where it has not been put in perspective by the continuous light of memory. Henchard falls theatrically because his life is presented theatrically, and not narratively.

But more than this, the downfall is not singly caused. The return of the furmity woman is only socially 'a startling fillip downwards' (31) – the descent is completed by an accompanying commercial loss of buoyancy which Hardy traces through in some detail as a combination of rashness and loss of credibility. Hardy now effects a remarkable withdrawal from the tragic potentialities of the story: 'the details of his failure were of the ordinary kind'. The 'scene' of his meeting with the creditors lacks the finality it might have on two counts. First, when he offers his watch, the creditors refuse and see his whole career 'pictured distinctly', thus aligning them with Elizabeth Jane, who watches the proceedings feeling 'quite tearful'. So that the event is realized within an ambience of awareness that both diminishes Henchard's dramatic importance and undermines judgement. At the same time, after he is examined, he himself is thrown 'into a reverie' when he catches sight of Elizabeth Jane.

In the following chapters we see traced out in detail two processes which make Henchard 'a changed man' (45). It is a further sign of Hardy's preoccupation with the aesthetic terms of his narrative that he should try to define this phrase: 'as far, that is, as change of emotional basis can justify such a radical phrase'. First, Henchard becomes one of a class, 'les misérables' (32). (Hugo had died in 1885, so that his practice as a novelist was much under discussion.) And secondly, from within the obscurity of that class he acquires reflectiveness. No longer the self-made man, in either the formal or the ideological senses of the word, he becomes the model of the new Hardy protagonist. As Mrs Yeobright, the mother, makes the ideological journey to the 'nevertheless' across man's place in nature, Henchard, the father who is not a father, makes the formal journey from the artificiality of the world historical figure, through the protected apartness of the middle of the road heroine, to the exposed, gesturing, trapped but not spectating protagonist who is not representative but who re-presents, makes representations.

The detail with which Hardy makes this transformation of his project is extraordinary. In chapter 32, Henchard comes, 'as other unfortunates had come before him' to the bridges whose 'speaking countenances' inscribe another history than that of the official record. Like the amphitheatre, they form an archaeology, but not one that is inexorably cut off from the present. On the contrary, in six paragraphs, Hardy creates a context for Henchard to become part of that which, on the one hand, establishes the generalized conditions of failure, and on the other names those who had preceded him. The distinction between the two bridges is, of course, vital. Hardy is by no means allowing Henchard to become working-class, but the only difference between the shabby and the shabby genteel failures is the attitude to publicity. What is crucial is that Henchard is one of many. When he goes to work at Farfrae's yard, his accommodation is described with a phrase, 'broken in', which recalls the opening of *A Laodicean*. When he thinks of Lucetta as being wise in her generation he is echoing a phrase from the gospels which contrasts the children of this world with the children of light in their attitude to God and Mammon. Henchard takes on himself the voice of the oppressed, and although the psalm he sings at the rescension of his oath is as theatrical as the oath itself, it is worth noting that it is a curse against oppressors.

Certainly to some extent what Hardy has moved towards is the kind of social realism which is beginning to be written in the slum novels of the eighties,[13] and this again would confirm this novel as an intervention in the era of discussion since its main protagonists were preoccupied with socially aware mimesis. But obviously Hardy is never that simple. The first phase of the third movement is ostensibly as theatrical as the first, and Elizabeth Jane's function is to watch helplessly from the sidelines. Henchard ends his curse, and plans not one but three 'grand catastrophes' (34), the reading of the letters to Farfrae, the humiliation of Lucetta in the ring, and the self-presentation to the royal personage. But note that these are *rejected* theatrical moments: 'in cold blood he could not do it. Such a wrecking of hearts appalled even him' (34). Awareness disables. In the following chapter, more specifically, with Lucetta (who of course has dressed down for the scene) he is 'unmanned'. By being unmanned, he achieves a solidarity with this other ill-used woman. Theatre is accompanied here by an insistently limiting vocabulary. The grand catastrophe is seen as the practical joke. Henchard says at the disoathing that he is a practical joker. Elizabeth Jane fears that he will play 'some practical joke' on Farfrae (34), and Henchard describes his reading of the letters as 'only a sort of practical joke'. It is limiting in two opposing ways. In these terms, it keeps the theatrical gesture at bay in the name of a supervening, non-theatrical pity. One remarkable extension of this is Newson's attitude to Henchard's deceit, which is so decisive for the respectable Elizabeth Jane and merely a joke for him. On the other hand, of course, in terms of the action, the major theatrical event, the skimmity ride, is also a joke. The difference is that it is not permissive, and thus for Jopp is not a joke but a retaliation. (Note Newson's response, however, which is one of amused tolerance. Elizabeth Jane, of course, owes her origins to the fact that Newson joined in Henchard's original joke. Hardy was very proud of belonging to the Rabelais Club.)

Thus, in this apparently casual denouement, a double and crucial process in inaugurated. On the one hand, Henchard learns to become a woman. Not only negatively, by being unmanned by pity and remorse, but also positively by solicitousness (he cooks Elizabeth Jane's breakfast, which will remind us of *The Hand of Ethelberta*), which also implies awareness. The final stages of the novel, explicitly taking Henchard from being a rebel to being one who lives in leaden gloom, also establishes him as a consciousness, whose final perception, of course, is precisely that which the novel has established on his own self-creation: 'He had no wish to make an arena a second time of a world that had become a mere painted scene to him' (44).

But this takes him far beyond that feminine awareness which is the education of Elizabeth Jane. Indeed she is marginalized by the triumph of the respectability to which in the first part of the novel she attends, so that when *she* triumphs at the end it is as one with an almost sardonic wisdom, that of Minerva. For what Henchard learns, as the biological father enters the story to defeat the value of the lesson, is that through the non-biological parenthood of the daughter he has rejected there is a possible dream of the future. Of course it cannot be contrived, but even in the self-obliteration of the end, his story is retained through one to whose parent he has been 'kind-like'. It is, of course, an echo of the Fool and Lear, but Henchard has not died as Mayor, only as the journeyman he once was, and there is no Cordelia with whom to share his death. Nothing to remember. But that contrast with Lear is positive too. At the end of Shakespeare's tragedy, the characters lament that they will never experience what the dead protagonist has known. The Hardy protagonist does not have that kind of privilege. Character is enacted on a painted stage, the chamber of the mind leads only to the conclusion that no one gets as much as they deserve. But beyond this there is the story itself, the general drama of pain.

Confronting the issues that confronted the novelists of his time emerging from the certainties of characterization into the problem of the relationship between perception and action, Hardy works out his own very distinctive solution, which is that the man of character becomes that only when he has no name, no gender, no social flag. 'Character' is at the heart of the novel's aesthetic, and it is right that having worked through to the overall ideological 'nevertheless', Hardy's first major narrative should open out the dualism embedded in the concept to evolve an entirely other sense of being. To look and be looked at are separate forms of subjective containment. There is a third term which is neither the fiction of a lost community nor the myth of universal individualism, but the returned question of the obscure life.

What Is and What Might Be: *The Woodlanders*

Near the beginning of *Père Goriot*, Balzac depicts the reader of his obscure Parisian tragedy complacently sitting in his armchair to be entertained by the human misery of the story, and in despair abandons him and gets on with the novel anyway. Hardy starts his equally obscure tale, set, indeed, outside the gates of the world, with a specific role for the reader – 'the rambler who for old association's sake should trace the forsaken coach road . . . from Bristol to the south shore of England'. Ramblers have leisure and can view the scenery from an unimpinging distance. Here, however, the view does not hold out: for the coach road is not empty but 'forsaken'. Swinburne's 'Forsaken Garden' is cut off from memory but the act of writing reconstructs a lost world of pain. The retarding language of Hardy's opening by which the rambler is transformed to 'loiterer' (which has in addition a trace of criminality) upon whose mind the gay charioteers, blistered soles and the tears that have wetted the road return, 'exchanges' a simple absence for the incubus of the forlorn.

Novel-readers are protected from what happens because it has happened. You can shake your head and understand and put the book down. Misery, as Benjamin said, becomes a commodity.[14] Forcing on his reader a role that carries its own opposing incubus, Hardy, by a double negative, the denial of the denial that is the reader's immunity, implicates us in what we witness. It is not only what we see, 'what is' (to which we can say, 'so be it, amen') but 'the contrast of what is with what might be' that we are forced to confront. *The Woodlanders* is the novel of an unfulfilled intention, of an action which is primarily to be defined by the exclusion of what might happen, leaving the reader with the question why. It is thus the prelude of the last novels. If *The Mayor of Casterbridge* reworks the intersubjective bases of human relationships, *The Woodlanders* enacts a transformation of the literary practice itself.

Not surprisingly, since it lacks a strong story and lacks focus on a single dominant character (that is, seems to invert the form of *The Mayor of Casterbridge*), it has become Hardy's gift to the dominant technique of literary analysis, practical criticism. Its metaphors and themes invite an organic, spatial reading confirmed by its apparent ambiguity and multifacetedness. Even those who resist finding it mellow, or elegiac or merely polysemic (getting comfort from a totalizing process which does not violate the complexity of its concerns) tend to decompose it into co-existing elements which merely turn the organic on its head.[15] My starting point is the recalcitrance of Hardy's fiction which the latter affirm, but I have to go further and argue that the later novels, of which this is the first, do not merely, like Giles's house, jut into the road, but, dismantled, create spaces in which phaetons are overturned. Hardy doesn't suddenly start showing things as they are, but shows them with an offensive strategy whose design is to make the reader take responsibility for what is happening.

Let us start with the famous imagery, which is usually taken to juxtapose a rich pastoral sense of the natural world against a Darwinian fear of its underlying struggle. It depends above all on sequence. Hardy opens with an exchange of one sense (simple absence) for another (incubus of the forlorn) which sets the pattern for the whole. Frequently it exchanges the picturesque for the grotesque. Thus chapter 4 opens with a positive and descriptive phrase, 'there was now a distinct manifestation of morning in the air', but leads the reader to a more precise and macabre simile, 'the bleared white image of a sunless winter day emerged like a dead born child'. We recover from this only to receive a second blow by starting with a slightly patronizing image of the animal life retreating before the arrival of humanity and moving it towards a disconcerting climax: 'owls that had been catching mice in the outhouses, rabbits that had been eating wintergreens in the gardens, and stoats that had been sucking the blood of the rabbits'. Later Fitzpiers and Giles driving under the trees see shapes like large tadpoles, which is gruesome enough, but when they are explained (as pheasants at roost) it is in the context of a report of a gun (16). Even summer fullness is associated with green sickness and pock marks (20). It seems characteristic that when Hardy contrasts the boredom of townee Fitzpiers with the 'interests' the woods hold for more knowledgeable people that those interests should be in 'the strange mistakes' made by the more sanguine trees and the 'sanguine errors of impulsive birds' (17). Again and again we return to the spectral, the gloomy, the deformed and the diseased. In April, the mother of the months, the moon (an allusion to the situation of woman, as in *The Revolt of Islam*[16]) appears through the leafless trees 'starved and bent to a mere skeleton' and at the end of summer, 'the smooth surfaces of glossy plants come out like weak lidless eyes'. If there is no hysterical storm, there is 'mesmeric passivity' (24). It is not a juxtaposition of ways of seeing. There is a constant strategy of disenchantment, an insistence that this most 'natural' of settings is latent with horror which is always there. Of all Hardy's novels it is the one which owes most to the post-Baudelairean decadence.[17]

My comparisons to Balzac and Baudelaire draw attention to the precise nature of this imagery, however, which is that of urban degeneration – infant mortality, malformation, madness, crime. That this is programmatic is clear from the much analysed passage introducing the tree auction:

> They went noiselessly over mats of starry moss, rustled through interspersed tracts of leaves, skirted trunks with spreading roots whose mossed rinds made them like hands wearing green gloves, elbowed old elms and ashes with great forks in which stood pools of water that overflowed on rainy days and ran down their stems in green cascades. On older trees still than these huge lobes of fungi grew like lungs. Here, as everywhere, the Unfulfilled Intention, which makes life what it is, was as obvious as it could be among the depraved crowds of a city slum. (7)

There is nothing indecisive about this passage. It deliberately lures us into the prettiness of the opening image to punish us with the increasingly grotesque detail which the penetration into the wood entails. And then it moves us from the specificity of the descriptive to 'everywhere'. Intention is an important word – it takes us back to forsaken and forlorn, from mere absence to the presence of waste and failure. If it is a totalizing concept taken from Schopenhauer or von Hartmann, it is none the less functional, important because it encapsulates a dual process of movement (intention) and moving on from defeat, abandonment, unfulfilment. This leads him to overthrow the pastoral frame explicitly by likening the waste of nature with the waste of the city – the *slum* (which is, if not a neologism, a very striking word in the context of all the literature about urban decay which appears in the mid-eighties).[18]

Finally this deformation is linked with *exploitation* – the lichen eating the vigour of the stalk, the ivy strangling the promising sapling. Later in the passage the Woodlanders' walking sticks are compared to the way in which the Chinese mould human forms into grotesque toys by constant compression (of course, Hardy is referring to the compression of girls' feet which specifically brings it within the terms of the exploitation of women). Nature is grotesque, then, because it recalls the depravity of the city and echoes the exploitation that is at the heart of that depravity.

Hardy is not suddenly turning on nature, for he never has sought the support the romantics found in it and Arnold lost. The non-human world is fully imaged in Knight's ordeal on the cliff, and the central affirmation, as we have seen, is the gospel of the body which is written in the language of successful agriculture, which means the intelligent control and exploitation of natural forces. In fact, so far from embodying post-Darwinian disillusion with nature, these images are, as we shall see, the basis of a radical new naturalism. At present we have a reversal of the relationship of man and nature on Egdon Heath where the intractibility of the landscape (which is not the real, but a point of view) reduces human endeavour to a trace. Here, the landscape bears all the marks of its humanization: the central image is of the trees subjected to social interactions – auctioning, planting, felling, barking: 'Each tree doomed to the flaying process was first attacked by Upjohn ... an operation comparable to the little toilette of the executioner's victim' (19). Contrast this with the sheep arising like Aphrodite from the foam of her shorn fleece. Agriculture here is violation, whereas in the earlier novel it is a form of enhancement. The effect of the reversal of the man/nature analogy is to throw back any distancing – to say that if society images nature, nature reflects society and there is no comfort in that. Human endeavour is not inadequate but all too effective.

More importantly, it brings to the centre implications that are marginal to the affirmation of work and love in *Far From the Madding Crowd*: that the communal nature of work is shadowed by actual conditions of production, that the wheat actually embodies itself not as food but as its exchange value, that the gospel of the body actually sends unmarried mothers to the workhouse. Above all they are presented dialectically. If the imagery reflects victimization, it is also a threat, as were the slums of London for the worried respectable classes of the 1880s. The images of the forlorn speak of the consequences of oppression – infant mortality, premature ageing, deformity, immorality and so on, but they also speak of crime and rebellion. When Giles is forced to use his old pack of cards, the pictures 'wore a decayed expression of feature, as if they were an impecunious decayed dynasty, *hiding in the obscure slums*' (10; my italics). Fitzpiers and Mrs Charmond disappear into the gloom of the lawn, and Fitzpiers is 'speedily absorbed into the duskiness of the trees' (34). Barber Percomb is lost, as are Félice and Grace. The obscurity generated by the exploitation, whether we are talking about the slums which are generated by capitalist industry, or the woods which are the site of capitalist agriculture (for Melbury is not the same as Oak or Bathsheba despite his memory of work), is always threateningly there. Later, when Grace looks out into the storm, the wind is like a rioting mob 'trampling and climbing over the roof, making branches creak, springing out of the trees upon the chimney, popping its head into the flue; and shrieking and blaspheming at every corner of the walls' (41). Naturalizing the slums (as the product of Social Darwinism) is a common way of accommodating them. To bring the slums back into nature reconstitutes them as a domain of obscurity, to reactivate them not merely as waste but as part of the process, disruptive, Other. It is as though Mixen Lane (itself a 'back slum') had ceased to be an area and become instead a force.

Once we have seen the process of image-making as a strategic sequence of discomfiture and not merely as a monumentalized metaphoric trace (there is no monument in *The Woodlanders*), the sequence of the narrative becomes strategic too. As Jacobus has shown,[19] the novel has a clear tripartite structure in which the first fifteen chapters deal with the relationship of Grace and Giles (Melbury's first unfilfilled intention to make reparation to Giles' father), chapters 16–30 with the relationship of Grace and Fitzpiers (or Melbury's second unfulfilled intention to make his daughter a lady) and chapters 31–48 with the dialectical consequences of that double failure. There is on the one hand the positive emergence of new kinds of relationship, and on the other the closure brought about by the deaths of Félice and Giles and the reassimilation of Grace and Fitzpiers in an ironized second start. At the end of the first movement, Giles 'retired into the background'; at the end of the second he is moved forward again as the new object of Grace's desire. Both movements end with an ineffective written message – the writing on the wall which is Marty's message edited by Grace, and Melbury's crumpled (that is, self-edited) letter to Félice. The third movement begins with Melbury's *going to speak* to Félice, and continues with a sequence of spoken confrontations. This shift is crucial, since it realigns the whole power structure of the relationships. More generally, each movement is a transformation of mode, not as in *The Mayor of Casterbridge* mutually exclusive of one another, but as products of one another. Thus the first movement is predominantly social – its dual themes are exploitation and alienation, and the completion of that pattern produces the 'mutual explorations of the world of fancy', the paid-for ego-trips of the prosperous triangle. Out of this grow the new modes of consciousness of the final movement.

The novel opens with Barber Percomb's visit to Marty to make a bid for her hair. Our first image of the society of Little Hintock, in the second and third chapters, moves from the extreme rusticity of the opening to a description that could well have come from one of the novels about the urban poor (Gissing or Margaret Harkness, for example) – a young girl in an apron too large for her is working late into the night to produce a sufficient number of spars to earn 2/3*d*. Her face has been brought to 'premature finality' by the 'necessity of taking thought at a too early period of her life'. Her hand, 'born to manual labour', bears witness to the injustice of her situation: 'Nothing but the cast of the die of destiny had decided that the girl should handle the tool.' The Barber offers her a free choice – to go on working in this exploitative situation, or to sell part of her body, for which he offers guineas which stare at her from the mirror. To be sure, the free choice is backed up by coercion since Mrs Charmond is her landlady, but like any working-class girl, Marty is at liberty to choose a more abject state if she prefers her reflection to the gaze of the money. The solitude of her rustic situation only stresses its opacity (she looks into the night as though she were on the 'very brink of an absolute void') and her vulnerability (since she is still caught up in the vestigial feudalism of agrarian paternalism). Later she will have to run up and down the lane to warm her frozen feet. Caught between the Ginnung-gap of the 'ante mundane' night and the rape of her locks by Loke, she is the first character of the actual community of the novel, and her life is exploited and deformed. It is a powerful opening sequence, but we soon learn that Marty is not alone in this victimization. Melbury pays for his self-made success with the rheumatic effect of divers strains and exertions 'required of him'. Giles is controlled by the leftover feudal power of Mrs Charmond. And most crucially, the class basis of the social action extends to the privileged woman Grace, whose education is an investment: 'You'll yield,' says Melbury, 'a better return'; and Grace recognizes that she is a mere chattel. Later the even more privileged Mrs Charmond will reveal that she is only in Hintock because the man she married brought her there: 'women,' she tells Fitzpiers, 'are always carried about like corks on the waves of masculine desires' (26). 'How can you think so much about that class of people?' Giles asks Grace after she has visited Mrs Charmond. But that is because he fails to realize that class relations incorporate a sexual politics.

The most pervasive effect of the exploitation is the alienation of consciousness. Most of the characters confront the opacity of the environment as a dream. At the tree auction, appropriately enough, even the auctioneer shows his absence of mind by bringing down his hammer on the head of a bystanding boy. Giles accidentally bids against Melbury. Previously, in Sherton Abbas, he has seen the eloquent look of the medieval buildings, 'but could not construe it' (the linguistic metaphors are significant – basically this means that there is no monument, although as we shall see this is by no means a negative point). Returning from Mrs Charmond's, Grace falls into an abstracted gaze, and the familiar look of her bedroom has a 'face estranged'. Things she has always known 'gazed at her in helpless stationariness' (6) and Mrs Charmond looking at Grace and herself in a mirror (mirrors are crucial – they image, among other things the alienation of the gaze), falls 'into a meditation'. Melbury is insomniac, Marty deeply pessimistic, Fitzpiers bored. All are rapt, and though, of course, they are not all exploited, and not in the same way, the pattern of exploitation is mechanical and thoughtless. It is a system which is in operation, not a conscious social intention. In fact, when characters are made aware of what they do to others, they tend to retract. Even Mrs Charmond's destruction of Giles is done in a fit of pique which appals her when she later recognizes its consequences.

Indeed, insofar as the power relations surface into consciousness, the novel keeps in play the tension between what is and what might be. Thus Marty recognizes that the cottages have gone 'with my hair' and Grace, far from allowing Giles's demise to confirm her rejection, actually moves towards him. So that at the end of the first movement, if her frail barque of fidelity is merely the writing on the wall, a writing that emends Marty's critical comment (for Marty too is reduced to silence by her father's death), nevertheless that writing embraces the three main victims of the power relations manifest in the first movement. Giles moves into the background, but insofar as he has a voice at all in the second movement it is to remind both Fitzpiers and Grace of the actual material base of their relationship. His response to Fitzpiers's aristocratic surprise about Grace's cultivation is 'won't money do anything?' (16) and later, when Grace patronizingly calls out from the Earl of Wessex, he angrily replies, 'isn't it enough that you see me here moiling and muddling for my daily bread while you are sitting there in your success?' (36). The novel does not forget the sense of class relations which, as Sherman says, are more clearly defined here than in any previous Hardy novel.[20]

In the second part of the novel those class relations operate to create a specifically defined space for romantic subjectivity. Fitzpiers, we are told, regarded 'his own personality as one of unbounded possibilities because it was his own – notwithstanding that the factors of his life had worked out a sorry product for thousands' (19), and his consciousness dominates the second part. The romanticism is obviously ironized. In spite of it, he lives in a neat box-like house, and before he can intervene in Grace's impending 'tragical self destruction' at the newly painted gate, he is held back by his inability to find the 'right' hat. Later we are told that he went for a 'ramble' which places him in the category that the disabused reader has been educated out of; and when he isn't bored, he sentimentalizes the woodlands, as when, at the tree barking, he sees himself as becoming 'welded in with this sylvan life'. His quotations from Shelley (notably from *The Revolt of Islam*, which is about highly politicized love) and Spinoza (who is the very opposite of a romantic egoist) place him as an egoist with strictly determined power. If the novel has moved to an arena of personal relations, it is one that is bounded by the social conditions that make it possible.

Moreover, Fitzpiers only comes into his own because the limitation of the social structure manifests itself partly in the alienation of the privileged woman forced into reverie, available for mutual explorations. This is explicitly noticed by Giles, who recognizes the 'curious parallelism' between Fitzpiers and Grace, who both stray 'into a discourse so engrossing to themselves that it made them forget that it was foreign to him' (16).

Egoism is neither a psychological trait nor a philosophical position, but the reflection of particular social conditions, as Hardy would have realized from his reading of Meredith. In this novel it is the result of the weakest link in the chain of exploitation, its effect on sexual politics. The weakest link affects the structure in two diametrically opposed ways. First, it most overtly constructs the victim as commodity: thus Fitzpiers's recognition of Grace is defined as 'Grace's exhibition of herself' as though she were in a shop window, although in fact she has no intention of being seen. She is thus to be appropriated, worked on, given in exchange. Fitzpiers is like 'a dram' to her, increasing her passivity, and this is reinforced by Melbury's pressure: 'you'll feel as if you've stepped into history' (23). She is as much an object of possession as Suke Damson. Equally, however, that objectifying appropriation leaves her subjectivity anomalously unsatisfied: 'but what an attenuation this cold pride was of the dream of her youth' (24). Moreover sexual politics cuts across immediate class relations. On the one hand, Fitzpiers can be attracted by Suke Damson, and on the other, he in turn can be made the victim of Mrs Charmond's enforced languor. Boumelha speaks of the naturalization of sexuality in the novel which she sees as the manifestation of the influence of contemporary French fiction, and it is true that the dissolution of personal relationships in the larger processes of desire is comparable to the treatment of sexuality in Maupassant's *Une Vie* and Zola's *La Faute de l'Abbé Mouret*, from which Hardy copied many passages into his notebook.[21] But this naturalization, like the nature of the first part, is carefully socialized.

Marriage, as Engels wrote in 1884 (basing his ideas on the work of an American anthropologist who was readily available), only means monogamy for the woman.[22] The shift from marriage to adultery in *The Woodlanders* is an instant reflex, not a liberation. It is also based on the hierarchy of power relations established in the first movement. Fitzpiers's shabby little romance with Félice in her appropriated hairpiece, and its formation through a tired nostalgia, reflects above all his dismay at being welded into the sylvan scene. Significantly, 'the words about his having spoiled his opportunities . . . haunted him *like a handwriting on a wall*' (25; my italics). Soon, he is 'believed in no more as a superior being hedged in by his own divinity'. Adultery is a response to the threat to the enclosed ('hedged') ego ('his own divinity') by the loss of social status.

Equally, however, it is caused by the woman's enclosed subjectivity which makes her the agent of inconsequence (this is the word which summarizes Félice but also accounts for the affair between Fitzpiers and Suke). The construction of the ironized egoistic space is the result of a phallocentric culture on the three levels of pursuit, possession through marriage and adulterous courtship. In the case of marriage it is specifically the conjuncture of the father and lover that reduces Grace to mesmerized passivity. Either side of this are the error of Suke and the ennui of Félice. Fitzpiers has his day within the spaces of the imprisoned female psyche. Equally, however, he is letting light into the dark cell.

For if Grace moves into marriage as in a dream, she will awaken into the novel's other values. 'Grace was amazed at the mildness of the anger which the suspicion engendered in her' (27). In the few pages following this, Hardy abandons completely the conventions of sexual love on which the English novel as a whole is based, that is the social ideology of monogamous marriage. Even where it extends to include romantic adultery, it is very difficult to think of a novel which does not assume that desire resides in its object so that (a) there is a right object, a single target of desire which it is the task of desire to find, (b) familiarity will increase the desire and

(c) transfer of the desire either means that the subject is superficial
or that it has made a mistake and that it is still looking for the right
object. Above all sexual desire is always looking for a place of
residence, even if it turns out to be Wuthering Heights. Houses are
very important in Hardy's novel, but mainly as windows to look
out of. The twenty-eighth and twenty-ninth chapters awaken
Grace into a world outside this structure.

The mildness of the anger defines the basis of her love for
Fitzpiers, which is 'mystery and strangeness'. 'This structure of
ideals' is 'demolished by intimacy of common life'. The housing
metaphor is very useful here and extends itself – 'a new foundation
was in demand' and it is not forthcoming. So Grace's marriage is
demolished a second time, by a non-event, as much as the event of
Fitzpiers's adultery. The metaphor picks up what has literally
happened to Giles. A house has been demolished and no new house
can be built. Grace is as outside emotionally as Giles is
economically.

But it is also an awakening. She actually *watches* Fitzpiers
disappear. It is significant that the natural setting (the gorgeous
autumn landscape) reminds her of an urban situation: 'the burst
husks of chestnuts lay exposing their auburn contents as if
arranged by anxious fruit sellers in the market' (though equally, of
course, the sexual connotations are obvious, even if Marty had not
had to sell her chestnut hair). She moves towards Marty's cosmic
pessimism: 'she wondered if there were one world in the universe
where the fruit had no worm and marriage no sorrow'. Fitzpiers
now becomes 'her Tannhäuser', the chivalric knight lost to the
buried Venus, his voice exercising its absurd Shelleyan vindication,
lost to her 'in silent spectacle'. His captivation, as the lines from
'Epipsychidion' make clear, frees her to consult her own vision.
What immediately arises, of course, is 'Autumn's very brother',
Giles.

It is a complex moment. The passage certainly stylizes Giles,
though to dismiss it as patronizing irony oversimplifies. However
inadequately, her heart rises 'like a released bough', her 'senses'
revel in a lapse back to nature unadorned. Hardy clearly wants to
establish the actual sensuality of the impression as well as its
conscious, controlled sublimation as pastoral. It is both illusion
and reality. Nature is not bountiful, we know, but the senses are
real. Her gloss precisely indicates the gap between impression and
the reception of the impression. Having lost her knight, 'another
being *impersonating* chivalrous and undiluted manliness had arisen
out of the earth' (my italics). The ambiguity of manliness
(implying both moral rectitude and physical strength) is to control

the outcome of the novel. It entails the non-event of Grace's new-found desire. Now looking into a sky which resembles a jewelled palace but beyond which is a bottomless medium of soft green fire (Whitmanic grass?) Giles kisses the flower on her bosom. It is enough to recall them both: 'I was not once like this.' The moment has been constructed from her structure of ideals, though its foundation is merely human. Having found the physical form of Giles to awaken her senses, she will hide in his hut. The gospel of the body is sacrificed to the need for houses.

But we must not dismiss what has been gained. In the following chapter Grace discovers the truth about Suke Damson but is 'possessed by none of the feline wildness it was her duty to experience'. 'Duty to experience' is an astonishing phrase – how can experience be a moral duty? Only because experience is socially constructed. Grace is not supposed to feel the way she does, and indeed consciously doesn't; otherwise she would have made the mistake of thinking that Fitzpiers did not love her. (That, I think, justifies the otherwise strange passage rationalizing Fitzpiers' philandering by a kind of evolutionary superiority.) She feels sorry for Suke as later she is to feel sorry for Félice, and climactically when all three stand round the bed, 'wives all', she is able to feel solidarity with them, which is the awakening of an unstructured emotion which needs one of the radicalizing key words Hardy has already begun to use in opposition to love: 'a tenderness spread over Grace like a dew' (35). The development in Grace is precise. Knowledge of her husband's promiscuity frees her from the passion of the wronged wife, absolves her from the prescribed experience of woman, turns her back to 'the crude country girl of her latent early instincts' (39) but holds this return in an ideological frame, or rather keeps it as a return, does not liberate it to move forward.

Giles is different. He kisses the flower and later, in the full knowledge that she can never marry him, steals a passionate kiss. It would be easy to dismiss this as underdevelopment or frigidity on Grace's part, but that oversimplifies. Hardy is not ambiguous about the way she feels, and indeed later she implies that the reason why she should not remain at the hut too long is that she doesn't feel she could resist the inevitable. What is more important is that the awakened senses cannot elude the ideology within which they are constructed. The primitive for Grace has to remain a concept: 'honesty, goodness, *manliness*, devotion, for her only existed in their purity now in the breasts of unvarnished men'. The actual Giles is resolved into a type.

This opens a gap which motivates the third movement. But to

avoid sentimentalizing, it is worth stressing that just as Melbury the father moved Grace towards romantic marriage, so to bring the gap into play it takes him living out vicariously the jealousy that it is her (failed) duty to experience. He goes, of course, on the advice of Giles so that it is a positive gesture to resolve the impasse he has tried previously to deal with by writing. Giving voice to his complaints precipitates the new level of relationships which result from it. But at the same time he creates terms which, to use a word Hardy is to use later in the text, *negative* their effect. As he goes to Félice, 'the scene to him was not the material environment of his person but a tragic vision that travelled with him like an envelope' (31). The reduction of the situation to tragic vision (tragedy is essentially a term of abuse in this novel, denoting the premature foreclosure of hegemonic egoism) is sufficient only to force Félice to recognize that she is becoming a passion incarnate, but that at least compels her to seek mental serenity in the woods. And in the woods, of course, she meets Grace. It is an episode in which for once the unfulfilled intention works positively. For confronting one another, Grace wins the victory of her insight into Fitzpiers and they separate. Getting lost, however, they are forced to cling to one another in that defensive alliance which Hardy has already suggested should form the new foundation of marriage. It is a physical, unbounded contact which straddles both the truth – 'O my great God . . . He's had you' – and the human solidarity which will not be denied by it: '"Are you rested?" she asked in a voice grown ten years older.'

The scene is repeated as farce between Melbury and Fitzpiers, when the material contingency compels a physical intimacy which momentarily overrides the regulation relationship of defensive father and offending husband. But, of course, it is limited, and its net effect is not to bring a new system of relationship between the men but only to act as a catalyst for the bed-scene and confirm the break-up of the marriage. Nevertheless the novel has explicitly rejected the structure of ideals in the name of material contingency. The pattern of exploitation in the opening movement has been overturned by the self-contradiction of the egoism it permits. The obscure woods, outside the houses of bourgeois relationships, have their revenges.

It is vital that at this point Hardy should turn back to the social issues. The opening section of the last movement merely brings the novel to a Meredithian affirmation – the subversion of the structures by natural forces. But we have already seen that nature is no match for the social world. The gospel of the body cannot be recovered: it must be made. Again it is Melbury, seeking by social action to rectify the error he has made, who motivates these issues. The briefly held out hope offered by the new divorce law precisely launches Grace and Giles into a *new* phase: 'surely the adamantine barrier of marriage with another could not be pierced like this. It did violence to custom. Yet a new law might do anything' (38). (The use of indirect free style here makes it very reminiscent of Zola.) Later, Giles recognizes that he is no longer speaking to 'the girl, Grace Melbury' but, in a topically resonant phrase, 'a new woman'.[23] Craving to be the country girl again means putting off the old Eve.

But this is placed as utopian on two grounds, external and internal. Externally, custom is truly adamantine. Lawyer Beaucock's claim that there is no longer one law for the rich and one for the poor is absurd, but it points to what would be needed to give institutional sanctity to the transfer of love, and the actual wooing of Giles and Grace is placed as affectionate comedy, a rehearsal of a future bounded by 'the gloomy atmosphere of the past and the still gloomy horizon of the present' (38). The boundary is 'the whole environment' and Grace and Giles are placed with a phrase whose immense significance we already know, as Arcadian *children* talking of imperial *law*, recalling General Principles and anticipating *Jude the Obscure*. The 'children' make a 'humane person' weep. Giles is as 'fearful as a child'. The law which the father tries to operate makes their love for one another irrelevant: 'I wish to keep the proprieties as well as I can.' Both, when disabused, feel that they have been 'simple'. 'The Simpletons' was the original title of *Jude the Obscure*. To be simple is both to be uncomplicated and foolish. Pastoral is not wrong, but it does not exist, nor ever has.

At the same time, as we have seen, Grace's feelings for Giles already have a potential structure that will make the law effective. This is the internal boundary. Her very feeling for him is made more romantic by the absence caused by her illness ('He rose upon her memory as the fruit god and wood god in alternation' (38).) Hers is a very theoretic paganism. She has to struggle with the 'unexpected vitality of that fastidiousness' and really is more in place in the Earl of Wessex. The failure of the divorce proceedings is 'almost tragical information' but only almost. Giles could only become her lover within a new structure of ideals.

Howe finds the hut episode working against Hardy's intention, at least for readers 'unvexed by aspirations to saintliness': 'no-one', he writes, 'neither man nor dog should have to be that loyal'.[24] But this does not undermine the coherence of the last movement, it merely fails to acknowledge the necessity which produces the absurd situation. Giles's '*strange* self sacrifice' is certainly not endorsed. Rather it is produced by the social law which has 'negatived for ever their opening paradise of the previous June' (41), and Grace's Daphnaean instinct. What is left to Giles but 'stoical pride'? I said at the beginning of this analysis that Hardy implicates the reader, makes him responsible, and Howe's response is precisely that responsibility demanding voice. It is another un-fulfilled intention. Grace has run away from a false position but is too bound by the proprieties to run to more than an ideal, and Giles is too used to the adverse way of the world to confront her with the truth of his situation. So that if in the wood the exploitation of the opening is overturned by the prospect of the future, it would only be by a new law that the prospect could be realized. For after all, Félice can hide *her* wounded mate in an obscure room in her house. Grace can only nurse Giles from his exposure. Not only is there one law for the rich and another for the poor, they have different narratives too.

'A dew of tenderness'; 'to make a humane person weep'; or, in an earlier phrase used to define Giles' insight into Grace, 'watchful loving kindness'. These are the only gains of a novel which demolishes the social forms of relationship. The ending is deliberately absurd. Grace makes Giles into the object of devotion, indulging in mournful fancies and reading from a psalter he has used to wipe his penknife on (do I need to spell out the marked conjuncture of ideal and material?). It is a climactic irony that Grace gets her skirt caught in the mantrap, which is in turn (and explicitly) a tribute to the ages of oppression against which loving kindness has to break new ground. It is not the past that has been destroyed, but the future. Memory is not pastoral. The praise of Giles which Marty has to keep alive is not a knowable community but a secret script:

> The casual glimpses which the ordinary population bestowed on that wondrous world of sap and leaves called the Hintock woods had been with these two, Giles and Marty, a clear gaze. They had been possessed of its finer mysteries as of commonplace knowledge; had been able to read its hiero-glyphs as ordinary writing . . . together they had, with the run of the years, mentally collected these remoter signs and symbols which seen in few were of runic obscurity, but all together made an alphabet . . . The artifices of the seasons were seen by them from the conjuror's own point of view, and not from that of the spectator. (44)

A writing age, the practice of an obscure art. Marty is left as an androgynous figure to celebrate Giles. She has 'rejected with *indifference* the attribute of sex for the loftier quality of abstract humanism' (my italics), and this is not a Positivist project (for Positivism has quite other roles for woman to play) but a Symbolist one. In a world in which the very landscape mirrors the power relations of a repressive society, the gospel of the body is an occult worship. *The Woodlanders* finally comes to rest in the absent future which is the forlorn. It is enough to make a humane person weep. The reader cannot ramble, but has to ask why to be good and do good things is not enough to stay alive.

The answer lies somewhere between the law of the unfulfilled intention which is everywhere and stupid divorce laws which are always changeable, and there is no evidence that Hardy ever comes nearer than that to defining his political position. But this novel places itself in a wider context which will have to be borne in mind as we approach the novels of the nineties. The final turn of *The Woodlanders* hangs on Grace's skirt. *She* is not caught in the mantrap, only her skirt. As Gregor reminds us, it is characteristic that as she goes off to restart her marriage she complains that she hasn't a brush and comb.[25] Her return to the fold is because she has not the enterprise to walk naked. The skirt has occurred twice before. It is mentioned as soon as she appears, for example:

> There was nothing remarkable in her dress just now . . . But, had it been quite striking it would have meant just as little. For there can hardly be anything less connected with a woman's personality than drapery which she has neither designed, manufactured, cut, sewed, nor even seen. (5)

The second is about her bridal gown:

> But there were preparations, imaginable enough by those who had special knowledge. In the remote and fashionable city of Exonbury something was growing up under the hands of several persons who had never seen Grace Melbury, never would see her, or care anything about her at all. (24)

The skirt which is caught in the trap is the product of the division of labour. Obviously the major source of such an idea is Ruskin, but in 1886 the most active development of it is that of William Morris. Morris, unlike Ruskin, acknowledged the conquest of nature (significantly in an essay called 'A Factory as It Might Be') and asked what we are going to do with all this power exept use it to exploit the weak. More importantly, he had just published his remarkable poem about the Commune, *The Pilgrims of Hope*, which describes unpossessive sexual relationships and non-property-based parental responsibility. The opening paragraph of Hardy's novel forces us to think about the way things are in the light of the way they might be. It is Morris's literary programme. Hardy will send a copy of his next novel to Morris. If his portrayal of the woods, belying Fennimore Cooper and Thoreau, maintains that nature is only the site of the historical struggles of man and not a shelter from them, it is not because he wishes to make a commodity of misery. It is because he wants to insist that there is a struggle, no matter how uneven it is. We admire Zola's *Germinal* and Gissing's *The Nether World* for their scrupulous and humane intelligence about poverty and oppression. *The Woodlanders* and its successors we take into battle with us.

4   The Offensive Truth: *Tess of the d'Urbervilles*

Purity and Faithfulness

Tess of the d'Urbervilles is one of the most discussed novels in the language. It was clearly intended to be. Everything about the presentation of the text calls on the reader to participate in its production: the subtitle, a *pure* woman *faithfully* presented, offers a double challenge, first to the moral values it expects to encounter and contest, and secondly to an aesthetic judgement – what is 'pure', what is 'faithful'? The division into 'phases' spatializes temporal change so that, at the moment of crisis, between 'The Consequence' and 'The Woman Pays' a decisive progression is made between the moment of speaking and the silence which follows, and makes it a deterministic growth so that 'pure' cannot be ascribed to a state of being 'untinctured by experience' (since the first 'phase' is not that of a 'woman' at all but of a 'maiden'), but most effectively to the moment of death ('fulfilment'). 'Untinctured' clearly differentiates itself from the moralistic 'untainted', but as clearly brings that possibility shamefully to mind. And the Preface confirms this dislocation of prevailing assumptions. Quoting St Jerome, the most unlikely defender of sexual growth, it links truth with offence.[1] Even its textual history confirms our sense of its designs upon us – there is no freezable text, only a constant exchange of revisions, particularly polemical sharpenings. It is possible that Hardy sent the novel to publishers certain to refuse it in order to generate an atmosphere of controversy before its publication.[2]

This discussability is resisted in various ways in order to inscribe the text within the institution of literature. In order to ascribe *meaning*, liberal analysts of the late 1960s and the 1970s met the disjunctions of the text as a confusion arising from a prior ideological commitment and an insurgent humanist identification with the protagonist.[3] They discarded the polemic altogether, so that what remains is a naturalized Tess, as though she is more than the words of the text, to be mourned, loved or otherwise possessed in the sacred refuge of the (usually male) reader's good nature. A later generation, seeing the danger of this, reconstructs the text as discontinuity or endless repetition of forms, and this is closer to my own analysis, but I think it reaches the impasse of Hillis Miller, by which the text is trapped in an infinite plurality of decipherings which are no more than the ruins of human song that blow about Egdon Heath.[4] And even P. Boumelha ends with a strangely despairing pluralism that does not question the gleeful appropriation of J. Bayley.[5] At least those readers who look in vain for coherence retain a sense of the novel's impact, which does not cease to be unified in the double anger of the subtitle – pure/faithful.

We should try to become the reader the book demands. If there is no comfort in coherence (we cannot put the book down, and say amen) it is no more merely an exhilarating exercise. We must acknowledge the novel's disjunctions as a particular strategy. On the one hand there is no form which is not discontinuous since signs only identify themselves as difference, but discontinuity cannot be a function of 'form' at all since the opposite to their differentiation is amorphic/amorphous (formless). I will stress a polemical design in which the discontinuities are seen as properties of the ideological discourses the text articulates. It is heteroglossic, in Bakhtin's real sense which is not the revisitation of polysemic ghosts as it is often treated, but the evaluation of verbal interactions.[6]

At the centre of critical debate is the correlation of two discourses, that of 'nature' and that of 'gender'. There is a third, that of the social relations of production. They form an ideological hierarchy which can be formed in the primary model of superstructure and base. The discourse of nature is effectively about 'reality' that is 'wisdom', the free play of concepts within the role of uncontaminated ideology. Gender too is ideological – it takes its origin from the assumptions about reality which are marshalled by ideology but it is not pure as nature is, for gender relations subserve a specific economic need – specifically marriage is a form to facilitate the production of surplus value, and organize its distribution. It mediates the 'natural' and the 'social', which are respectively the concerns of ideology (the super-structure) and the relations of production (the base). The presence of these discourses is not in doubt. What I want to establish is that they open out into one another. Or rather as the look such discourses bestow on life is returned from the contradiction within them, their intended foreclosure is subverted, not endlessly, but ending on a question. For each discourse is manifest as a way of looking which is at the same time looking at looking. Although the ideological discourse of nature and the discourse of the social relations of production correspond to the opposed metonymies of the return and the gesture (as being aligned with the repeated 'rhythms' of life and the 'march' of history respectively) and the discovery of gender constructing the object of love as symptom with the metaphor of human making, so that it manifests itself finally on the sacrificial stone, the identifying signal is the gaze, either appropriated or at last returned.

Nature's Holy Plan

Critical assimilation of the text finds its most perplexed and assimilating effort directed at the discourse of nature, for it is the site of what appears to be a manifest authorial confusion.[7] It is the discourse of double vision. 'Simple Tess Durbeyfield stood at gaze' (5). We enter her perspective, since what she is gazing at is the slopes which we encounter with her, but the 'simple' prompts a second view. She is astounded by what we understand. The double vision is most explicit in the famous flight of point of view as Tess crosses into the vale of Great Dairies when the irresistible, universal, automatic tendency to find sweet pleasure somewhere lures her into mingling her hopes with the sunshine in an ideal photosphere (16). She finds herself on the carpeted level which stretched to the east and west as far as the eye could reach but is herself like a fly on a billiard table and of no more consequence to the surroundings than that fly. Our vision is that of 'nature's cruel law' which she has by her nature lost (though she had it when she recognized that we live on a blighted planet). It is merely unexpended youth, and will no more find a way to reconcile the will to enjoy and 'the circumstantial will against enjoyment' than her life hitherto has done more than illustrate 'the ill judged execution of the well judged plan of things' (5).

   This animus against the natural spans the whole novel and it is real and no mere lament. Trying to explain Tess's victimization as the law of the sins of the fathers, the author blasphemously calls it a morality good enough for divinities, but scorned by average human nature. It resembles Darwin's outburst, 'What a book a devil's chaplain might write on the clumsy, wasteful, blundering,

low and horribly cruel works of nature' (which Hardy would not
have known); and it consciously involves Swinburne's 'Time's
satiric psalm' with a text from his *Atalanta in Calydon*, whose crucial
line is 'the supreme evil, God'.[8] But it is held in manifest
contradiction with another way of reading 'the natural' which is to
oppose it to the 'social rubric', and locate the disjunction in Tess's
moral upbringing, 'a cloud of moral hobgoblins' (13). It is often
said that Hardy cannot make up his mind between a Darwinian
pessimism and a romantic embrace of the natural as against
convention. But this is precisely the point. That double vision is
the product of an absence. Between the carpeted level of
unexpended youth and the billiard table of the unsympathetic First
Cause there is an unvoiced average human nature which might say
that Tess has not been ruined, that her passing corporeal blight
could be her mental harvest.[9] But there is nobody to say it, no
shared human experience that can mediate between the inert
passivity of it was to be, 'tis nater . . . and what do please God' and
the cloud of moral hobgoblins which christens the child of
shameless nature Sorrow. Nothing is so clear as that Tess and her
family and the maidens following the sun of their hope, which may
starve to nothing, live in a dream; but the evil which is done to
men, whether it is the death of Prince, or the yielding of her body
to one who has no more love for her than she for him, is the
product of exhaustion. Nature's cruel law is cruel because
providence is not for the improvident, but who can fail to
understand the release of the habitués of Rollivers, and how is it
that a critic as astute as Gregor can think the drunken revelry of
the Trantridge workers is not appalling (not morally, of course, but
socially)?[10] All is worse than vanity for those who have not means
or understanding. 'Nature's holy plan' is an ideology mocked by
improvident procreation.

A curious sentence in the middle of the early paragraph about
the ill-judged execution of the well-judged plan of things should
alert us to this absence: 'We may wonder whether at the acme and
summit of the human progress these anachronisms will be
corrected by a finer intuition, a closer interaction of the social
machinery than that which jolts us round and along; but such
completeness is not to be prophesied, or even conceived as possible'
(5). Of course, the mere mention of it cannot fail to make us
conceive it as possible. That it is not says something about the
power relations which obtain.

There is, first, a contradictory ideological input which so far
from being a residual romanticism overtaken by Darwin, is on the
contrary a modulation of the evolutionary law. As we have seen,

nature in Hardy is predominantly ideological – it is a landscape literally, a *view*. Insofar as there is a Hardyan 'real' – the interstices of a hard prosaic reality – it is the material necessity subserved by agriculture. The most important transition we have noted so far is from the silent gaze of Knight on the cliff or Yeobright on Egdon Heath at an implacable other to the Paterian inflection that circumstance is within us as well as around us. The *further* possibility of that recognition is to accept its impulses as the basis of a 'new faith'. The phrase is from Havelock Ellis, but it is present in a number of writers Hardy admired: in Swinburne's 'Hertha', for example, or throughout the work of Meredith. It is, Ellis wrote in 1890, to turn from Socrates to Heraclitus, to be ready to throw away all prepossessions and to follow nature withersoever her caprices lead and he specifies three elements in 'the new spirit' this engenders – the influence of science upon life ('an accomplished fact') the influence of women (on the eve of attaining its outward consummation) and the influence of democracy ('much more vague, complex and uncertain'). In other words, without deserting the Darwinian account of natural processes, it becomes possible to see not the Paterian trap but 'the reasonable path of progress': 'We know at last that it must be among our chief ethical rules to see that we build the lofty structure of human society on the sure and simple foundations of man's organism.'[11] It totally reverses nature's holy plan: rather than making it fit a moral law, it argues for a moral law which follows its 'caprices'. The location of this possibility in the 'entire freedom of development' of women argues the possibility not of a contradictory discourse in the novel but rather of a shift in values. In a different order, an order determined by the new spirit, science, women, democracy, nature's cruel law would cease to be anything other than an instinct of self-delight.

This shifts the centre of gravity from the 'natural' as an account of the real to the natural as a reflection of the social structures, which we have seen Hardy moving towards in *The Woodlanders*, and which is more emphatically evident here. The effect of the presence of this duality in the novel is very precise. The cruel law perspective is increasingly located in the mind of Tess, who comes more and more to enunciate it in place of the author. That is the product of her 'experience', which obviously reflects the efficacy of the dominant power relationship. The positive possibility is one she is never allowed to know, not by some deprivation of the narrative but by the events which limit her 'single opportunity of existence'. The blight of her planet is predominantly social. Thus the angry retort about Wordsworth's phrase 'Nature's holy plan' is a comment on the population problem among the poor (the Ship of the Durbeyfields). When Tess specifies what she would mean by an unblighted planet, it is one unvexed by social limitations of her poverty: 'Well, father wouldn't have coughed and creeped about on the floor, and wouldn't have got too tipsy to go this journey; and mother wouldn't always have been washing, and never getting finished' (4). The pessimism is bound up with exhaustion. Quoting Asham at the beginning of chapter 15, the author comments 'Our long wandering unfits us for further travel, and what use is our experience to us then?' It is, of course, a remark that anticipates the whole narrative but by then the context of wandering is the explicitly historical context of rural migration.

The issue is very clearly marked when this cosmic pessimism is located by Angel as he sees it in Tess as 'The Ache of Modernism'. He is bewildered to find such a sophisticated consciousness in so simple a nature. She, however, is equally bewildered to find the same ache in one so privileged. His reading of her comes out of a purely ideological history – it is Arnold's account of the modern spirit.[12] Hers of him is already a social comment. This is essential to the dynamics of the plot. By the time Tess has confessed to Angel and been rejected the issue of whether nature's cruel law is cosmic or social has become purely abstract. The world of nature for Tess is historically constructed by the fact that she is a woman and the fact that she is working-class. Indeed to talk of Tess's sexuality as though it were a possibility repressed is to ignore the way in which she is consructed as a subject by her gender and class – for by that stage, 'nature' as any kind of measure has been appropriated by this middle-class rule. Hardy certainly does not avoid the 'vulgarism of the natural woman'[13] – he confronts it as one dimension of a patriarchal and capitalist ideology.

One of the most intense moments of the interplay between the instinct for self-delight and nature's cruel law is the much analysed passage in which Tess drawn to the music of Angel's harp moves through the unkempt garden at Talbothay's with its 'profusion of growth' and the offensive smells of the weeds and the ambiguous stains left by the cuckoo spittle and the blights left on Tess's arm as she passes through (19). Lodge has discussed its ambiguity in detail and the only question raised about it is whether Hardy is confused or ambivalent.[14] I think he is neither, or rather that the primary preoccupation of the passage is not 'nature' at all, but the way in which Tess's subjectivity is constructed by the patriarchal hegemony that calls it into being. The ideological context is very important. What calls her is Angel's music, not heard for the first time, but heard now in the garden, where in contrast to the 'dim, flattened, constrained' notes confined in the attic, it may now appear 'with a stark quality like that of nudity'. Music has from the beginning played a special role both for Tess and her mother. In the opening chapter her mother is singing as she rocks the cradle with one foot and plunges her arm into the washtub. It is one of those passages in Hardy which starts from a comfortable irony – the incongruity of song in these automatic actions, and particularly a song whose subject is romantic sexuality. But as he develops this double image to a generalization, Joan's passionate love of tune, we see less the sub-Dickensian grotesque than what underlies it: 'There still faintly beamed from the woman's features something of the freshness, and even the prettiness, of her youth' (3). It is as though music acknowledges a lost potential of womanhood. Certainly that is how it is used in Tess's case. In the depths of her misery, after her 'ruin' when she has to creep to church unseen, she is momentarily taken out of the sense of shame by the 'old double chant – 'Langdon': 'she thought, without exactly wording the thought, how strange and godlike was a composer's power, who from the grave could lead through sequences of emotion, which he alone had felt at first, a girl like her who had never heard of his name, and never would have a clue to his personality' (13). And thirdly, and most importantly as she crosses into the vale of the great dairies, she searches about for a tune that will embody the irresistible, universal, automatic tendency to find sweet pleasure somewhere, which pervades all life, and sings an old 'Benedicite' which does two distinct things: it celebrates the ongoing world *and* praises the Lord. Note that as the song moves to this second point Tess stops and *murmurs*, 'But perhaps I don't quite know the Lord as yet' (16). Hardy endorses her judgement with a Positivist vocabulary – it is, he says, a 'fetishistic utterance in a monotheistic setting'. Fetishism for Comte is the first stage of religion when the mind is roused from its torpor but before it is inserted into the *law* of monotheism.[15] In other words music is a double signifier of the human impulse for survival and the order into which it is inserted. The passage elaborates the implications further: 'Let the truth be told – women do as a rule live through such humiliations, and regain their spirits.' The whole Victorian fictional discourse of the fallen woman is thus put aside in the moment of musical response to the external world. All art, Pater had said, aspires to the condition of music, because music is the least vulnerable to the moral order which constrains art. And art, as we have seen, is the equivalent at least for a sense of freedom for the modern mind endangered not only by circumstances but by its own forces.[16] Tess in the garden, called through the entangled natural world by the promise of a paradisal nudity, materially acts out this idea. Of course, too, we are reminded that the attic constraint is not an abandoned accidental. *Absolutely*, Angel's art is 'poor' but, to use another Paterian discrimination, 'the relative is all'. Thus the whole context of the passage in the garden is both about the 'truth' of woman and the imprisonment of that truth in the stain of experience.

But equally that stain is socially constructed. The profusion of growth emanates from the fact that the garden is unkempt. The tall flowering weeds, where colours are as dazzling as those of cultivated flowers, nevertheless emit 'offensive' smells. Its very power is at once reminiscent of and in contrast to Paradise. The very light is 'like a piece of day left behind by accident'. Angel does not go on playing as she hopes but speaks to her. And what follows is the dialogue to which we have already referred when Tess enunciates the lesson of her knowledge without Angel being able to understand its significance (later he assumes that such a daughter of the soil could only have caught up the sentiment by rote). For there is not one nature but three. There is the naturalist nature of Darwinian struggle ('crushing snails that were underfoot'), and the instinct of self-delight which makes a mental harvest of that passing corporeal blight. But instead of leading to the kind of transcendent humanism that is glimpsed by Tess in connection with the Langdon, it leads only to Angel's double appropriation. He is precisely drawn to Tess by her 'ache of modernism', but then he has to make of her a 'daughter of the soil' constructed in terms of a nature that has already been doubly denied both by blighted planet and by mental harvest. She, on the other hand, thinks that the maker of music is godlike (Langdon) and that he can raise up dreams. In more ways than one she does not know the Lord as yet.

What confirms this reading is its comparability to the natural-istic paradise of *La Faute de L'Abbé Mouret*. There too the garden has been overgrown, and it becomes the site of woman as subject and object of sexual desire in which, in an interval of forgetting the law to which he is bound, the young priest enters only to betray it and destroy her. For if Tess is moving around in a garden which has moved and is moving forward in time, Angel has *by choice* gone back to nature, to this 'obscure dairy'. It is significantly limiting that he learns there no more than the lesson of Gray's elegy ('some acutely Miltonic, some potentially Cromwellian'). The ideological disjunction of nature's cruel law and the instinct for self-delight is contained by the possession of the discourse of nature by the male.

An Almost Standard Woman

A powerful and controversial essay of 1890, 'The Morality of Marriage' by the distinguished feminist Mona Caird,[17] appeared in the leading liberal journal, the *Fortnightly Review*. It provides a clarifying model of the transitions of discourse that we see in Hardy's novel. 'It is too late,' she writes, 'to press "nature" into service.' Women are beginning to try their own experiments with Nature.' She also provides an ironic version of the harvest theme, saying that it is not true that women reap what they have sown: 'we reap what other people have sown for us' (p. 328) – the woman pays. But above all she raises the question of 'purity':

> What after all is 'purity'? Does it not come very close to charity which vaunteth not itself, is not puffed up, seeketh not her own, thinketh no evil? The 'purity' that sits up aloft under the presidency of Mrs Grundy vaunteth itself exceedingly, is puffed up very much indeed, to the entire forgetfulness of the manner in which she acquires it, and occupies all her leisure in thinking evil. This kind of purity has a beautiful sister who unquestioningly adopts the elder's rules, but obeys them in a devotional spirit, believing them to come straight from heaven with the light of holiness still upon them. And for these she is ready to suffer – and often has to suffer – martyrdom. Both these forms of purity grate against fact. There is another kind.
>
> This purity came into being with the love of nature. The vivid modern sense of the splendour of life, 'the beauty of the world'. She is fostered by that passionate love of liberty, of health, sunlight, freshness which is becoming one of the regenerative and moving forces of the century . . . This is the purity of an age of science. (pp. 329–30)

The revisions of purity pick up the relationship between the nature discourse and the gender discourse in the light of post-Darwinian naturalism. Caird takes us through precisely the procedures that Hardy's novel demands. Its general argument is that marriage is immoral because it puts human nature in possession of 'almost irresponsible power'. 'Can we forget,' she continues, 'how much the allotted scapegoats of society have to endure in the interests of purity among the elect?' (p. 321). The ineffectual Angel, bringer of light without heat, is the child of a Calvinist father. David, as Swinburne called Arnold, was son of Goliath.[18]

It is precisely in the space generated by the double Darwinian vision of nature that the discourse of gender which is the mediant between the isolated superstructure of wisdom and the base of the social relations of production is formulated, first by Alec and then, more significantly, by Angel. Note too that it involves the metonymy of the return. If we look carefully at the end of chapter 18 we can see how exactly Hardy delineates the transitions. 'What a fresh and virginal daughter of Nature that milkmaid is' is the historical reversal of pastoral in general and it is locked into the motifs of the return: 'And then he seemed to discern in her something that was familiar, something which *carried him back* to a joyous and unforeseeing past.' For Angel it is the atavistic illusion of Clym. But through the trace of his consciousness the ironic contingency of Darwinian nature asserts itself: '*A casual* encounter during some country *ramble* it certainly had been and he was not greatly curious about it. But the circumstance was sufficient to *select* Tess.' We recognize the resonance of the vocabulary – 'casual' takes us back to 'Hap', 'ramble' to the undermined complacency of the opening of *The Woodlanders*, 'select' straight to Darwin himself. We recall that the tourist is advised to view Blackmoor 'from the summits of the hills that surround it . . . An *unguided ramble* into the recesses in bad weather is apt to engender dissatisfaction with its narrow, tortuous and miry ways' (2). At the same time, *in reality*, Angel, retreating from curiosity into image, plays his part in nature's cruel law by *selecting* Tess, as Alec, scion of the socially selected Stoke d'Urbervilles, has selected her once before. The function of the garden episode which immediately follows has been, as we have said, to establish Tess's own attraction to him as the raiser of dreams, not to escape from the 'real' but to 'drive such horrid fancies away'. Tess is right, that is she speaks here coherently with the authorial discourse of nature, since we know that the 'inquisitive eyes' of the trees are mere moral hobgoblins. Angel, however, will take that desire and make it the predicate of his own subjectivity.

In the following section, Clare takes home with him an image of 'the impassioned, summer steeped heathens in the Var Vale, their rosy faces court-patched with cow droppings', (25) and this is linked to the opposition to his father's Pauline rigour with Hellenism. It is interesting that these chapters should show his attempt to balance his independence with a need to accommodate his father: in the alterations to the text, Hardy plays down the paganism of Angel so that he 'waxed quite earnest on that orthodoxy in his beloved Tess which . . . he had been prone to slight when observing it practised by her and the other milkmaids,

because of its obvious unreality amid beliefs essentially naturalistic'
(26).[19] The essential point is that it is not the 'natural' that he
espouses, but an ideological version of the natural which organizes
it in terms of the patriarchal (literally, of course, Angel is going to
make peace with his father). The issue becomes plain at the end of
the chapter in which he returns. As he tells Tess of Alec's attack on
his father, he is so preoccupied with his father he does not notice
her reaction. What he sees instead is a remarkably significant
image:

> All the girls drew onward to the spot where the cows were
> grazing in the further mead, the bevy advancing with the
> grace of wild animals – the reckless, unchastened motion of
> women accustomed to unlimited space – in which many
> abandoned themselves to the air as a swimmer to the wave. It
> seemed natural enough to him, now that Tess was again in
> sight, to choose a mate from unconstrained Nature, and not
> from the abodes of Art. (37)

Again it is the invincible instinct but we note that 'naturally' and
'Nature' are part of Angel's vocabulary and that this is linked with
'choosing a mate'. Thus the unchastened motion of the group is
inserted into the monogamous institution of marriage. Throughout
the Talbothays section, of course, there is the sense of a corporate
sexuality that has to be denied in the interests of an institution.
And this is confirmed in a different dimension in the following
chapter when, in the context of Angel pressing his suit, we are told
that love-making in this relatively ungoverned world is 'more often
accepted inconsiderately for its own sweet sake than in the carking
homes of the ambitious' (28). *Choosing* a mate, *making* an entreaty
are the 'natural' reflections of a patriarchal culture. When the
confessions are made, Angel is to refer to Alec as 'your husband in
nature' and what convinces Tess that he is right is his allusion to
possible children. We are moving from the nature of nature to the
nature of marriage. Monogamy, as Engels argued, is only
necessary for woman since there is no other way of ensuring that
her progeny have a single father and hence no other way of
preserving the values of property.[20] It is not merely a double
standard that Tess encounters when she matches Angel's confession with hers but also a culturally necessary double standard.

All I have done so far is to establish the clear link between the
divided discourse of nature and the gender discourse that arises in
its gap. But we have already noted that these issues proceed from

looking. It is part of Hardy's strategy to constitute the woman as symptom, as object of sexual desire and only in very limited ways as subject of it, and this has led some feminist critics to see the novel as confused and disjointed.[21] However, if we keep in mind the analysis of the nature discourse which shows it to be divided but not multiple, we can see more clearly the way in which the gender discourse is set up.

It is useful here to think of Joyce's distinction between kinetic and static art. In *Portrait of the Artist as a Young Man*, Stephen distinguishes two levels of kinetic art – didacticism and pornography. As the discourse of wisdom, the nature theme is certainly didactic, predominantly causing us to stand away from the life portrayed. Conversely, the sexual discourse contains a very definite invitation to possess the image. It comes out clearly in chapter 14, in which the reader is invited to select Tess from two other field women. It becomes a pretext for erotic melancholy:

> It was a thousand pities, indeed; it was impossible for even an enemy to feel otherwise on looking at Tess as she sat there, with her flower-like mouth and large tender eyes, neither black nor blue nor grey, nor violet; rather all those shades together, and a hundred others, which could be seen if one looked into their irises – shade behind shade – tint beyond tint – around pupils that had no bottom; an almost standard woman, but for the slight incautiousness of character inherited from her race. (14)

This description certainly gets carried away by its own rhetoric. Immediately after it, we are given details about her skirts lifted by the breeze and the 'bits of naked arm' whose feminine smoothness becomes scratched by the stubble. The pity is real, harsh detail specific, but this context makes these very responses erotic in themselves. We have only to ask why the colour of Tess's eyes makes her story more pitiful to see that something more is going on than mere sympathy. However, we must note two points. In the first place if we attend to the episodic context of the passage we note that it is established in terms of the clear gaze of masculine appropriation. The chapter opens with the sunrise, and grants the sun a sentient look 'demanding the masculine pronoun for its adequate expression'. It is an affirmative moment of the 'old-time idolatries' and we must not make the mistake of thinking it ironic. Nevertheless it is specific, and that specificity is echoed by the threshing machine which sounds like the love-making of the grasshopper (the male grasshopper of course makes that noise) and a significantly possessive mutation of the novel's subtitle, 'an almost *standard* woman'.

What is equally important is the focus on the eyes. For the gaze of the discourse of gender is appropriative – not looking at a way of looking but taking over the agents of looking as a possession in its own right. At several points Tess is described as having 'eloquent eyes' and that exactly recapitulates the possessive gaze. For in the eyes of the woman are found the words which she is presumed not to need to speak.

Silencing Tess is not a function of the novel but of the masculine domination of its reality. 'That's what every woman says,' Alec retorts to Tess's claim that she did not understand his intention; and Tess replies, 'How can you dare to use such words . . . Did it never strike your mind that what every woman says some women may feel?' (12). The struggle of woman in the novel becomes identified as it already has been as long ago as *A Pair of Blue Eyes* and *Far From the Madding Crowd* as a struggle over language and voice. Immediately after this challenge to Alec, she meets the writer of texts and calls his words 'crushing, killing' and says, 'I don't believe God said such things.' When she baptizes Sorrow she utters the ceremony 'boldly and triumphantly in the stopt-diapason note which her voice acquired while her heart was in her speech, and which will never be forgotten by those that knew her'. On one of the few occasions in their courtship when Angel actually listens to her, after he has been calling her by the 'fanciful names' of pagan goddesses, she asks him to call her Tess. He does and this makes her features 'simply feminine' by which Hardy explicitly means 'they had changed from that of a divinity who could confer bliss' (the masculine image of the beautiful woman) to 'those of a being who *craved* it' (my italics).

Hardy, it is true, does not give us the words of her confession, but this does not silence her. On the contrary it is the moment in which she takes voice that destroys Angel's virginal image. It is a very painful moment to read because we know that it is precisely her sense of justice and honesty that is going to betray her – 'because 'tis just the same. I will tell you now', 'murmuring the words without flinching,' 'no exculpatory phrase of any kind' – these phrases do not repress what she says.

The scene which follows is a sequence of voicings and silencings, linguistic interactions, in which power is made manifest through the control of language. 'The complexion of even eternal things seemed to suffer transmutation as her *announcement* progressed', 'the auricular impressions from *previous endearments*', 'repeating them-selves as *echoes* from a time of supremely purblind foolishness' (my italics). He eventually speaks 'in the most inadequate common-place voice'. The fact that she has spoken reverses the previous gap between image and consciousness. His 'words' realize her own apprehensive foreboding. And when she *voices*, repeats his claim that she is no longer the same woman, the image raised causes her to take pity on herself. Later she 'remains mute' knowing that he was smothering his affection for her. And later still, she 'could not help addressing him'. The whole relationship in short is in terms of the linguistic interaction between them. And that interaction is determined in the final instance by the structure of power that language inherently embodies (as Bathsheba has realized). When she defends herself in terms of his double standard, he feels no need to refute her but merely says 'don't argue'. Then he asks her to say that it is not true, and she repeats that it is true, 'every word'. Again when she offers to commit suicide he says 'do not speak so absurdly . . . ' (rather than saying 'don't do it'). And he finally resorts to the eloquent eyes structure because Tess 'had no advocate': 'Could it be possible, he continued, that eyes which as they gazed, never expressed any divergence from what the tongue was telling were yet ever seeing another world behind her ostensible one?'

From then on a system of power is asserted by which she is compelled to silence by his determination but by which he also risks being changed by her 'confession' that she has attempted suicide, and by her sobs. Indeed we are explicitly told that more worldliness on her part would win him but 'she took everything as her deserts, and hardly opened her mouth'. This silence is linked as well to his idealizing nature which is more fond of her in her absence than in her presence. 'She found that her personality did not *plead* her cause so forcibly as she anticipated. The *figurative phrase* was true' (my italics.) The only way in which Tess has become 'another woman' is through the power construct of language. She perceives in his words her apprehensive foreboding in former times, but we have been told that the perception is wrong, a cloud of moral hobgoblins. What she perceives, if we read the passage properly, is 'his view of her' and it is nothing short of a capital offence that, literally having destroyed her, made her another woman, he should execute her with gentleness: '"You are ill; *and it is natural that you should be so*"' (my italics).

I have attended to the process by which Tess becomes for Angel 'another woman' in such detail (though not enough, as the passage continues to accumulate ironies) first to stress the centrality of language, the actual linguistic relationships that are embodied especially in the illocutionary vocabulary (confuse, plead and so on). Secondly, I want to stress that it is not the text which silences Tess but the patriarchal hegemony within which she is constructed and that this means that there is a voice, linked with music, which keeps in touch with the unaccommodated woman. Thirdly, and as a consequence of this, it moves us into a double action whereby Tess less and less becomes the visible vessel of experience – the eloquent eyes – and more and more the voice of her own experience ('as one who was ill-used') either to us or to the characters she meets. I am thinking specifically of her disconversion of Alec which, although it uses Angel's words,[22] belongs to a discourse which Tess has discovered for herself. Indeed she has put it to a shocked Angel when she rejected history – the narrative of wisdom, being one of a line – in the name of a rationalism that asks why the sun should fall on the just and the unjust alike. But more importantly it is growingly evident in the letters to Angel. It is significant that they should be letters because insofar as she is allowed to articulate her own dilemma ('once victim always a victim, that's the law'), she becomes less and less visible as a selected object of sexual appropriation. As she comes closer to the reader she also becomes part of a process which at once alienates her – 'we see her a lonely woman with a basket and a bundle in her own porterage' – and at the same time part of a social class: 'Thus Tess walked on; a figure which is part of a landscape; a fieldwoman pure and simple' (41). Only if we fail to see her as a textual manipulation will we make the mistake of thinking that she becomes a different woman.[23] She has never been a woman anyway – only a grammatical construct whose shift from predicate to subject is part of the shift from an almost standard woman to a fieldwoman pure and simple. For this novel is not about Tess's sexuality – it is about the articulation of the sexual politics which the ideological gap exposes and of its incorporation into the social relations of production. The theme of purity, to put it another way, is incorporated into the question of justice.

But justice is not merely ideological. Strangely enough, although Mona Caird cites the great Russian realist Cherneshevski, she explicitly ignores the economic dimension of her subject.[24] But the explicitness calls attention, of course, to its necessity; and Hardy demands that his Christian, male, middle-class reader enter the *double* bind of the working-class woman.[25]

Justice Was Done

The gaze of wisdom is the double gaze, the gaze of sexual oppression is the appropriated gaze, the gaze of the social relations of production is reciprocated – the gaze in exchange. It appears most dramatically when Tess and Angel take the milk to the trains:

> The light of the engine flashed for a second upon Tess Durbyfield's figure, motionless under the great holly-tree. No object could have looked more foreign to the gleaming cranks and wheels than this unsophisticated girl, with the round bare arms, the rainy face and hair, the suspended attitude of a friendly leopard at pause, the print gown of no date or fashion, and the cotton bonnet drooping on her brow. (30)

Like the fly on the billiard table, and the girl in the pink cotton jacket, this is an image of Tess which momentarily turns the novel inside out so that we gain a certain determined distancing from the experiential narrative. But it is very different from these. For our intimacy with Tess at this point is much greater since it is mediated through Angel's company, so that the change in perspective is not merely from her to an opposing gaze, but her visibility to the opposing gaze of something outside the novel (and therefore outside the illusion in which it holds us). Moreover it is not the eye of the painter who picks out a girl from a landscape, or of a god, but the eye of the gleaming cranks and wheels of a locomotive. This estrangement of Tess involves therefore the construction of the reader's eye in terms of a specific social and cultural medium. We have to transpose ourselves to an unspecified passenger seeing Tess as an image lit only by the form of transport in which we are carried. Our vision in other words does not liberate the viewer in the manner to which he is accustomed in the construction of images. 'Foreign' also discards any possibility of an absolute possessing assessment – she is not simple or beautiful but only different (and 'unsophisticated' doesn't give a positive purchase). The moment is further troubled by the simile 'the suspended attitude of a friendly leopard at pause'. Again it is redolent of a strange paradox – it is a moment which returns the gaze we try to hold it in.

In terms of the novel's structure, the function of this passage is to remind us of the social specificity of the story that is being told. And it is not the image taken away by the train that is developed (the reader is whisked away by it and has to be returned to the text); it is a moment whose meaning is *voiced* by the 'receptive Tess'. What follows is her observation of the immensity of the social gap specifically in relation to the Ruskin–Morris critique of the division of labour: 'Londoners will drink it at their breakfasts tomorrow won't they . . . Strange people that we have never seen.' Angel who, as we know, reduces social experience to cultural choices (the ache of modernism is something that may be learnt by rote) vaguely comments on the adulteration of milk (note that his response is on behalf of the consumer), but is totally unable to grasp the social relations which Tess is defining. As she insists and elaborates, *he* takes refuge in the humorous potential of her unsophistication ('particularly centurions') and as she continues, he tries to silence her by reminding her of the private function of their presence at the station. We have seen this before as well when Angel, 'privateering' at the garlic picking, singles out Tess. But what is different here is that he is not artificially selecting Tess but suppressing the real social relationship by which she relates, and thinks of herself as relating, to the world as a whole. More specifically, since the relationship is defined in the reciprocal gaze (the train watching Tess watching the train), I mean *our* world, the world of the consuming reader who will not only drink milk without ever having seen a cow but consumes Tess's story without having to undergo it.

The process recurs – at the climax of what for Tess is an epoch of letting things be. Moving in a photosphere (of her 'excess of honour' for Angel) and knowing that her past sorrows 'were waiting like wolves just outside the circumscribing light', she desires 'perpetual betrothal' so as not to tie time to an institutional structure. Angel presses her for a date in the presence of gnats knowing nothing of their brief glorification. It is another image of dualistic possibility of Darwinian nature since, although it includes the wisdom that knows of their coming extinction, it does not diminish their ecological identity ('irradiated as if they bore fire within them'). At the same time, the transition in the cows lying-in hospital reminds us of the actual economics of Talbothays, and it is in the context of her coming redundancy that Angel presses his hint: 'I don't think you ought to have felt good, Angel.' Note also in this chapter how Angel plans to stay with her to continue the process whereby she learns to talk like him. In other words there is a process of socialization going on which looks like chivalry to her and is actually a form of possession for him.

Significantly again Tess, off her guard, is responsive to the social world as a whole. Listening to the waters of the vale forces on their fancy that a great city lies below them. But it is she who speaks: 'It seems like tens of thousands of them . . . holding public meetings in their market places, arguing, preaching, quarrelling, sobbing, groaning, praying and cursing.' Again Tess reaches out through her imagination to the populous world from which she is held apart by her fictionality and we note how that reaching out is by her own linguistic awareness. For not only is this a novel in which ways of speaking define relationships but one in which, too, the *potential awareness* of its protagonist is in terms of linguistic interaction. It links her to the world of the reader, the communal and the linguistic. But again it is repressed: 'Clare was not particularly heeding' – and he reminds her that she is about to be made redundant.

Now obviously the vision of the train does not inaugurate the discourse of the social relations of production. It has been present from the beginning and it motivates in the last instance both the discourse of nature and the discourse of gender. But what is important about this passage is the reciprocity of the gaze, and this may seem an odd thing to insist on in a context in which the determinations exercise a non-self-contradictory control. But just as the privileging of the voice over the eyes is a token of the evolution of the discourse of gender, so this return of the gaze across the social divide indicates the whole strategy of the novel. For the discourse of the social relations of production is present at first as the one-way gaze of the anthropologist and sociologist, Parson Tringham's thoughtless genealogy, or 'the yellow melancholy of this one-candled spectacle'. But the attack on nature's holy plan is an anger that arises from a securely distant cliché, 'All these young souls were passengers in the Durbeyfield ship.' And, at its most dislocating, the 'picture' of the Durbeyfields merely switches from the flippant to the serious: thus the lurching of the drunken John Durbeyfield between his wife and his daughter 'produced a comical effect, frequent enough in families on nocturnal home-goings: and, like most comical effects, not quite so comic after all'. We only get *into* this world with the controlled terms of Tess's selection from it. Her emergence, and her consequent availability to the less determined ideologies of wisdom and love is the condition of the reader's involvement. But what happens during the passage from Tess's acquiesence in Angel's courtship and his rejection of her is that her mind is developed and her voice *audibly repressed*, so that we can no longer revert to the comfortably distanced realism of the opening. And yet that is precisely and explicitly what Hardy does – he sends Tess back into the world of the social structure from which both Alec and Angel have temporarily, and violatingly, separated her.

Thus when Tess re-enters the novel in chapter 41, she is both a solitary and a social phenomenon: 'We see her a lonely woman with a basket and a bundle in her own porterage.' Later, of course, when the already disastrous consequences of her selectability become a general danger she has deliberately to violate her beauty to survive and become, in a savagely ironic transformation of the title, 'a fieldwoman pure and simple'. It is the more ironic because it picks up and confirms in a bitter way the 'improvement' Clare has made to Tess by decking her with jewels and lowering her neckline: 'The beauty of the midnight crush would often cut but a sorry figure if placed inside the fieldwoman's wrapper upon a monstrous acreage of turnips on a dull day.'

But what we have is a double movement. In the first place, of course, there is a vividly realized sequence of contexts in which Tess is made to pay as a working-class woman for the desire of the middle-class males. Feeling 'hunted', she takes refuge in a copse where wounded partridges take refuge and she has to kill them to put them out of their misery. From then on we have the totally realized starveacre Flintcomb Farm, which produces the most extreme alienation in the woman forced to work there (Marian tells Tess that they can see 'the gleam of a hill' to remind them of Talbothays). Then follows the journey to Emminster, the battle with Alec, and the threshing machine which reduces Tess from the selected object in the pink coat in the previous threshing episode to a mere vibration. Finally the whole episode of the death of the father and the Lady Day eviction reduces her to a sociological phenomenon. (Hardy actually, of course, quotes from his own essay.) I don't need to spell out the vivid realism of this narrative – unlike some of its contemporary naturalistic representations of how the poor live, it is fully presented from the inside as a realm of experience. We only need to read ten pages of George Moore's *Esther Waters*, which Bayley amazingly considers to be superior in some ways to Hardy's novel, to understand the difference between a writer who can present working-class reality and one who relies on 'local colour'. But at the same time, it picks up and modifies the range of perspectives offered. To begin with, it puts Tess in her class again. She may be Mrs Clare but she is one of the girls who are trying to survive on casual labour and dreams. This is not only true of Flintcomb Ash but also, in a more significant way, at Marlott, when she works the vegetable plot in the twilight. 'She was oddly dressed tonight, and presented a somewhat *staring aspect*, her attire being a gown bleached by many washings . . . The women further back more white aprons . . . ' (50; my italics, stressing the gaze returned). The focus on Tess dissolves into the group. So much, Hardy had commented earlier, for Norman blood unaided by Victorian lucre. Selection is a condition of the economic structure. Of course here she is about to be selected again by Alec working alongside her, but it will be a selection whose condition is solely economic.

Secondly, the process explicitly revalues the discourse of nature. When the Durbeyfields are exposed to the Lady Day eviction it is broached with that evolutionary wisdom that has tried to place the oppression of Marian and Tess within 'the two forces'. But just as that is undermined by the immediate comment that Marian's will to enjoy has to be aided with drink, so this is openly contradicted. 'So do flux and reflux – the rhythm of change – alternate and persist in everything under the sky' (50). The Lady Day migrations are part of the life of the countryside. But, he recalls, 'a depopulation was also going on'. This is a historical and not merely a sociological event. Flux and reflux do not account for the irreversible change. This refocusing of gender, from almost standard woman to fieldwoman, and of nature, from the rhythms of life to the history of agriculture is half of the process by which ideological discourses open up into the discourse of the base.

The other dialectically contradicts the generalizing tendency of the first. As she is absorbed more and more into the landscape, becoming a documentary case, as she becomes more and more the object of a text whose concern is less 'with' her than with the social process she represents, she emerges contradictorily as a woman capable of telling her story in her own voice, more than by her eloquent eyes. The 'somewhat staring aspect' responds to her historical placing as a question about the just and the unjust. There is a powerful transition to this return when a little earlier in the chapter she is watched by Alec in the barn. She appears on his altar as a 'Cyprian image' which well nigh extinguishes the fire of the priest. The reconstruction of Tess as *femme fatale* at this stage is a reminder of how far away we have moved from that appropriation, since there is no way, having seen Tess bent double over a field of stones, and hobbling back from Emminster because Mercy had taken her boots, that we can identify with Alec's idealization. But it also leads to an astonishing passage in which the erotic gaze is assimilated into her consciousness as an act of exploitation: 'She went on without turning her head. Her back seemed to be endowed with a sensitiveness to ocular beams – even her clothing – so alive was she to a fancied gaze that might be resting on her from the outside of the barn' (45). It takes her hunger for affection and replaces it with an 'almost physical sense of an implacable past'. The gaze that is returned is the gaze of the

victim who knows that victimization is the law, who knows that the
question she asks about justice is not going to be answered.

This has two consequences. In the first place, precisely insofar as
she is absorbed into a social setting which silences her as one of
many in a long line of many changes, she acquires a voice for the
reader. Thus, after she has spent the night in the copse, she kills
the birds 'tenderly' and feels ashamed of her 'gloom of the night,
based on nothing more tangible than a sense of condemnation
under an arbitrary law of society which had no foundation in
Nature'. We should obviously compare this with the end of chapter
11 – what is said there by the author against Tess's erroneous
consciousness is now her consciousness. Later it becomes impossible to tell whether Hardy is echoing her consciousness or
commenting on it: 'Then she grieved for the beloved man whose
conventional standard of judgement had caused her all these latter
sorrows.' The disconversion of Alec, the letters to Angel, the
complaints about being a victim, the comment that life is vanity –
these are not isolated outbursts but aspects of a structured
development of a voice which does not accept the socialization
which is inevitable. So that we are both presented with a picture of
Tess's life and times, and made to hear the voice that the picture
silences. Obviously the fact that she has to speak through *writing*
has its own kind of resonance and this is confirmed by the fact that
Hardy reprints the second letter at its arrival. The only *voice* she is
allowed is the imitation of Angel but nothing stops her from
making a text. And, of course, this is exactly what is happening in
relation to the reader. For we no more hear Tess than we see her:
what we have is a textualization which offers us (in theory) the
choice. Clearly we only make the choice that is made necessary by
the event but what is important is that Tess is a heroine for the
writing age. She is 'fulfilled' in the space between the social rubric
and the offensive truth.

This dialectical movement is intensified and it means that the
novel has no satisfying end. But it does not mean that it has no
end. What the reader is forced to do is to take on the inexorable
logic of the socialization of Tess in the context of her increased
articulateness. Thus, for example, the way in which she talks to
Alec – not the arguments learnt from Clare, but the comments she
makes in terms of her own experience ('and then it is a fine thing,
when you have had enough of that, to think of securing your
pleasure in heaven by becoming converted', 'He won't hurt me.
He's not in love with me'; 'Why, you can have the religion of loving
kindness at least.') – have a very different effect on the reader from
what is actually happening. That is, she is allowed to reach a
certain kind of wisdom based on her experience which promises to

reconstruct her as a voice rather than as eyes for the reader. Above all, the voice textualized in the letters to Angel makes a stand against his values, so that they effectively for the first time 'faithfully' represent the affirmed integrity of the subtitle: 'I am the same woman, Angel, who you fell in love with.' The second thus recognizes the cruelty of his rejection, and labels it with a word which casts a radical ironic shadow over the end as injustice. The last gives up on justice altogether and calls out that term which we have already seen constitutes the collective gesture in response to the reproach of the law: 'please, please, not to be just; only a little kind to me' (53). The more authority she gains with the reader, the more she is deleted by oppressive forces: as Tess 'learns' by experience, the lessons serve no purpose except to make her aware of what will happen to her anyway.

The action of the text *puts the reader through* the primary working-class experience: the truth does not make you free, it simply exposes your chains. There are other novels which show this. But I know of none that actually thusts it on the reader. This is strengthened by the fact that her two decisions – to go with Alec and to murder him, which each in their turn trap her into the system whose consequences they attempt to subvert – echo Angel's 'truth': 'Yet a consciousness that in a physical sense this man alone was her husband seemed to weigh on her more and more.' We want to ascribe this to the ideology which her whole development has denied. But in the end it is what is left her. Prostitution is the ultimate capitalist relationship for the woman. Her whole economic being is the sale of her body – the violation of the threshing machine is clearly coherent with the occupation of her body. In this perspective the murder is not an escape from this closure. 'How can we live together,' Angel had asked, 'while that man lives?' (36). The rational answer is obvious as Tess's first letter makes clear. Rationality, however, is not that she has an answer but the same as power to rule the world – the only way it is possible to live together is to end Alec's life. Again the effect on the reader is to make him (yes) protest. She doesn't have to go that far! 'What bodily? Is he dead?'

Angel's silly question here echoes one dimension of the reader's response – that is the desire to naturalize the situation, to reserve it in terms of a personal survival. His consequent reflections spell out the other dimension of his logic, the inscription of the reciprocated gaze:

> His horror at her impulse was mixed with amazement at the strength of her affection for himself; and at the strangeness of

> its quality, which had apparently extinguished the moral
> sense altogether. Unable to realize the gravity of her conduct
> she seemed at last content; and he looked at her . . . and
> wondered what obscure strain in the d'Urberville blood had
> led to this aberration – if it were an aberration. (57)

'Amazement', 'obscure strain', 'aberration – if it were an
aberration', 'nothing could be more foreign': Angel's trip to Brazil
has taught him relativity but it is not enough to take him over to
her. And this applies to us as well, since he is the reader's main
agent in the last phase, the narrative centrality of Tess having been
brought to an end with the unexplained decision to go off with
Alec. That is why, in spite of the dialectic of experience and
circumstance by which the reader is increasingly frustrated as the
novel progresses, what we have to acknowledge in the end is the
reciprocation of the gaze. From that reciprocation grows, however,
not some privatized privileging of experience (by which we could
possess 'Tess' as an act of love) but the unviolated signifier of the
returned gaze as question and dream.

First let us look at the moment of recognition itself and then try
to pick up its reverberations in the text.

> They stood, fixed, their baffled hearts looking out of their
> eyes with a joylessness pitiful to see. Both seemed to implore
> something to shelter them from reality.
> 'Ah – it is my fault!' said Clare.
> But he could not get on. Speech was as inexpressive as
> silence. But he had a vague consciousness of one thing,
> though it was not clear to him till later; that his original Tess
> had spiritually ceased to recognize the body before him as
> hers – allowing it to drift, like a corpse upon the current, in a
> direction dissociate from its living will. (55)

On one level, the reciprocation of the gaze here is the recognition of
how the truth is a form of bondage: they stand *fixed*, their hearts
look out of their eyes (as though out of a cell), and the joylessness
(the negative of the recognition after absence, the very reverse of
what should be) is effecting a positive force (like the later
'existlessness'). Seeking 'shelter' (the word is proleptic) from
'realms', Angel tries to resolve it by *language*, but is unable to
continue. Note that Hardy says not what one would expect, 'go
on', but 'get on' – it is as though language would be a way of
progress, but it is devoid of its power now. (This may have
something to do with the expressive power of Tess's own 'realism'

– 'he bought me', 'these clothes are what he's put on me. The step back to him was not so great as it seems. He had been as husband to me: you never had.') What remains to him is 'a vague consciousness' of the implications of the reciprocated gaze. Note how carefully Hardy sets up this sentence (an addition of 1892; he must have felt it necessary to establish Tess's specific presence). She ceases to recognize (see) her body, which is the body in his gaze, her body before him, as hers. Throughout what we have seen is her body – here at the moment of epiphany (which is what it ironically is). It is on offer as a property of someone else. He *bought* me. This confirms the imprisoned look which they exchange, but leaves two openings. In the first place, the new Angel is *conscious* that the look makes this separation, and secondly it is like a corpse to a current (Ophelia) dissociated from *its living will*. So that there is an other that has vacated this purchased body clothed by its owner. An other that the new Angel is forced to recognize.

The terms of this recognition are worked out in such detail that we have for the moment merely to follow the text. Of course Angel, for whose ideology the murder is done, thinks she has gone mad: 'As well as his confused and excited ideas could reason, he supposed that in the moment of mad grief of which she spoke her mind had *lost its balance*, and plunged her into this abyss' (my italics). It reminds us of 'you are ill; and it is natural'. The gesture Tess makes which embodies the full force of her emancipation from Alex and her commitment to Angel is bound to appear like an act of insanity. There is a point beyond which the eloquence of woman, in her own voice, is always *insane*. Obviously you don't need to go around killing the men who possess you. That is going too far. 'What, bodily? Is he dead?' But just as Angel is able to stop speaking and be vaguely conscious, so here his ideas are confused and excited and are inadequate ideas (in Spinoza's sense). And a remarkable transition takes place, prepared for by the relativism of Brazil, foreseen in the gentle way he carried her across the steams:

It was very terrible [read tragic] if true: if a temporary hallucination [women are hysterical. He never meant bodily dead!], sad [I'll look after her till we get her to a hospital]. But, anyhow [this is confusing] here was this [here, no other but this one, not a constructed generality] deserted wife of his, this passionately fond [she terrifies me] woman, clinging to him without suspicion that he would be anything but her protector [poor thing has forgotten that there is a law. She seeks shelter from reality!].

Angel is still the old ineffectual Angel beating in his void. But also new. Thus:

> He saw that for him to be otherwise was not, in her mind, within the region of the possible. Tenderness was absolutely dominant in Clare at last.

After all those confused ideas and shifting responses, HE SAW. But what he sees is not that she is mad or sad or any other objectifiable predicate. He sees what in her mind is the region of the possible. He sees her as subject of her own sentence. And the word that Hardy reaches for in this context is, of course, 'tenderness'. It is a word that has previously occurred in the sleepwalking sequence: 'The revelation of his tenderness by the incident of the night raised dreams of a *possible future* with him.'

This last is, of course, a private thought of Tess. In fact she has deliberately suppressed it because it might imply that she was laughing at this compromised dignity, and she is not sure that he won't think her calculating. That privacy, that silence, however, constitute a trace in the novel that is not the novel for the novel is the law. But there is also a not-the-law, '*dreams of a possible future*'. Two moments at Talbothays indicate this. The first is the negative, silent response Tess makes to the story of Jack Dollop: 'This question of a woman telling her story – the heaviest of crosses to herself – seemed but amusement to others.' Almost immediately after, she varies that other in response to his individuation and selectivity:

> 'Our tremulous lives are so different from theirs, are they not?' . . .
> 'No so very different, I think . . . There are very few women's lives that are not tremulous.'

The significance of these statements becomes clear in the last but two chapters of the novel. Ideologically what is important is that they reach out to other subjectivities. There are instants of tenderness, but which go against the uttered phrase. However, they are important because they are of the text as well as in it. This question of a woman telling her story is precisely the question of the novel which is compelled by the silence of her oppression to tell it for her, and tell it as an amusement, since that is what novels are, for others. Moreover her process of selection – this is Tess's story and not anybody else's – is part of the condition of the novel too. But, as we are constantly reminded, the distance between Tess and the other girls is not always so very great. There are other stories. Other women's lives are just as tremulous. The whole pragmatic effect of the novel is called by this into question. Boumelha says that Hardy cannot make up his mind whether Tess is exceptional or representative. But we must try to distinguish the effect of the text from its commodity value. For the process of representativeness itself is a process of exceptionalizing. To write a novel is always to lift the single story out of the social picture and for precisely that reason it is bound by its very nature to lure the reader towards the private solution. In other words we ought to be feeling very strongly that Tess needn't have actually murdered Alec and that she and Angel could have worked it out. And maybe if they had been actual living human beings they could have worked at some kind of private solution to the contradictions with which they engage. But it is precisely this kind of confusion that Ellen in Morris's *News from Nowhere* objects to in the novel and which Hardy, motivating Tess at the end as *actress* (in both senses of the word) avoids. He opens out the book not in the sense of leaving it available but in a sense that pushes it back into life, into the general. So that if we do feel very strongly that Tess didn't need to murder Alec, we ought in the end to understand that to feel that way is irrelevant.

It is irrelevant because Tess has understood what constructs her and the murder makes possible a parenthesis within the sentence (in both senses) in which she is inscribed. For actually, like Sancho Panza, she is given an island, not in space but in time, during which she is allowed to learn from her experience.

We have to return to this running commentary on the text; it is so necessary to be careful. She has killed Alec because it has come to her as a shining light that she 'will get you back that way' (57). Her response to Angel's decentring of love (not for its own sweet sake but for the sake of the species and the institution) is to turn him into a god (she mistakes his lack of fervour for chivalry, remember?): 'I was unable to bear your not loving me.' 'I will not desert you' (whatever you have done!). She, however, takes possession of the novel's campaign key word: 'the one man on earth who had loved her purely, and who had believed in her as pure'. (Note she has told Alec that it is possible to retain *loving kindness* and *purity*'.) There is, however, an unalienated version of this worship: 'the thought of going through the world with him as her own familiar friend . . . the laugh of a woman in company with the man she loves'. Out of this she creates Utopia. We note now that for this space, it is *Tess who looks at him* (he was still her Antinous, her Apollo even) and he is no longer at the service of his own consciousness but of hers. They move not to the station but into the woods. Briefly they recover a national rhythm: 'They promenaded over the dry bed of fir needles, thrown into a vague intoxicating atmosphere at the consciousness of being together at last, with no living soul between them; ignoring that there was a corpse.' I call it 'natural' here simply because the only significance of the corpse is the law – in 'nature' there is no reason why you should take any notice of a corpse. (Utopias are by their nature natural.) Moreover it is a journey into the 'interior' (Angel's word), which makes us forget for a while that we are actually talking about England.

They follow 'obscure paths' – it is to a new terrain, a new life they tread. And yet the journey is not fugitive but innocent: 'Their every idea was temporary and unforefending, like the plans of two children.' The perspective created by these phrases gives them a parenthesis. They are in movement rather than flight. Later, coming to an abandoned house, Tess interprets it socially: 'All these rooms empty, and we without a roof over our heads.' So it is her comment as much as Angel's decision that takes them back. Hardy, of course, reminds us of the actual state of affairs by having the housekeeper leave them alone because of the fine quality of the clothes Tess has been wearing – which, were, of course given her by Alec. In case we miss the point, she thinks of it as a genteel elopement – that is, she inserts it into a romantic love story. 'Rest at last' – an epoch of rest – news from nowhere. 'Why should one put an end to all that's sweet and lovely? . . . All is trouble outside there; inside here content' (58). She is looking out and he looks out *after* her. Later, when she hears the *music* of Stonehenge, he will listen – in contrast with his unheeding responses earlier. Moreover, he finds what she says is true – 'Within was affection, union, error forgiven: outside was inexorable.' The happy house, a dream of rest, of union, which cannot last for really it is not just there but part of a social system – a property, like Tess herself. The contrast between what is and what might be.

The utopian interval makes the novel's end completely uncathartic. Passing through the intercepting medieval city to the heathen temple of Stonehenge they reach a theatre of containment Stonehenge is clearly the monument but it is full of problems. Angel thinks it monstrous but she hears there the music of a gigantic harp. She asks to stay, but he says it is too *visible*. She replies that it is an ancestral home (through the mother). She asks whether it has been used as a sacrifice to God and he replies no, 'I believe to the Sun.' So that it is a heathen and matrilinear, and it is also the site of her question about Liza Lu. Neither Boumelha nor

Bayley find this acceptable. But it is neither fantasy nor childish. What Tess is asking Angel to do is marry his deceased wife's sister, which is not merely blasphemous but specifically is the occasion of Matthew Arnold's most vituperative attack on modern liberalism in *Culture and Anarchy*. Tess is once again challenging the hegemony, this time in terms of the customs of her country. So although it is right for the site of sacrifice it is not the sacrifice of the present order. She is too fit, as one of my undergraduates pointed out, to die at Stonehenge. Hardy stresses her capacity for walking and effort. What we have instead is a line of policemen crossing a plain to take her back into her sentence.

I have read and reread *Tess of the d'Urbervilles* many times during twenty years, and I still find the end impossible to read. Throughout I have warned against naturalizing Tess, but, of course, it is part of the strategy of the novel that we should do so. The novelist aims at an illusion. But this novelist aiming at it and succeeding only does so to punish us for our complacency. How many other English novels end with the execution of the female protagonist, who has already been raped? To have her die would enable us to say amen – terrible and sad but so be it. But she is hanged by the neck until she is dead. 'Justice' is in inverted commas, both because it is a legal term carried over into aesthetic discourse (hence the savagely ironic invocation of the Aeschylean phrase). We know what average human nature thinks of divine morality, and we know that Tess understands the meaning of sport: 'she had occasionally caught glimpses of these men in girlhood . . . strangely accoutred, a bloodthirsty look in their eyes'. Our ruling classes, like gods, administering justice as sport. But notice how it continues – gaze and speech again – 'the two speechless gazers bent themselves down to earth, as if in prayer, and remained thus in prayer absolutely motionless.' But the flag, the only signifier of narrative left, continues like some distant friend to 'wave silently'. Invocations of *Paradise Lost* are not adequate here (though they are relevant). Hardy is making us read about the response to the *hanging* of a loved one. As soon as they had strength they arose. Nothing, of course, is left to reciprocate their gaze. They are not silent, but speechless. The only language is the flag's. But is is also the novelist's. 'Justice' is torn between legal action and poetic fitness, but, as we know Hardy sent *Tess* to Morris, and the original newspaper of the Social Democratic Federation was called *Justice*. Justice is more than the prevailing law. It is something that is fought for, a truth that is on the offensive.

5   Hardy's Fist

What has Providence done to Mr Hardy that he should rise up in his arable land of Wessex and shake his fist at his creator?

Edmund Gosse

That is the voice of the educated proletariat speaking more distinctly than it has ever spoken before in the English Literature

H. G. Wells[1]

One Cannot Choose One's Readers

Of course, no text, however hard it tries, stands free within its frame. But *Jude the Obscure* rejoices in its entanglement:

> Growing up brought responsibilities, he found. Events did not rhyme quite as he had thought. Nature's logic was too horrid for him to care for. That mercy towards one set of creatures was cruelty to another sickened his sense of harmony. As you got older, and felt yourself to be at the centre of your time, and not at a point in its circumference, as you had felt when you were little, you were seized with a sort of shuddering, he perceived. All around you there seemed to be something glaring, garish, rattling, and the noises and glares hit upon the little cell called your life, and shook it and warped it. (I. 2)

Lying down behind the pigsty, sacked for having been kind to the birds he is paid to scare, this hitherto safely ironized innocent, failing to find a coherent discourse (discourses seek to rhyme, to harmonize) is granted instead that authoritative second person as though the ' of speech remains unclosed. For 'he perceived' is tagged on too late to keep the third and fourth sentences in the frame of free indirect style, and the perception is not only as sophisticated as the implied author, but deliberately inverts the traditional development of knowledge, which is that you learn to be part of a larger whole. Growing up is an ordeal of centring and you, the reader, are dragged in to be made part of that ordeal. It happens again in Part I, chapter 4: 'but nobody did come because nobody does'. We are supposed to be watching the development of a poor young boy, but he keeps taking charge of our end of the syntax and our tense. The particular is not generalized, it is universalized. The very language pulls you in to the picture: Jude is not one of many (typical) – he is one of us.

Again and again the novel breaks out of its frame. Another, more representative, example follows the death of the children:

> 'I am a pitiable creature' she said, 'good neither for earth nor heaven any more! What ought to be done?'
> She stared at Jude and tightly held his hand.
> 'Nothing can be done,' he replied. 'Things are as they are and will be brought to their destined issue.'
> She paused. 'Yes! Who said that?' she asked heavily.
> 'It comes in the chorus of the *Agamemnon*. It has been on my mind continually since this happened.'
> 'My poor Jude – how you've missed everything! – you more than I, for I did get you! to think you should know that by your unassisted reading, and yet be in poverty and despair.' (VI. 2)

It's all in the worst possible taste. The children have been found hanging on the back of the door, and not only does Jude produce an apt quotation which shows his knowledge more than it illuminates the situation, but Sue suddenly looks out of her understandable hysteria and both awards him an accolade and tells the reader how to assess his quotation. The novel frequently annoys the reader in this way, preventing him from 'identifying' with the situation (by which I really mean keeping it out there as a self-contained game, for this is so 'unbelievable', isn't it?) and, what is worse, doing the critic out of a job, since analysis and comparison are, as Eliot says, the critic's tools, and Sue and Jude frequently do both.

Worse still, the novel bedecks itself with precedents either by quotation, or allusion or direct comparison: '"it makes me feel as if a tragic doom overhung our family, as it did the house of Atreus." "Or the house of Jeroboam," said the quondam theologian.' (V. 4). The novel not only ruins the prospects of interpretation by explicit discussion but also offers its own system of literary allegiances, which makes it difficult for the critic to determine influences or place it in a tradition (though this has not deterred many from doing it). And it breaches decorum in other ways such as when, again at the centre of a highly charged scene that any respectable writer would let us enjoy for all it was worth, Jude warns Phillotson that it is dangerous to sit on stone without a covering and offers him some sacking, presumably so that his rival does not get piles. Obviously it reminds us that Jude is more intimate with material contingency than the schoolteacher, but it still seems an oddly affectionate and 'irrelevant' gesture. Hardy keeps preventing us from reading this novel as 'story' – as illusion, as fable, as vision. *The Woodlanders* and *Tess of the d'Urbervilles* subvert the reader they call into being. *Jude the Obscure* does not even acknowledge the reader as a self-defined and separate subject. It is simply not fit for consumption.[2]

Or to put it positively, it is a text that can only be called into being as an event. It certainly *was* an event, as the reviews and letters about it to Hardy show. The *Life* mainly stresses the hostile response, and the 1912 Preface says that this cured him of novel-writing. But this flagrantly misrepresents what happened. If the Bishop of Wakefield publicly burnt the novel and Mrs Oliphant took it as evidence of Hardy's membership of an anti-marriage league, a whole group of reviewers – Gosse, Ellis, Wells, Hannigan, Le Gallienne – wrote about it with a passionate commitment which effectively embraced the text more as a cause than as the object of a professional judgement. Nor can Hardy have had any other intention (despite the disingenuous protests of aesthetic disinterestedness) than to make an intervention in highly controversial issues of the day, most notably that of marriage. As soon as Jude is married, he makes an explicit comment about the nature of marriage which is directly linked not only with the host of novels which dealt with 'the new woman' but also with the prolonged debate of 1891–3 about marriage which dominated the journals and to which Hardy himself contributed.[3] If he could justifiably claim that the novel is not merely about marriage but also about education, that theme is presented within the parameters of

theology, which links it with the current polemic about religion
(see the correspondence with Clodd).[4] And bearing in mind that
the big sensation in fiction of the previous decade was precisely a
novel, Mrs Humphrey Ward's *Robert Elsmere*, which dealt with the
contact between education and theology particularly in the way an
Oxford intellectual's theological doubts can be made positive by
his recognition that working-class people are likely to be blasphemous and revolutionary without some religious values, the Bishop of
Wakefield was surely right to burn Hardy's novel. Beside anything
it said about sex, it also portrayed the absolute failure of
Christianity to provide any ethical or ontological guidance.

This is doing scant justice to the topicality of the novel,[5] but I
only want to indicate that it is conceived as an intervention, and
that it is in those terms that we still read it. Education and the
family, in Althusser's phrase, form the ideological couple of late
capitalism, and that is the concern of this novel (that is, not one
and the other but the coupling of them): it is the double call of the
self into the world that determines and constructs it. The effect of
the disframing is precisely that it negotiates the eventfulness of the
text's reference as an eventfulness of its action or the act of reading
it. We are agitated by its vulgarity. This is guaranteed by two
formal devices, a structural strategy and an intertextuality.

We are used by now to Hardy's triadic structure, whether as
sequence, as in *The Mayor of Casterbridge* and *The Woodlanders* or as
the overlaying and refocusing of levels of discourse as in *Tess of the
d'Urbervilles*. *Jude the Obscure* develops this in an extreme way,
constructing a triadic 'series of seemings' which I take to mean not
the charting of a mental history, since the novel is much too bound
up with the contingent and the necessary for that, but a sequence
of illusory modes which comment on one another. Specifically, it is
structured according to a determinative role of place which
presents us with a precise graph of the socialization of the
characters. 'At', the word which links the title of each part, implies
a double negation of the subject since although it defines a location
it does not suggest, in fact in most cases positively denies
accommodation – thus at various stages the characters are placed
but have no place. Moreover, there is a shift in the significance of
place progressively from the purely given (Marygreen) to the
chosen by gesture (Christminster), the chosen by compromise,
blocked gesture (Melchester and even more Shaston), the determined solely by economic necessity (Aldbrickham and elsewhere).
The arbitrariness is vital: they both have to go to these places and
these places have no meaning for them. Thus finally the arbitrarily
asserted return is the locative equivalent of the nevertheless which

we have encountered as the key action of the late fiction, but significantly *as* return and not as a gestural metonymy.

This gives us a triadic structure in two ways. First it constitutes an onion, since Marygreen and Christminster again both universalize their predicaments in metaphysical terms. Christminster and Aldbrickham are both about the condition of the working class, and at the centre, Melchester and Shaston, preoccupied as they are with training and marriage respectively, personalize, so that there is a vortex of particularization. But in terms of a linear structure it also means that the first and the last sections act as a symbolic frame for the realistic narrative (which is one reason why the novel seems to have no frame, since frames should not really be in the picture). That use of the second person which I indicated as important earlier is the keynote of Marygreen, which centres on the field and which in spite of sharp social observation, works out to a highly generalized level.[6] 'But nobody did come because nobody does' indicates a shift from the condition of Jude to the condition of man: the field is the ontology of the unnecessary life. As soon as he moves to Christminster, Jude embarks on a history marked by the specific institutions of his time and the specific relationship to them he has as working man (and Sue as woman). It is not the field and God's gardener, but the city, the stonemason's yard and the Master of Bibliol, the marriage bed and the husband. At the end, however, the novel is transformed again. Just as the metonymy of the gesture ('thither J.F.') lifts the novel out of its field and into the urban life of the nineteenth century, so the metonymy of the return is to 'the centre of my dream' – to 'the *reflected* sunshine of its crumbling walls' (my italics). It is a return to a symbolic mode but not a symbolism generated by the metaphoric eye of the narrator (making the actual field the field of life), but a theatrical gesture generated out of the protagonists' despair of dealing with life 'realistically'. Jude's speech, Father Time's euthanasic infanticide, Sue's conversion and histrionic remarriage make the text a performance. The novel restates itself – as 'myth', as social problem novel, and as (avant-garde) theatre.

The intertextuality functions also both to alienate the text (in a Brechtian sense) and to radicalize its effect. This is an area I have to dispute with critics with whom I am broadly in sympathy but who, I think, take 'the letter killeth' as too global and one-dimensional an instruction about what to do with the literature incorporated.[7] First, we should recall that Hardy's relationship to writing is dialectical – it is both an institution which has to be negotiated and an agency of self-improvement. The letter killeth is after all a perception only available to the literate who know their

Bible.[8] Moreover, killing isn't only a bad thing. Some things need to be killed, and one thing the literature that is invoked in this text can kill is the unquestioning acceptance of authority emanating from Bibliol and the marriage laws. Moreover, the actual context in 2 Corinthians indicates that by letter is meant the law, the scripture, as voiced, to invoke Derrida once more. To suggest that the display of learning merely signifies the dead illusion that Jude is betrayed by is to read the allusiveness undialectically (although I accept that if you follow many of the quotations through they cast an ironic light on the text, as Ingham in her excellent Introduction indicates).

The key to this is the episode of the grammars. Jude is to think that the possession of the grammars will give him instant access to the ancient languages and therefore to a distinguished career as a bishop (though to regard him as hypocritical because he fancies having money is a middle-class judgement). He is disabused, of course, but two things follow from it. In the first place, Hardy let us know that partly Jude is only under an illusion because he has no access to modern linguistics, Grimm's Law. This theme pervades the whole learning process. It is not just that Christminster is difficult to enter, it is also that it is a place of ignorance, like the British elite in general, not only impervious but second-rate. Thus there is a way of learning which Jude is denied. But secondly, he takes on the pedestrian grammars and works his way through them, which is what brings him to Christminster, and if not to the University to Sue, and the echo of the undergraduate and the enlightened liberation from the darkness of theology and marriage. The written may be identical with the walls (see II.2, as Wotton points out[9]) but it is also the obscured signpost, J.F.

The texts of Jude form their own antagonistic canon, which is deliberately a contradiction in terms, because what opposes itself to rubric and cardinal is an apocrypha, and in more ways than one the textual allegiances of this novel are apocryphal.

In the first place, there is a highly polemical secularization of the sacred text itself. Not only are there frequent references to the actual Apocrypha (including, for example, the Gospel of Nicodemus, which actually presents Pilate in a sympathetic light) but also Sue calls attention to the absurd way the Song of Songs is canonized, and the book most frequently quoted from is the Book of Job, which Leslie Stephen had described as the agnostic's book of the Bible and which had been the subject of a great deal of non-Christian commentary such as that of Renan and Mark Rutherford.[10] Even the New Testament citations which occur more frequently as we should expect when Sue begins to retreat into the

Church, tend to privilege the epistles to the Corinthians, which are actually not very Pauline in their liberal attitude to dogma.[11] So the Bible is evoked not as a sanctified authority but as a document of human experience that privileges love, sex and the resistance to oppression.

There is also a secular use of a poetic succession. The poets most often cited are Shelley, who was sent down from Oxford for atheism, Browning, who became disillusioned with higher education and who was radicalized by his reading of Shelley, and Swinburne, who was a notorious rebel at Oxford and whose most immediate mentor was Browning. And Hardy too, of course, was immediately inspired by Swinburne, and exchanged letters with him comparing the reception of *Jude the Obscure* with that of *Poems and Ballads*. All of them at some point oppose Christianity and marriage. And they can in this respect be linked with the other recurrent presence, Gibbon, whose fifteenth chapter is cited several times and who is, of course, one of the inspirations of the poem quoted about Julian the Apostate.

But this leads to the dialectical effect of these citations. On the one hand there is a radical agnostic tradition which underwrites the intellectual emancipation of the novel. On the other hand, of course, all these writers, including Gibbon, had the privilege to go to the University, even if, through their integrity, they rejected its values.

Gibbon's account of the rise of Christianity in his fifteenth and sixteenth chapters makes continual use of the words 'obscure' and 'obscurity' to describe both Judaism and early Christianity. For him a fundamentally rational polytheistic civilization hardly noticed the rise of this grubby little religion from Palestine. In the sixteenth chapter he relates how the grandsons of St Jude, supposedly the brother of Christ, were arrested in Rome because they were thought to be pretenders to the mantle of King David. To prove their innocence, they showed their hands, 'hardened with daily labour'. 'The obscurity,' Gibbon contemptuously remarks, 'of the house of David might protect them from the suspicions of a tyrant'. Hardy's novel enters a tradition of a radical discourse knowing it to be socially apart. The reaction to Gibbonian rationalism implicit in its evocation is parallel to Marx's response to Feuerbach. Ideologically Feuerbach explained the deformative effect of religion but failed to understand its material foundation. The 'theoretic unconventionality' which the intertext invokes is not denied, on the contrary it is very important, but its limits are seen.[12]

In terms of his own immediate cultural situation, Hardy knows that he can call on what we can accurately term an avant-garde (the case of Shelley, for example, is partly mediated through Dowden's biography, which provoked the reactionary essay of Arnold in 1886).[13] Theoretically, avant-gardes are not elites, since there is nothing to prevent anybody who cares to master the intellectual parameters of such groups from entering them. But, of course, only certain privileged groups are ever in a position to choose. *Jude the Obscure* exists exactly at this interface. In a letter, ironically to Mrs Henniker, one of Hardy's society ladies, he pointed out that his novel was written for those into whose soul the iron had entered, and would not be appreciated by frequenters of drawing-rooms. But, he added, one cannot choose one's readers.[14] A little earlier, the eminently bourgeois feminist Millicent Fawcett, admiring *Tess of the d'Urbervilles*, asked him to write a novel warning working people of the disastrous consequences of hasty marriage. Hardy declined, but it is tempting to think that his last novel is a considered ironic response to that banal request.[15] For all that it was written with a certain support assured, there is a level on which Hardy is writing for the future.

Of course, that future is observed in Wells's review. But the educated proletariat, sharp as the phrase is, is a contradiction in terms. For in this world, to be educated (led out) is to cease to be proletarian. It is a way out of the field to which there is no return. *Jude the Obscure* rallies the avant-garde in the name of the excluded, and it remains an event because that means it poses the question of knowledge and its ideology, knowledge as education and carnality, the wall and the garden of bourgeois order. For to open them out is to admit the obscure, and that is the decline and fall of an empire.

Ingham argues that the outcry against the novel was the recognition of a revolutionary novel.[16] I agree with the spirit and not the letter of this, for if the novel distances itself from the official public it does so under cover of the avant-garde. The question is whether the avant-garde relates to the proletariat, those whose soul the iron has entered and in terms of the historical formation of the novel, its existence as a totality, surely not. Significantly the word Ingham reaches for is 'subversive'. The *revolutionary* novel is still to be made, out of the recalling of the reader into a double reading. Having dragged in the reader, it devises a sequence of concrete universals. The field is the result of labours but becomes the symbol of the human condition; Christminster is both the wall against the self-taught and the ideological formation of the nineteenth century; marriage is about the new woman but is actually about the family. We need two readings, one representational, which is the field and leads to the coming universal wish not to live, and the other representative of the voices unsilenced within it. We can thus transform the totality that the novel represents to the totalization of which it is a representative, or, to put it another way, to understand the agency of its structuration.

My Scheme or Dream

'At' doubly decentres – it is an exclusion, since none of the places demand your presence, and an imprisonment since only by being domiciled at that place can you get work. This is to become a novel, literally about finding a lodging: knowing your place means knowing you have no place. Yours is an unnecessary life because its necessities are not reciprocated. The cell called your life is at once an incarceration, the thick wall, as Pater puts it, of personality,[17] and always, at the same time, part of a whole. It turns the organic inside out – instead of the part being itself and being part of a greater self, the part is cut off from the whole and for all that is not free to be itself.

Marygreen thus inverts the obvious fictional structures to which it makes reference. Classically enough it begins with a departure, but this is not the setting out of the protagonist, but his abandonment – he is left behind, alone but not on the road. Sent to the well, which is as ancient as the village itself, he finds only 'a long circular perspective ending in a shining disk of unquivering water' which offers him no mirror, but merely assimilates the tear of his desolation into its depths. His thoughts are *interrupted* by his aunt. Three possibilities of relationship are at once denied. The only link with a present, with the teacher who is leaving is reduced to the stored, unplayed piano. The link with the past and the quivering water is denied by the reversal and absorption of the well process (that is, instead of drawing water from it, he drops a tear into it which is never to be heard of again, which makes no mark). And finally his aunt disrupts even his relationship to his own thought, so that when he does operate the well it is overshadowed by the negations of fear and stress.

I term the section mythic only because of its quality of generalized explanation, 'how it came to pass'. It clearly parodies the opening of *Tom Sawyer*, where the importunity of the aunt provokes the division of labour. Jude has no such resources – this will not be a comic novel about the origins of capitalism or about the retarding interval of childhood. What he finds instead of a negotiable world is the apparently transcendent presence of the field:

The brown surface of the field went right up towards the sky all round, where it was lost by degrees in the mist that shut out the actual verge and accentuated the solitude. The only marks on the uniformity of the scene were a rick of last year's produce standing in the midst of the arable, the rooks that rose at his approach, and the path athwart the fallow by which he had come, trodden now by he hardly knew whom, though once by many of his own dead family.

'How ugly it is here!' he murmured.

The fresh harrow-lines seemed to stretch like the channellings in a piece of new corduroy, lending a meanly utilitarian air to the expanse, taking away its graduations, and depriving it of all history beyond that of the few recent months, though to every clod and stone there really attached associations enough and to spare – echoes of songs from ancient harvest-days, of spoken words, and of sturdy deeds. Every inch of ground had been the site first or last of energy, gaiety, horse-play, bickerings, weariness. (I. 2).

There are two manifest forms of obscurity here. First the obscurity of social marginalization which is how it is dominantly used throughout the text (obscure means poor, as Ingham says).[18] Also, however, there is an obscurity of mind. The field of vision (though, of course, it is also a field in which he works and a battlefield of Darwinian nature), doubly darkens Jude's view: first by stretching up to the horizon and obliterating its verge; equally, as the second paragraph makes clear, the brown utilitarian surface obscures its history which has to be supposed by a self-advertising, omniscient narrator ('though to every clod and stone . . . '). Thus the self is abandoned to this apparently unbounded real without a history, though in fact, as the text keeps telling us, there is nothing exceptional about it since he is one among the many which he cannot see. This gives him nothing, for the many are obliterated. Only the well survives as an ancient relic and the church is 'erected on a new piece of ground by a certain obliterator of historic records'. Not, either, that the historic records hold much comfort, since insofar as the invisible past is authorially voiced it is largely a history of deceit and oppression.

None the less it has its marks, and thus a third kind of obscurity: a rick of last year's *standing*, a path *athwart* the fallow, and the rooks, '*inky* spots on the nut brown soil'. They are marks of a kind of opposition, residual, transversal, despoiling. The obscurity of Gibbon's little sect is about to overwhelm the world and it will be Julian's philosophy that will be described as obscure.[19] Now look at Jude's response – 'how ugly it is here!' It is a strange way for a young boy to respond to his oppression. The objection is aesthetic, and the only gesture he makes imaginative: 'his heart grew sympathetic with the bird's thwarted desires . . . A magic thread of fellow feeling united his life with theirs.' 'Thwarted' recalls the path athwart and the thwarted aspirations of the unseen buried. The magic thread, which clearly echoes the Paterian web, comes from the perception that their life 'much resembled' his own. Later, he will see Christminster as phantasmogoria, 'either directly seen or miraged', and he will look at his learning as at a magic lantern. I do not mean that this novel has a teleology, though at the point of his death Jude will operate a theatrical representation, having tried to survive through the creation of images, first in stone and then in cake. Rather it constitutes a mode of relationship for the reader of what would otherwise be a self who disappeared into the field. Jude too, by his voice (note), which is opposed to the noise he is paid to make, is a mark, unedited by the world he inhabits since he has no value, no family, no community, only the prospect of 'the fall of the curtain' on his unnecessary life. Hardy has called you into the being of what Virginia Woolf will later call the obscure life. The obscure life is the subject without a predicate, the margin that calls into question the page from which it is excluded.

The field carries only marks, to which we shall return; but the opening momentum is the necessity of moving out of the field, which can obviously only happen in disorganic ways (since organically, the field would have to open itself to the subject athwart it, which would be absurd). Verges are boundaries, here lost in mist. They propose both limits and edges that the Marygreen section defines, thus achieving its ontological status. The dialectic of limits and edges is narratively embodied in the marriage to Arabella and the grammars respectively, though neither of these are simply assigned to one concept (since edges are always limits and vice versa). But their confrontation is dramatized in the walk during which Jude stares at his future and is struck with a prick.

The limits are stated by the two women in Jude's life as a quadrilateral which could enclose a field. They are presented as four syntactically axiomatic statements:

1   'Pigs must be killed. Poor folks must live' (Arabella)
2   'She or he "who lets the world, or his own portion of it choose his plan of life for him, has no need of any other faculty than the ape like one of imitation" ' (Sue, quoting J. S. Mill)

3   'Feelings are feelings' (Arabella)
4   'We should mortify the flesh, the terrible flesh' (Sue – this
    is not strictly axiomatic, but it is her inductive logic
    consequent on 'because we are too meny')

These are all true and borne out by the narrative, but obviously
they contradict one another. There is a primary opposition
between Arabella and Sue. Statements 1 and 2 embody the
polarities of evolution, since on the one hand evolution is the
struggle for survival and on the other the recognition of the
development of species and choice becomes part of the definition of
being human. Statements 3 and 4 embody the polarity of emotion,
since the only way to protect the feelings is to mortify the flesh and
the only means of mortification is the privileging of feeling over
other demands. Thus these pairs might seem to deal antinomously
with the objective and subjective respectively. Moreover, they
respectively represent working-class and middle-class verges, since
Arabella's are realistic (natural and sexual selection as the binary
form of ''tis nature and what do please God') and Sue's
aspirational, postulating the world as the field of the self – self-
fulfilment, self-discipline. For, of course, the working class is the
predicate of the middle-class subject, which is why if we do not
sentimentalize, working-class culture can too often look like a
programme of acceptance and evasion. Equally however 1 and 3
and 2 and 4 are as incompatible with one another as 1 and 2 and 3
and 4. In this opposition within the character, Arabella would have
to be taken as representing 'nature' (Darwinian and romantic
respectively) and Sue 'culture' as the illusion of free will and
equality and the superior choice of spirituality respectively.

There is nothing *really* natural about Arabella, but she uses this
term frequently (for example about her grief for little Jude) and
tries in several ways to imitate natural processes like pregnancy
and hair growing. Of course the Other of Arabella is only another
mode of assertion into the symbolic order, since what she offers is a
trap to make a marriage. Arabella's sexuality is never separated
from conventionality: the barmaid becomes the landlady.
Lawrence's later reading of Arabella as some kind of natural
energy only shows that he was as vulnerable to barmaids as the
rest of us. But her dimple making and hair enhancing are not
qualifications of her sexuality – they are part of it. Even the Other
trajectory (literal) of the pig's prick is bound up with the economic
system it serves. After all it is not mere realism that locates the
enticement and breakdown in the dismemberment and demolition
respectively of the pig. Not only is Jude's sexuality at variance with

his theological ambition, it is the sign of his proper place within the economy of pig killing – that is, lower-class marriage. 'Feelings are feelings', Arabella's furthest excursion from the symbolic order, is a return. It has nothing to do with the loving kindness of Jude's sympathies in the field. When she expresses her grief over the death of the children she admits that she feels much more for Father Time 'as is natural'. Sue and Jude have already shown us something very different from this natural which serves the social. The natural is the symbolic order. The Other is only what the structure licenses – carnivals are not revolutions, but ways by which revolutions are avoided.

Nor is there anything intrinsically civilized about Sue, who recognizes that she is pre-medieval, but nevertheless is forced to retreat into urban ideologies, theoretic unconventionality or ritualism (the Anglo-Catholic arena she disappears into was a very urban movement). Thus, she schematically voices the extremes of civilization – liberty (via Mill who rejects 'Nature') and repression.

Along these axes Arabella moves from a zero by which the natural law is made to serve the existing order of things to an affirmation by which human desire is brought within the compass of nature to justify not a disruption of the order (since although she is about to reseduce Jude it is so that she can reobtain a husband) but its manipulation (which is a subversion, it is true, but one which finally strengthens what it subverts). Sue on the contrary moves from an affirmation which is as chronologically modern as Arabella's zero (since the text from which she quotes was published very shortly before the story takes place)[20] to a negation (which is precisely medieval, or medievalist). Her zero is the ontology of the railway station (where you choose your journey and where you experience, as Sue does, the overwhelming sense of the vast train stopping just for you) as the negation is that of the cathedral in which personal aspiration is abolished. Both women move between the symbolic order and the Other but on opposing levels (nature and culture) and in opposing directions (plus and minus). Although these statements are articulated for Jude by his women (and that has a bearing on the sexual politics of the novel), they can be traced to his original ordeal at Marygreen. Thus the Arabella axis is absolutely defined (though only the zero statement is made) within the field, since what Jude has to learn is that what was good for God's gardeners was not good for God's birds *but* the only mode of inclusion offered is the magic thread of feeling. The field obliterates human continuity but can only do so because that continuity underlies it and leaves the marks without which Jude would have no place in them at all: or, to put it more starkly, if the inky blots of the birds were not there Jude would not be employed, though he is employed to enforce their absence. Jude's work is thus his own cancellation as it will be at Christminster where he repairs the walls that keep him out. After he has decided that he does not want to be a man, 'then like the natural boy, he forgot his despondence and sprang up' (I. 2). The natural keeps you going in order to rule you out – the only way he can prevent being a man is by not being a natural boy (an omen that is clearly fulfilled).

The Sue axis is hardly present since Jude's contact with civilization is minimal. Nevertheless the section opens and closes with the choice of a departure – Phillotson's scheme or dream – and Jude's own signpost. 'He who chooses his *plan* of life for himself,' Mill's text goes on, 'develops all his faculties.'[21] All the planning and scheming and dreaming belongs with Sue's affirmation, but also, at the end of the paragraph from which this quotation comes, Mill compares human nature to a tree 'which requires to grow and develop itself on all sides, according to the tendency of the inward forces which make it a living thing'. I don't know how consciously Mill is appropriating that organistic image of human society as a tree which is central to Burke and Carlyle (and later to Yeats) but it is clear that he does exactly the opposite with it, for instead of it becoming a metaphor of subordination, it becomes a metaphor of self-development (inward forces). Sue is as axiomatic as Arabella because she gives voice to the inward forces which remain as much a part of the field as the utilitarian surface. Thus it shares a common base with 'feelings are feelings' since although both are affirmations they are as determinate as the negations. To be me at all I have to develop myself irrespective of the social order which demands that I come into being. Sue's negation, that we should mortify the flesh, obviously recalls the way in which sexuality literally puts a stop to Jude's dream when Arabella throws a 'piece of flesh' at his self-dedication to being the *beloved son* of Christminister, in other words at the point at which he sees himself entering the symbolic order. (Given his orphanage, Jude's address to the Alma Mater adds another resonance to the merely trivial ambition of which he is wrongly accused.)

Thus the field is defined by the inclusive oppositions of survival, love, freedom and self-discipline. They are modes of being all of which are modes of determination. There aren't any ways out through them. They are the invisible verges.

Unless we understand the inexorability of this landscape we cannot understand the extraordinary inclusiveness of Jude's own journey. Let me recapitulate the sequence. Jude's sense of justice loses him his place. Having reported this to his aunt, he lies down

behind the pigsty (which is, as we know, a very significant place to
be behind) and meditates on the flaw in the terrestrial scheme of
things. This leads him to reject the prospect of growth, but 'the
natural boy' springs up and forgets (it is anti-Wordsworthian since
in Wordsworth the child is father to the man and wishes his days
to be bound each to each). Jude, on the contrary, *steals* out of the
hamlet and returns to his field not to work but to follow the path
athwart. At the edge of the ploughing, another ironic echo, this
time of the end of *Paradise Lost*, marks off the field from the world,
but the world is only a bleak open down, *crossed* by a solitary road
at right angles to the neglected Icknield Way (the monumental
significance will be obvious). It is a flat, low-lying country 'under
the very verge' of his upland world, so his ascent merely gives
access to a drop, and the only way to move is via a cross. Until,
that is, he finds a *ladder* which can literally lift him to a point of
vision from which he can see Christminster or its mirage. He
obliterates his despondence, he climbs out of his field and sees,
whether truthfully or not is indeterminate, what is at least light.
The whole process is disruption, misery and the way out (to echo
Morris's title).[22]

Christminster is the last monument. As with the Barrow, the
amphitheatre and Stonehenge it persists as the record of endeavour
and oppression. Jude successively becomes aware of each of these
dimensions. At night, he hears the broken voices of the inmates
who, under the umbrella of his naïvety, or (to exercise the principle
of the grammars again) the reductive anthologization which is
history, speak in a succession which glosses over their actual
incompatibility. There is an obvious irony in juxtaposing, say,
Gibbon with Newman, or Arnold with Peel, and it reflects Jude's
indiscriminate awe, *or* the fate which awaits polemic in time. By
day, in the meantime, he recognizes the walls' barbarian
oppression (thus echoing the term Arnold used for the aristocracy
and summing up the irony of Christminster which, designed for the
poor, is the citadel of the ruling class), and feels a bond not with
the voices of the past, but 'as an artizan and comrade' (this latter
word is crucial in the novel, and is obviously chosen by Hardy
throughout with deliberate care) who made and remake the walls,
as we now recognize, into pages that can be read. The monuments
are petrified residuums of the Barn, or rather the Barn blended
with Church and Castle from which it is distinguished in the
precarious utopianism of *Far From the Madding Crowd*. But unlike
the other monuments, Christminster is still active, and reminds us
that the novel as a whole relates as a grotesque mirror of *Far From
the Madding Crowd*, and its activity is to do with work including the

intellectual work (Jude's invocation of the ghosts is imagined to have been heard by a student working late), but work here does not bring people together – it is precisely a separating process. 'Artizans and comrades' recalls the cancelled tension of the novel which follows *Far From the Madding Crowd*, in which the heroine's brother, also a stonemason, maintains a recalcitrantly radical position in the face of her entryism.

Of course, Christminster is merely a place of fetishists and ghost seers, and this leads radical critics to see Jude's aspiration as mere illusion. Ingham, for example, correctly notes that it is neither coherent nor disinterested.[23] It is merely the mirage of social integration which is confirmed by the parodic names which echo its petrifaction. But if Jude is merely to confront an illusion, what is the point of the universalizing of the opening section? It is as though a wide-angled narrative, which drags the reader in as unseparated subject, is suddenly narrowed down to a patronizing tale of lost illusions. The negative answer is already clear from the analysis of the movement out of the field. Jude is not offered a place which he chooses to leave as Sorel leaves his village, or Rastignac his country home or even Pip his forge. As we have seen he is both abandoned and constrained. His 'illusion' is not an illusion in respect of the identity which awaits him. It is the primary condition of his obscurity that there is no true self for him to find. Christminster is at least a place where there are no farmers. Phillotson refers to 'my scheme or dream', which aptly encapsulates the double bind of the obscure life. For how can you be human without choice, and yet how can this choice be anything other than a dream? Jude picks up Phillotson's word when he realizes he has trapped himself into marriage which is the field, 'a social ritual which made necessary a cancelling of well-formed schemes involving years of thought and labour' (I. 9).

We know that the well-formed scheme involves illusions that will be quickly disabused. Doesn't the first breakthrough in classical learning teach him a poem which induces 'a polytheistic fancy' inconsistent with the 'ecclesiastical romance in stone' but which voices precisely the need that will initially deprive him of it? His only resource is system, just as with the grammars it has been doggedness. When he has abandoned the pagan classics, his resolution to go to the city of light and lore is approached with a logic as abstract as his ethical decision to abandon the sheer love of reading: 'What was required by the citizen? Food, clothing, and shelter. An income from preparing the first would be too meagre; for making the second he felt a distaste . . . They built in a city: therefore he would learn to build' (I. 5). To work out a programme

of action in such terms is a sign of your unnecessary life. There is
no reason why *you* should follow this course. Jude seeks in
Christminster not merely enlightenment but 'a place' – 'it has been
the yearning of his heart for something to anchor on' (I. 3). The
yearning has to embody itself therefore through a sense of order.
Jude is not trying to escape from his place, because he has no
place. He has no choice but to make a choice to improve himself
and that is no choice at all. That is why the dream is a scheme or
the scheme a dream. The only 'place' for Jude is displacement.

Jude is to find that the order which Christminster is, is not
orderly in terms of his own consciousness but only in terms which
exclude him. That is a condition of his specific social construction.
But the specific social construction is not realized as such until that
construction has become normative – the product of the ethical
decision, the logical assessment of possibilities. That is why I stress
the universalizing rhetoric of the first section. It is not a question of
Jude's typicality but of the universalized terms of his situation –
Jude's field is the field of life, which does not make the novel more
representative but more importunate. He may absurdly see
Christminster as the New Jerusalem but the way of seeing it is
contrasted by way of Gibbon with St John the Divine who sees it
with the eye of a diamond merchant. This partly just relativizes
our judgement (that is, if Jude aspires towards an illusion, it is at
least more morally just than that of the author of Revelation). But
also it is related to the fact that the contradiction in Jude's
encounter with Christminster is not singular but double. There is
the contradiction within the superstructure that Christminster
represents, between learning and culture which the Horatian Ode
foreshadows and the contradiction between superstructure and
base, that is the historical deformation of Christminster as an
institution – 'You are one of the very men Christminster was
intended for when the colleges were founded' (III. 4).
Christminster is a place full of fetishists where you are elbowed off
the pavement by millionaires' sons. This is not two contradictions,
but one. On the one hand there is the pagan proletarian, on the
other the established bourgeois. It is a question of knowing your
place, remaining in your own sphere, which is terribly sensible
advice but a hard slap after ten years of labour. And what else is
the sphere of the labourer?

Christminster is the city of Light and the Tree of Knowledge
grows there. But the celestial city is the giver of order and the tree
of knowledge a forbidden fruit. Education is about the training of
traditional intellectuals and universities are the modes of organizing them into socially acceptable, if not useful, cadres (for in

bourgeois society one way of handling the intellectual is to shut him away in an institution – see Pater's *Emerald Uthwart* if you think I am importing a 1960s accent). This raises a problem of how to read Christminster which, unlike anything earlier in Hardy, must be read parodically. You cannot think of Christminster as you must of Casterbridge as an entirely independent name (for Casterbridge has nothing to do with Dorchester, that is clear). But Jude hears the voices of real people all but one of whom are associated not with Christminster but with Oxford. So we cannot but think of the history of Oxford, and the history of Oxford is complex and revealing. Given the structure of his learning, what Jude goes to find is the Tractarian movement. What he finds there, insofar as he gets anywhere near, is the second-hand residue of the undergraduate's scepticism which resembles the climate of criticism of the scriptures which surfaced in the publication in 1860 of *Essays and Reviews* and which had led to Pusey's unsuccessful persecution of Jowett, and to some extent the heterodox Hellenism presided over by Pater.

The master of Bibliol's terribly sensible advice is a good instance both of the way in which the text works parodically and of the complex relationship between criticism and containment in the debates of the sixties. Bibliol clearly reminds us of Balliol whose *Master*, Jowett, who died in 1893, was the subject of articles by Swinburne and Stephen (and therefore topical both to the time of the story and the time of the production of the text). As a contributor to *Essays and Reviews* and as a general liberal presence he was a valued ally of the kind of enlightened opinion to which Hardy's novel owes its admittedly ambiguous allegiance. In a letter of 1867, Jowett defined 'the object of reading for the schools' as 'to elevate and strengthen the character for life'. The three ways of attaining this have a clear bearing on Jude. First and second respectively are hard work and 'a real regard for truth and independence of opinion'. On the other hand, alas, we also need 'a consciousness that we are put here in different positions of life to carry out the will of God, although this is rather to be felt than expressed in words'.[24] A wall of silence thus intervenes between what is rational for the ruling class and sensible for the worker. In his radical essay 'on the Interpretation of Scripture', Jowett makes it clear that no amount of truth is sufficient to alter institutions:

> An ideal is, by its very nature, far removed from actual life. It is enshrined not in the material things of the external, but in the heart and conscience. Mankind are dissatisfied at this separation. They fancy that they can make the inward

kingdom and outward one also. But this is not possible. The frame of civilisation, that is to say, institutions and laws, the usages of business, the customs of society, these are for the most part mechanical, capable only in a certain degree of the higher spiritual life. Christian motives have never existed in such strength, as to make it safe or possible to entrust them with preservation of the social order . . . For in religion as in philosophy there are two opposite poles; of truth and action, of doctrine and practice, of idea and fact.[25]

The way in which it appropriates a rational materialism (laws and institutions are not absolute) for a deeply conservative end (they are mechanical and therefore not accountable to the intelligence) is beautiful and its detailed appropriateness to Jude's ordeal is obvious (we note how many practices are dispersed to the 'frame' so that very little is left on which 'mankind' can have any effect). Thus the Tractarian aspiration towards an organic totality (an anchor) is displaced by a dialectically educating and excluding liberalism.

Moreover, Jude is deprived of the reconciliation of culture and learning that emerges in the dominant, reorganizing figures of the interim between the story and the text (the seventies and eighties) who were busy recuperating the learning roaming unfettered and dangerously through the ruins of theology. I think not only of Ruskin, who became Slade Professor in 1870, and Arnold, who had been professor of poetry from 1857 to 1867 but also the English Hegelians, above all Bradley and Green, who used a highly radical philosophical system to provide new strategies of containment. Bradley demolished any basis for conduct other than 'my station and its duties', and is another presence in the terribly sensible advice. Green worked apparently more progressively by the dialectical elaboration and practical application of the trans-individual consciousness.[26] Jude is never allowed into the city of light; but through the mediation of Sue, that is through the woman, he is allowed to eat of the forbidden fruit. He cannot, however, make this a fortunate Fall because, as we have seen, the world is not all before him where to choose. On the contrary, the world beyond the field, that is beyond his station and its duties, is an open plain below the verges marked only by a cross and a forgotten Roman way. Moreover, he only begins to benefit from the actual current of ideas when he is displaced from Christminster to Melchester.

Robert Elsmere, on which Hardy made extensive notes, clearly demonstrates the straight ideological version of this and is deeply relevant to the novel. It was the great success of the 1880s if you take success to be a matter both of sales and respectability. For a novel to be a bestseller (my copy of 1889 claims to be the twenty-fourth edition) and to have received favourable reviews from Gladstone and Pater it has to be quite special. Furthermore it has a remarkable pedigree, being written by Matthew Arnold's niece, and dedicated to the memory of T. H. Green. The hero, who is a paragon of learning but suffers from a strange physical condition, comes down from Oxford to inherit his father's rural living. This is on the estate of a Gibbonesque scholar who after a long series of complex confrontations finally induces a religious crisis by way of the Higher Criticism which leaves him unable to go on seeing Christ as a God or working as a rector. (Elsmere has no trouble with Darwinism though he does decide to keep quiet about it to his wife; the Higher Criticism alienates him completely from her – it is very stirring stuff.) Through the influence of a character who is a thinly disguised version of T. H. Green, he takes up instead a secular pastorship in working-class London. Both as rector and pastor, he works largely by telling stories to the lower orders (thus resembling ironically enough Hardy's Ethelberta). But what is important for us is that he re-embraces Jesus (not as God but as the ultimate image of human purity) in reaction to a series of blasphemous cartoons circulated by radical artisans depicting Mary Magdalen speaking obscenities to the crucified Christ. You see where this scepticism leads to!

The Tractarians and the Oxford Hegelians offer some kind of break with Utilitarianism. They offer the Tree of Knowledge as the City of Light. *Robert Elsmere* shows how careful such an ideology has to be, since it cannot be offered to the working class without becoming subversive of society as a whole and the family in particular. The undergraduate helps Sue, and thus Jude, to a pagan joyousness which grows out of pagan learning and the de-canonization of scripture. Green, on the other hand, sees the Greeks as merely selfish and regards Institutions as 'facts beyond' to which consciousness should submit.[27] The agents of emancipation are the walls that contain, the verges which are invisible in the mists. The 'new idea' of going to an obscure hamlet which takes him to Melchester is both Tractarian and Hegelian and depends on Jude not listening to Sue (Jude praying).

Education is an anchor, a leading out which holds him in place. The second dislocation which locates is sex. Like knowledge, it is both self-escape and repair. If it opposes the career of learning through Arabella, it also through Sue opposes the dislearning of theology. Jude recognizes that twice his path athwart has been thwarted by women. In the case of Arabella, this is 'the natural' reclaiming him to the symbolic order and it is not ironic merely that he is helped out of that by Spinoza, for the escape from Arabella is a version of his endeavour.[28] Sue is more complex since both Jude and Phillotson seek to bring her within the symbolic order. On one level she continues the radical theme of education and exposes its containment. She is free of the Jerusalem but can accommodate intellectually by reproduction. She does not seek the City of Light – she has it already. In the Training-School episode she clarifies the social control latent in the emancipatory agency of education, literally, as later she exposes marriage, by jumping out of the window.

Sue gets caught between image and utterance. It is the requirement of clothes and image that she leaps out of. The clothes episode recalls the climax of Sarah Grand's *The Heavenly Twins*, the apparently feminist bestseller of the nineties, in which the female twin Angelica, who has maintained in drag an intimate but sexless relationship with a wonderful tenor, nearly drowns in the river and has to be rescued and stripped by him. As it is all in the dark her naked body is not actually revealed, but it does lead to a recognition which ends the relationship. Luckily he dies of pneumonia and she returns to the husband who, being twenty years her senior, she calls 'Daddy' and achieves equality with him by writing his speeches. Such chaste and liberal fantasies must have struck Hardy with an irony picked up in the image of Phillotson fondly contemplating Sue's handwriting.

In marriage, Sue becomes a voice. It is her imprisonment and his torture. Just as the education motive is inevitable but part of the field – a way out which is a walling in, so here not only is marriage the inevitable, but so too is the end of marriage. Feelings are feelings and this binds Sue and Jude into their fate, though briefly they have something different.

The key figure here is Father Time. In another novel extensively extracted by Hardy and having many links with *Jude the Obscure*, Pater's *Marius the Epicurean*, the hero in a journal he keeps at the end shows that no philosophy can work. A return to the golden age (to the simplicity Jude and Sue feel they have found at Stoke Barehills) would not eradicate 'that root of evil, certainly of sorrow, of outraged human sense in things, which one must carefully distinguish from all preventable accidents . . . were all the rest of man's life framed entirely to his liking, he would straightway begin to sadden himself over the fate, say of the flowers'.[29] Jude's son clearly shares the same response. Marius's final vision is shaped by looking at the lives of the poor and the way in which what is valuable for them is the love they feel for one another (especially children) and how likely that love is to be destroyed by death. Watching a boy who has brought his labouring father lunch he foreshadows both the young Jude and the consciousness of his logical successor: 'He is regarding wistfully his own place in the world there before him. His mind, as he watches, is grown up for a moment; and he foresees, as it were, in that moment, all the long tale of days, of early awakenings, of his own coming drudgery at work like this.'[30]

Marius's only solution to the 'inexplicable shortcoming' on the part of nature is a 'candid discontent' in the face of the very highest achievement, but a 'minor peace' in the acceptance of a Christian martyrdom that privileges 'humanity standing free of self pity', and it is not really suicide (though Marius does not believe in Christianity), since its function is to preserve another character who will voice 'the plea which humanity would ever possess against any wholly mechanical and disheartening theory of itself'.

For Marius the children who dominate the latter part of the novel relieve the iron outline of the horizon about him 'with soft light beyond'. Of course, the children provide no soft light for Jude: their hanging bodies speak only for the outline, clarify the verges which had been lost in a mist. The logic of both novels is towards the Schopenhauerian opposition to the will to live. This is not incompatible with the evocation of Christ, which is apparently incongruous in a novel which so firmly rejects theology. Each of the re-organizing ideologies it encounters – Hegelianism, Arnoldism, Aestheticism – come back to Christ as model (even Marius). Even Schopenhauer himself, who might seem to negate Christianity by proclaiming the unforgivable sin as the supreme virtue, sees his own work as a New Testament in that it 'declares that the Law is insufficient, and indeed absolves man from obedience to it, and that the soul of the New Testament is undoubtedly the spirit of asceticism'.[31] This is abandoning the letter (he cites Romans 7) and mortifying the flesh; moreover, asceticism is 'precisely the denial of the will to live'. Sue and Father Time between them take the novel from the Old Testament of 'merely moral virtue' to the new gospel of the will not to live.

Nevertheless they are only voices, and both are heard not as the novel but as voices within it whose performative context includes ironic distance (not to say grotesqueness, since the suicide note is a grotesque pun). Even the doctor's explanation is the report of an opinion and immediately placed as a historical phenomenon. In other words the last section of the field is decentred. It has been closed up by the events of the middle which have led to that something external which, despite its lack of specific identity, is very specific in its triadic negation of learning, labour and love. It is not falsified but it is not a place of rest. It does not say amen to the novel. Hardy seems to want to stress this by the way in which the word tragedy is employed in the final section in a deliberately journalistic manner to refer to the death of the children, and not to the total situation of Jude and Sue. It confers no literary status on the totality of events. Even as he reports the doctor's 'explanation' Jude collapses into grief: 'He's an advanced man the doctor, but he can give no constatation to . . . '

The field is unanswerable. Its positives – choice and feelings – are the functions of its zeros – self-denial and survival. If we underestimate the pessimism of the novel's intelligence we shall not be able to embrace the optimism of its will. The only way out of the field structured at the beginning is the reflected illusions which are finally endorsed at the end. This impasse derives from specific conditions in the base but those conditions are not made typical, and not given a historical term but universalized. Nothing works to change them. The educated proletariat becomes the species man – the iniquity of the system is 'something external'. But the voice of the obscure articulates this and thus it calls out the replies it does not seek. Jude is condemned to repair and imitation, but 'how ugly it is here' is a sign athwart his furrow.

The Authority of Failure[32]

Of course, 'how ugly it is here' is a very weak and naïve response to the utilitarian field. Nevertheless it is close to what got J. S. Mill, whose *Autobiography* is certainly one of the most significant spiritual histories in nineteenth-century England, out of his dejection:

> I sought no comfort by speaking to others of what I felt. If I had loved any one sufficiently to make confiding my griefs a necessity, I should not have been in the condition I was. I felt too, that mine was not an interesting, or in any way respectable distress. There was nothing in it to attract sympathy. But there was no one on whom I could build the faintest hope of such assistance . . .
>
> I felt the flaw in my life must be a flaw in life itself.[33]

His way out is the poems of Wordsworth: 'they expressed states of feeling and of thought coloured by feeling, under the excitement of beauty'. He does not reject analysis – this is not an opposition between utilitarian and organicist ways of thought – 'with culture of this sort there was nothing to dread from the most confirmed habit of analysis'. Mill shows himself to be sufficiently in command of the history of institutions to oppose the kind of wisdom we have also seen Hardy escaping. What it inspires instead is the continual progression in Mill's work towards more radical positions – from Liberty to the Subjection of Woman, and from the Subjection of Woman to the later editions of Political Economy. Hardy's novel also, I think, articulates a form of opposition to primitive utilitarianism which by no means abrogates its commitment to rationality.

But we have a text that cannot be consumed and a story whose metonymies of gesture turn out to be metonymies of return and thus cannot be transcended, seeming itself to be transcendent like the metaphor of the field in which it sets forth. It is only in the voices that are raised against its closure, which on a formal level constitute the agencies of its narration, that the novel breaks with its own inexorability.

The critique of the given is doomed to closure by its very socialization, either as a form of light (mirrage) or as a programme for action (thither obscured). It is as the text moves from the representational to the representative (from its totality to its totalization) that it ends its circuit of avant-garde protest. The voice of the proletariat, the representative on behalf of.

In 'Democratic Art' J. A. Symonds wrote of the man of letters that 'it is his function to *find a voice* which shall be on a par with nature delivered from unscientific *canons* of interpretation' (my italics).[34] The fiction of the break requires a delivery from 'character' as a finite outline, from nature as order, the law (as opposed to the occult) and the production of speech out of silence (at least through writing). In other words it is a programme of obscurity, voices against the canon. Three voices leave their mark as inky spots. Sue's theoretic unconventionality breaks down but not before it has invoked paganism as a real alternative to theology (or rather re-invoked, since Jude hit upon it in the course of his dogged learning only to be hit in the middle of his dream by a prick thrown by another as though he were a working-class Tannhäuser). Nor before it has called upon the immediate beneficiary of that breakdown, Phillotson, to listen to Sue's *cry* for help and to construct a superior rationality against the order in support of which he 'as schoolmaster', lives his life, in support of a superior rationality. And most of all not until it has urged Jude towards speech which is neither graffito (thither J.F. and the writing on the wall) nor mere parody (reciting the creeds).

Such voices are not within the confines of character. Having for twenty years searched for a protagonist, and found her in need of authorial rescue as he has done with Tess, Hardy produces the voice that does not reside in the persona but the text of the obscure. The voices of the heath, before the ideological break, are naturalized into winds in a recalcitrant landscape, or silenced into monumental residualness, but now become not merely represented but are made the very articulators of the text. I am not speaking any longer of *a* text since *Jude the Obscure* speaks for all of them, as they speak through it. It mirrors *Far From the Madding Crowd*; it centralizes the anxious margins of *The Return of the Native*; it calls the man of character to the centre not of his single self as in a degenerative myth but as the self of *les misérables*; it re-establishes the occult couple at the centre of speech and drives them across the world of work and mobility. Both in the sense that it is a story narrated beyond the confines of character and beyond its immediate textualization, this is a collective text.

Hardy constructs Sue's Hellenisms, Arnoldian sweetness and light and Swinburnian paganism. She is an image of the former to Jude, who seeks in her as he seeks in Christminster an anchor; or rather she is an image haloed. We, of course, have already seen the Swinburnian purchase of the statues of Apollo and Venus, the latter of which she peeps at in an obscure street like the one in which Jude thinks he has found his light. The theoretic unconventionality breaks down because it has no anchor itself and thus can only project towards Greek joyousness which Pater in his response to Arnold argued was an inadequate expression of Greek religion.[35] But also Sue keeps escaping the image it is necessary to become by her insistence on utterance, or finally her insistence on the notes she passes to Phillotson, which precisely reflect the implied dispute between Arnold and Mill. So that her sexual availability is thwarted by her refusal to stop debate with order-loving men.

The novel ceases to be the simpletons.[36] Sue only exists in the last instance as part of Jude's ordeal. The divorce and the revolutionary marriage are part of the field, since they break from one contingency only to invoke a further set (predominantly economic, which is the final motivating force of 'At Aldbrickham and Elsewhere'). But Phillotson's allusion to Laon and Cythna (which is not casual, since Shelley's poem is the most important text for the novel after the Book of Job) gives an intellectual context for all the discussion that emerges from their admittedly doomed break. And that context is revolutionary as Shelley's poem is revolutionary. It raises the voice to the level of the text before it is silenced by the structures of power, the something external which says thou shalt not learn, thou shalt not labour, thou shalt not love. And the text by our reading of it becomes an instrument of ideological formation. Again I have to invoke *News from Nowhere*. Morris's utopian text is highly questionable as a representation but the function of literary production for Morris is 'making socialists'. This means actually refusing to be tied in by representation, which ultimately can only signify the absence of what it represents. Sue makes gestures and statements which defy the reality not only of what she confronts but of what she is. Sue and Jude as a couple clearly mount an impossible campaign, a coupling that opposes all the conditions of the coupling instituted by the dominant order, that expresses itself by the word 'comrade', that takes parentage on the basis of loving kindness and not biologically endorsed property relations, that shares work and ideas (explicitly in contrast with the idealized marriage of the Elsmeres which relies on the division of labour and chaste silence in the face of reason). That is what being a simpleton means, thinking all this could be true: it reminds us of Grace and Giles ... But thinking this way, more importantly talking together this way, and more importantly still having that talk written down and written as apocrypha rather than canon (which we can all read for ourselves) means that if the truth does not make us free, it can be made to make us free.

Whatever ideological end Sue travels to she leaves two residual traces, the most surprising of which is Phillotson, whose original role is that of order. When Jude calls himself an order-loving man he is referring to Sue's revulsion from her husband, and Phillotson himself complains that 'there's no regularity in your sentiments', complaining when she quotes J. S. Mill that he only wants to lead a quiet life. The point becomes clear if we contrast Phillotson with Casaubon in *Middlemarch*: he never confronts Dorothea's lack of attraction to him and tries to forestall her happiness beyond death. Phillotson goes through an ordeal of recognition – 'bent a dazed regard upon her through the glazed partition, and he felt as lonely as when he had not known her' (IV. 4). Later, walking back to the house where he has left her, he senses the 'increasing obscurity of evening'. Phillotson shares in the shadow of the field. 'Feelings are feelings' means that what is good for God's gardeners is not good for his birds – sexual selection is as ruthless as natural selection.

But this means also that he shares the voice in the dark. Note that the split is effected by an exchange of writing. The first sign of Phillotson's willingness to negotiate is that he does not want to 'thwart' her, and her final appeal (which works) is for him to be 'kind', so that he is inserted into the vocabulary of the resistance. One of the subtextual ironies here is that Sue not only cites J. S. Mill but 'your von Humboldt' who was, of course, the school-master of Prussia. Mill cites him as an authority for liberty but Arnold in *Culture and Anarchy* tries by a circuitous argument to re-enlist what he calls, with characteristic bluff, 'the most beautiful of souls' in the cause of culture against individuality; he points out that von Humboldt organized education in Prussia after he had written the text from which Mill (and Sue) quotes. Hardy works the other way round – the text deschools the schoolmaster. Though he sees Sue's relationship with Jude as 'riddle', he responds to its 'curious *tender* solicitude' and feels it would be 'inhuman' to torture her any longer. These are all words that we know have radical connotations in Hardy. He goes on to say that he cannot defend his action 'logically or religiously' but has to act 'by instinct and let principles take care of themselves'. The instinct is a response to a voice: 'if a person who had blindly walked into a quagmire cries for help, I am inclined to give it if possible'. The important point is that his *instinct* leads him to kindness even though it thwarts his desire, and worse. Offering her her desire, he loses his place. It is a strangely bitter irony that the schoolmaster should be defended by the itinerant gypsies.

But this is not merely sentimental decency – it becomes for Phillotson the basis of a new social outlook. The instinct may go against logic (for logically, as Gillingham says, it will bring the house down) but it leads him to a kind of reason: 'I was, and am, the most old-fashioned man in the world on the question of marriage – in fact I had never thought *critically* about its ethics at all. But *certain facts* stared me in the face, and I couldn't go against them' (IV. 4; my italics). On the one hand, logic, religion, the need to 'harmonize' (cf. I. 2) and on the other instinct, thinking critically, facts. The instinct is not the product of a feeling – the passion is still the other way round 'to adorn her in somebody else's eyes'. Not to give in to the passion, as Gillingham points out, would lead to a general domestic disintegration. 'The family would no longer be the social unit.' Phillotson in response goes through to the end: 'I don't see why the woman and the children should not be the unit without the man.' He out Sues Sue. When Millicent Fawcett later approached Hardy for his support for the suffrage, he made it clear that he thought it a trivial change but that he would support it because it might help to bring down the whole repressive social fabric, notably the family.[37] It is no wonder that Phillotson cannot go on being a schoolmaster. Mere decency demands he overthrow the social order.

His retreat from this position is carefully marked with the inky blot of his line of reason. Note that he re-enters the narrative by *reading* the account of the death of the children and feeling pained and puzzled by it. He is updated by Arabella, which signifies the return of the working-class verge (pigs must be killed, and feelings are feelings). On his return to the schoolroom he *pictures* Sue and thus there is a return to images, or inadequate ideas.[38] He is explained with what is effectively a Gibbonian irony: 'No man ever suffered more inconvenience from his own charity, Christian or Heathen . . . He had been knocked about from pillar to post at the hands of the virtuous almost beyond endurance' (VI. 4). The regression is not a retreat to order but the reversal of a reversal, just as Sue has not moved back to religion but forward to religiosity (which is more modern even than paganism and indeed a common enough fate of theoretic unconventionality). Phillotson's stand is 'subverted by feeling' as feeling had subverted his previous position – he 'makes use' of Sue's new views of marriage but does not believe in them, but in his 'wish' for her. Moreover, he vindicates her in exactly the terms that Hardy has pleaded early on for Tess – 'it has done little more for her than complete her education'. The reader is placed in a very strange position here. Obviously no one is going to feel anything but revulsion against Sue's remarriage, but in doing that the reader is not only aligning himself sentimentally with Jude, but also with Gillingham, who wants decency and order. Phillotson enlists Sue's reaction and his own liberalism in the cause of a return – not to order, since the right order envisaged by Gillingham is that Sue should settle down and marry Jude – but to a grotesque parody of it. As her religion is absurd, so her remarriage is a masochistic parody. And moreover, it is totally depersonalized. Hardy makes it impossible to blame either of them. Both have paid too heavily for their honesty and both are humiliated by the wages of return. Of course, it is mostly degrading for the woman but it is no more than a joyless self-relief for him.

Nothing mitigates the nauseating wrongness of Sue's return, and Hardy escalates the reader's discomfort by refusing to stop with the wedding and taking us to the consummation, which is enacted in painful detail. It is made worse by the sympathy we are forced to have with Phillotson and by the fact that he had done nothing to force the consummation. The detail is powerfully physical. He is snoring and stops and she hopes for a minute that he is dead; then she confesses to him, giving him the extra pain he does not need, and in this atmosphere of mortification she submits (her word is 'supplicates'). Worse still, Phillotson tries to dissuade her but in a sentence of remarkable mutual humiliation says, 'I owe you nothing after those signs', while she says, 'It's my duty.' Licensed to be loved on the premises, crude loving kindness has to be left to look after itself. It is not silenced, however, even in the hour of its deletion, for there is Widow Edlin (even her title comes to seem significant) worried that 'the little thing' is disturbed by the wind and rain, recognizing that a wedding funeral has taken place. The voice of the obscure speaks out of the past, but of course speaks to no listener so that it has no performative value, and is only available because the novelist has written it down.

The residual mark of resistance is made clear only in the written text, for Hardy makes us privy to an unedited version of Phillotson's letter which has a passage deleted in order not to jar on the rhadamanthine strictures calculated to appeal to her emotional temperament, and which shows the persistence of his 'heterodox' feelings:

> To indulge one's instinctive and uncontrolled sense of justice and right, was not, he had found, permitted with impunity in an old civilization like ours. It was necessary to act under an acquired and cultivated sense of the same, if you wished to enjoy an average share of comfort and honour; and to let crude loving kindness take care of itself. (VI. 4)

The vocabulary of these *cancelled words* is absolutely accurate. 'Justice' and 'right', as we have seen, are linked with instinct and de-control; our old civilization cultivates instinct not for the sake of happiness but for the sake of comfort and honour, the pair of bourgeois slippers. Above all 'loving kindness' is explicitly linked with heterodox views which have to be abandoned to the future.

To this context belongs the written pun of Father Time's suicide note, which in its grotesqueness makes no concessions to an appropriateness other than verbal and calls attention instead to a problem which in real terms could only be solved by a major change in attitudes to sexuality. It is not insignificant that Annie Besant, one of the true life new women, left the Malthusian Society in 1893 under the influence of Madame Blavatsky.[39]

Sue's theoretical unconventionality, Phillotson's cancelled words, the widow's unheard loving kindness, stand with this as echoes within the closed world of the novel's representation; but in the text they are marks athwart. The theoretical unconventionality does break down, the heterodox views are cancelled words, the voice of the future is dead and that of the folk wisdom past is solitary. What brings them together and makes the novel different from the representation it practises is that the final image of these issues is not *in place* as the novel is for the most part, but in the place of a chosen return, where the dying Jude and his disintegrating family receive the reflection of the sunshine from the wasting walls of Christminster. The phrase has two aspects. First, the sunshine is reflected: we are about to enter not a mimetic illusion but the image of a mimetic illusion, the magic lantern itself. The novel releases itself from the field not in truth but in fiction, by making Christminster a theatre in which all the actions will outshine the necessity that provokes them: 'Nevertheless it is the centre of the universe for me because of my early dream.' (V. 8) Note, however, that the reflection comes from wasting walls. The walls exclude – they are the ultimate confirmation of the field, and we should note that this passage comes at the end of 'At Aldbrickham and Elsewhere' which in its title already suggested the nomadic margins to which Jude is reduced, especially as all he can do now is imitate the dream in cake, thus reverting to the provision of food which he had rejected in the first part as not providing a living. He is by necessity forced to become like the itinerant gypsies. But it is not a timeless outside. The walls are wasting, the theatre becomes, I want finally to argue, the fictive arena of the uncalled-for voice which is also the prolepsis of a different world.

Jude dies reciting the Book of Job to the accompaniment of cheers: the episode surely parodies the climactic funeral of Mr Gray at Oxford in *Robert Elsmere*, for he who had sought continuity from within the walls has a proper attention paid to his death. Jude has not even his wife to attend him. But the Book of Job has as powerful a role to play in the novel as *The Revolt of Islam*. It enters the novel significantly as Aunt Drusilla calls into question the relative prosperity of Farmer Troutham and is first invoked by Jude himself after his rejection from Christminster as his writing on the wall. It is the sequel to the obscured sign of 'thither J.F.' the residual protest against the forced return to the field of his labours. Thus it becomes Jude's voice of protest; among the many invocations of the Bible, it is the privileged text of protest. Ingham correctly points out that Jesus is evoked as often as Job, but this merely confirms the importance it has. The Dean of Westminster in 1887 gave a series of lectures which came to the conclusion that Job reaches the point of darkness through which no light can come save that of Jesus.

The writing on the wall is from chapter 12 in which Job replies to his comforters that God has wrought evil as well as good and that 'Men grope in the dark without light and maketh them to stagger like a drunken man' (which is exactly what happens to Jude). But most importantly it is a residual act of defiance in the context of a heterodox perception: 'he began to see that the town was a book of humanity'. The later Aldbrickham citation is also a support for Jude's increasing heterodoxy, since it comes in the middle of the discussion about paternity and communal responsibility for children. The Job world view is seen to be a protest from which they wish to save Father Time. What is more generally important is that the whole of the Book of Job is about language. Bildad tries to silence Job, his comforters try to 'break me in pieces with words', God is rebuked for his silence. The silence of God which is the refusal to judge (to sort out Job's life in terms of justice) is imaged in two phrases which have obvious resonance for Hardy's novel. God, Job says, 'has fenced up my way' and 'set darkness in my path'. Verges and walls, obscurity – Job's words speak out against this. But 'speak' is not accurate enough. After a long, uncomforted enumeration of his wrongs, Job suddenly says: 'Oh that my words were written. Oh that they were printed in a book.' For that grants him a certain immortality and it is from this point that he becomes affirmative. The whole book centres on voices, the right to voices and the textualization of voices. For, of course, the voices can be silenced in time, it is that act of writing them down that retains them as an uncalled-for reply. Nobody hears Jude's words, but we read them.

This does not marginalize them because by now the novel is turned inside out. Instead of looking into a picture in a frame we are being addressed by the picture. The heterodox voice obtains its privilege as text (as the vote is a voice on paper in a secret box: it is the vote of the novel, not its speech, that we attend to now). This is the way from the avant-garde novel to the educated proletariat. Let me summarize where we are. Hardy writes within a radical discourse that immediately responded to the ethical vision of the novel but the novel differs from that discourse insofar as it links the ideological themes with the social relations of production, or in other words deals with an anomaly even more acute than the new woman, the educated proletariat. This certainly includes women since whatever Sue's education and origin, in her relationship with Jude she is simply a female worker who is rightly called his comrade, and we must not forget that the one proletarian action of the novel is the strike of the girls in the Training-College.

In these terms the field is closed but it is possible to climb, if not into the light, into a position from which the light can be seen or imagined either by the path athwart which is the free action, or by the spots of ink which however sentimentally call forth kindred, by which I take it is implied the emancipatory value of the written, the shred of writing. This is given its theatre in the last section, which is the theatre in which the heterodox voices play their part, as direct speech to the crowd, as theatrical conversion, or as 'tragic' euthanasia. This last instructs us how to read at this point. 'Tragedy' is a debased word in this section of the novel – though it is frequently repeated, it is in the journalistic sense (the tragedy of the children's deaths). We are thus alerted to the ironic disjunction between our involved proximity to the actual situation and the immediately containing distance of its public recognition. Insofar as the story surfaces into the public realm, it is special only in the sense that it is an oddity. But it is also presented as an actuality with which to identify. In that gap, the reader is remade.

The heterodox is only marginally Other since it cannot exist without the orthodox, and indeed, as Wotton argues, seen merely as a representation, Jude might seem reduced to the naked individual at the end.[40] But Job 3, on which the novel ends, goes beyond lament to Utopia. Job wishes for death because 'there the prisoners rest together, they hear not the voice of the oppressor' (it becomes a detailed celebration of an ideal society). Jude's speech to the crowd earlier likewise makes it inadequate merely to deal with the last section as the context of heterodoxy. First it parodies what goes on in the walls (Jude is called the tutor of St Slums), and parody by its nature assimilates what it ironizes: verbally conquers it, occupies it. The context and content of the speech are the very reverse of individualism. Jude says he is 'not inclined to shrink from open declaration' and speaks in 'a loud voice to the listening throng *generally*' (VI. 1; my italics). More importantly, it is addressed as a written text to the reader. We might contrast it with Clym, whose sermons are presented as reported speech, part of the picture within pictorial distance. The only comparison I can readily make is with the powerful long speech of Dinah Morris in *Adam Bede*, which also embodies directly an unauthorized account of working-class experience. (Obviously it is not really unauthorized, but it imitates an unauthorized speech. All art is imitation, not least revolutionary art.) For it is not inserted into the ongoing discourse, but disrupts it as an occasion and is a commentary on what we have been reading.

Above all, Jude refuses to discuss his life in isolation: 'that question I had to grapple with and which thousands are weighing at the present moment in these uprising times'. It is an instance of history, in a context of unrest. Secondly, it speaks against the totality of Social Darwinism – hence the allusion to 'accidental outcomes' and the identification of 'nature' and 'fancy' in Jude's parody of the responses to him – they become identical. Thirdly, of course, he firmly blames his failure on poverty. Then he engages with the Carlylean/Ruskinian discourse which has already been voiced in the novel, 'a paltry victim to the spirit of mental and social restlessness'. Sue rejects this but we can see that Jude is inscribing himself within a discourse that tries to account for the modern man. Finally he offers himself to the crowd, a sick and poor man, even worse than he seems, in a chaos of principles. It is another definition of his obscurity, groping in the dark; but more importantly he is reduced to acting by instinct, not in contrast with reason, but by contrast with example. Thus, far from maintaining a heterodox voice on an individualistic basis, Mill's mere example of unconventionalism, Jude has to seek his individuality in a non-existent community (the conflict is not absent from Mill's 'Civilization'). Nobody does come. He is *reduced* to liberal agnosticism ('following inclinations which do me and nobody else any harm, and actually give pleasure to those I love best'), but this is no position. On the contrary it is a sign that there is a flaw in the social formulas that make this inevitable. Jude's individualism is not an ideological resource but a social problem, not because of some vestige of organicism but because individuality is tied in to economic stratification. The only way we ever could be free is by being equal.

Jude now quotes from Ecclesiastes which is, of course, largely about the eternal vanity of human life. He moves to it from a sequence of concessions. There is something wrong though it can only be discovered by men and women with greater insight than mine. Perhaps it is undiscoverable but, he has already said, 'at least in our time'. One thread that runs throughout the novel, especially in the last section, is that the heterodox voice is the voice of the future tied dependently into the discourse of the present. Thus Jude, in his speech, socializes and then historicizes his life. He may speak, as the novel does, within the discourse of the radical inside the domain of the ideology, but its very quotation marks come out of the social relations manifest in the novel and between the novel and its readers.

What follows Jude's speech is the preposterous story, the 'tragedy' of the children and Sue's relapse. Speech, murder, conversion, self-sacrifice – theatrical gestures that voice denial of the order within which the novel remains closed, but which call down the alternative future. Hardy wrote no more novels and nobody can say precisely why, but one thing is very clear, and that is that this is a novel which calls for a reply, and still awaits it.

Notes

Chapter 1 A Scientific Game

1 E. Macdonald (ed.), *Phoenix: The Posthumous Papers of D. H. Lawrence*, 1936, p. 304.

2 F. E. Hardy *The Life of Thomas Hardy, 1840–1928*, 1965, p. 104. Henceforward referred to as *Life*. This highly coded text, emulating the 'life and letters' format of official Victorian biographies, is universally regarded as Hardy's equivalent of an autobiography.

3 There is no standard edition of Hardy's novels, so I have, throughout, indicated the chapter to which reference is made. Where possible I have checked my quotations against the Oxford editions. Roman numerals are used for Part or Book numbers, arabic for chapter numbers. Unspecified numbers in parentheses in the text are such references to the work under discussion.

4 The theoretical foundations of this chapter are taken from J. Derrida, especially *Of Grammatology*, trans G. C. Spivak, 1974.

5 Again and again in the *Life* it is made clear that poetry is a privileged and desirable medium only not available because of economic considerations. See pp. 48–9, 291.

6 S. Hynes (ed.) *The Complete Poetical Works of Thomas Hardy*, 1982–5, (henceforward, *Poetical Works*), I, pp. 11, 12, 18–20.

7 Once you have read Jacques Lacan, the resonances of these early texts seem amazing. But they are not inexplicable when you recall how much Freud and Lacan resort to nineteenth-century literary texts. Hardy would surely, for example, have responded very fully to Edgar Allan Poe.

8 Knight is certainly not Hardy. The most interesting contexts for Knight are to be found in J. Holloway, *The Victorian Sage*, 1962 (1st edn 1953), esp. p. 252; and J. Gross *The Rise and Fall of the English Man of Letters*, 1973, pp. 75–112. For Knight, Hardy and Victorian science see T. Cosslett, *The 'Scientific Movement' and Victorian Literature*, 1982,

pp. 140–8. For Hardy and Victorian biology in general see G. Beer's indispensable *Darwin's Plots*, 1985. Holloway's introductory chapter precisely defines the difference in certain Victorian polemicists between an appeal to 'wisdom' and rational argument. He shows that Hardy's novels are influenced by that mode and this can be and has been corroborated many times over. But like many who have succeeded him, Holloway fails, in my view, to see that Hardy is just as influenced by an opposing rationality, and, more importantly, that he *represents* these discourses quite as much as he represents the world of visible action.

9 T. Carlyle, *Heroes and Hero Worship*, 1841, Lecture V, 'The Hero as Man of Letters'.

10 Most obviously 'Hap', *Poetical Works*, I, p. 10.

11 Irving Howe, *Thomas Hardy*, 1968, p. 38, notes this in a characteristically memorable manner.

12 Juliet Mitchell, *Psychoanalysis and Feminism*, 1975, p. 372.

13 It has this in common with *The Waste Land* but, as Cosslett, p. 151, notes, it was also T. H. Huxley's image of the struggle for existence.

14 Shelagh Hunter *Victorian Idyllic Fiction*, 1984, pp. 167–208, is the best recent account of Hardy's deployment of the conventions available to the pastoral mode.

15 *A Study of Thomas Hardy and Other Essays*, ed. Bruce Steele, 1985. It is none the less true that Lawrence's critique remains the best starting point for an analysis of Hardy.

16 'In Tenebris', *Poetical Works*, I, pp. 206–10.

17 See Ian Gregor, *The Great Web*, 1974, p. 71; John Bayley, Introduction to *Far From the Madding Crowd*, 1974, p. 28. See also his *An Essay on Thomas Hardy*, 1978, pp. 99–123. Gregor's book is the best sustained analysis of Hardy's fiction within the terms of literary criticism, and I would not wish to minimize my own debt to it. Bayley's book is perceptive about detail but seems anxious to marginalize everything but Hardy's charm.

18 J. Ruskin, *The Complete Works of John Ruskin*, ed. E. T. Cook and Alexander Wedderburn, 1903–1909, X, pp. 180–269.

19 Raymond Williams *The Country and the City*, 1985, pp. 197–215. Originally published in 1973, this is without doubt the best single essay on Hardy as a whole.

20 Ruskin, *Complete Works*, XI, p. 151. See also V, pp. 130–48.

21 Gregor, *Great Web*, p. 55; Williams, *Country and City*, pp. 211–13. This is an extended discussion from the earlier version in *The English Novel from Dickens to Lawrence*, 1971, p. 116, from which Gregor quotes. Williams makes it clear in this later text that he is not thinking of work as a 'human' activity abstracted from its social conditions. But the distinction needs to be spelt out.

22 M. Bakhtin, *The Dialogic Imagination: Four Essays*, ed. Michael Holquist, trans. Caroline Emerson and Michael Holquist, 1981, p. 224.

23 That this phrase is echoed in Hardy's letter to Stephen written after the difficulties of writing for the magazines, that he wanted to be

considered a good hand at a serial, permits us for once, and once only, to make a biographical connection. The nearest he ever comes to an autobiographical character is this disguised woman. See *The Collected Letters of Thomas Hardy*, ed. Richard Little Purdy and Michael Millgate, vol. I, 1840–1892, p. 28. Henceforward, *Letters*.

24   J.-P. Sartre, *What is Literature?*, 1986, pp. 60–1. The second chapter, 'For whom does one write?', especially his comments on Richard Wright, have a clear bearing on Hardy and the issues rehearsed in *Life*.

25   For the concept of metaphor and metonymy, see R. Jakobson: 'Two aspects of language', *Selected Writings*, 1971, II, pp. 247–59; J. Lacan: 'The insistence of the letter in the unconscious', *Ecrits: A Selection*, trans. Alan Sheridan, 1977, pp. 157–9.

Chapter 2   Defects of the Natural Law: 1878–1886

1   John Paterson, *The Making of The Return of the Native*, 1960.

2   Gregor, *Great Web*, p. 101.

3   Penny Boumelha, *Thomas Hardy and Women: Sexual Ideology and Narrative Form*, 1982, p. 60. This book is more than just an authoritative treatment of a particular central issue in Hardy's work. It is the first sustained post-structuralist analysis of Hardy.

4   Ruskin, *Complete Works*, IV, p. 182.

5   Perry Meisal: *The Return of the Repressed*, 1972, pp. 88–9.

6   V. Shklovski, 'The connection between devices of *Syuzhet* construction and general stylistic devices (1919)', *Twentieth Century Studies*, 7/8 (December 1972), 48.

7   T. Huxley, *Evidence as to Man's Place in Nature*, 1863.

8   I am not, of course, arguing that Darwin is an ideological writer. On the contrary, *The Origin of Species* is correctly regarded as a blow to ideology. But there are closures available to Darwinians, and I think Darwin effectively inaugurates them both in some of the revisions to his original text and in *The Descent of Man*.

9   M. Arnold, *Essays in Criticism* (1865). See *The Complete Prose Works of Matthew Arnold*, ed. R. H. Super, vol. III, 1962, pp. 109–10. Subsequent references to Arnold's prose are designated 'Super' followed by volume and page.

10   J. A. Symonds, *Studies of The Greek Poets*, 1873.

11   M. Arnold, *Merope, Collected Poems* ed. Allott, 1965, pp. 398–443; A. Swinburne, *Atalanta in Calydon*.

12   The opposition of responses to the tragic vision in Yeats bears a close resemblance to that in Hardy's novel. Cf. 'Some burn damp faggots others consume / The whole combustible world in one small room' ('In memory of Major Robert Gregory'). The point is important because Hardy is, as I argue, to grow out of this opposition, whereas Yeats deploys it to the last (knowingly, in order to make poems that resist the political commitment they gesture towards).

13   C. Darwin, *The Origin of Species*, ed. J. W. Burrow, 1968, p. 459.

14   See T. Eagleton, 'Nature as language in Thomas Hardy' *Critical Quarterly*, 13 (1971), 155–72.

15   F. Max Müller: *Lectures on the Science of Language*, 2 vols, 6th edn, 1871. For the dispute with Darwin, see preface to 6th edn, I, p. ix. The Canon of Westminster, F. W. Farrar, intervened in the debate, having already published *The Origin of Language* in 1860. See *Language and Languages*, 1878, a reprint of two earlier texts. I mention this to stress the ideological centrality of the history of language, but also because his comments on metaphor are highly relevant. Agreeing with Mill that metaphor is a constant source of ambiguity and error, he goes on, 'but for this very reason they are best suited to our limited human condition . . . The gracious shadows, the beneficent imperfections of language save us from being scorched up by a fulness of truth for which we are yet but ill-adapted' (pp. 210–11).

16   M. Arnold 'On the Celtic element in literature', Super, III, p. 303.

17   M. Arnold, *Merope* II. 1093–6, Kenneth Allott (ed.), *Poems of Matthew Arnold*, 1965, p. 425.

18   F. Jameson, *The Political Unconscious: Narrative as a Socially Symbolic Act*, 1981, p. 53. This local reference does not do justice to the pervasive assistance I have recieved from Jameson's important text in thinking about the theoretical implications of my approach to Hardy.

19   See A. Gramsci, *Selections from the Prison Notebooks*, ed. and trans. Quintin Hoare and Geoffrey Nowell Smith, 1971, p. 7.

20   This is to interpret Locke's epistemology in the light of his theory of government following the argument of C. B. Macpherson's important study, *The Theory of Possessive Individualism in England*, 1962. For a different view of Hardy and empiricism, see T. Paulin, *Thomas Hardy and the Poetry of Perception*, 2nd edn, 1986, pp. 16–26; and J. B. Bullen, *The Expressive Eye: Fiction and Perception in the Work of Thomas Hardy*, 1986, pp. 79–82.

21   Cf. Edward Larrissy, *William Blake*, 1985, p. 41. Interestingly, Larrissy explaining Blake's rejection of dualism enlists Pater (p. 87).

22   K. Marx, *Capital*, I. 7. ii.

23   T. Eagleton, *Criticism and Ideology*, 1976, pp. 102–61.

24   F. B. Smith, *The Making of the Second Reform Bill*, 1965.

25   William Morris, *Collected Works*, vol. XXII, 1966, p. 65.

26   Cf. Eagleton, *Criticism and Ideology*, pp. 102–10.

27   I am referring to the ideological project of Eliot's novel and not to its aesthetic effect which is more complex and radical. See my 'The affections clad with knowledge', *Literature and History*, 9 (Spring 1983), 38–51. I am also taking a deliberately simplistic view of Bradley, on whom see R. Wolheim, *F. H. Bradley*, 1959, p. 267.

28   John Stuart Mill, 'On Nature', *Collected Works of John Stuart Mill*, ed. J. A. Robson, 1969, X, pp. 373–402.

29   Thomas Hardy, *The Literary Notebooks*, edited by Lennørt A. Bjork, 2 vols, 1985. The notebooks are a valuable guide to the cultural context of Hardy's writing, though they should be used with care. Hardy

gives no indication whether he endorses the quotations he copies out, and, of course, none of what he read and did not copy. They nevertheless remain much more reliable guides to what underlies the novels than any of the sparse biographical material that has been allowed to survive, and much more informative than the impenetrable mask of the letters.

30   F. Mulhern, *The Moment of Scrutiny*, 1979, p. 307; see also pp. 10–14.
31   W. Pater, *The Renaissance: Studies in Art and Poetry*, ed. Donald Hill, 1980, p. 185. This edition reprints the 1893 text, but it has relevant variants. It may seem surprising to enlist Pater in the service of a radical ideological disjuncture, and there is no doubt that Pater himself coded his ideas very carefully and then tried to disown them in the late eighties. What is important, however, is the effect he had (on Wilde and Symons, for example, as well as in complex ways Yeats and Hardy). On the revolutionary possibilities inherent in Pater see my 'The decadent producer', I. Fletcher (ed.) *Decadence and the 1890's*, 1979, pp. 109–29. D. Delaura, *Hebrew and Hellene in Victorian England: Newman, Arnold and Pater*, 1969, pp. 198–302, demonstrates how interdependent Pater's texts are with Arnold's. Delaura does not in my view demonstrate emphatically enough that it is an interdependence cultivated in order to establish implicit but radical dissent.
32   J.-P. Sartre, *Critique of Dialectical Reason*, trans. Alan Sheridan Smith, ed. Jonathan Ree, 1976, pp. 45–7.
33   Williams, *Country and City*, pp. 120–6; J. Barrel: *English Literature in History, 1780–1830: A Wide Equal Survey*, 1985, pp. 51–65.
34   *Life*, p. 149.
35   Ibid, p. 161.
36   Hardy, 'A Tradition of 1804' (*Wessex Tales*).
37   *Life*, p. 153.
38   M. Millgate, *Thomas Hardy: A Biography*, 1982, p. 237. This is by far the most sensible biographical work on Hardy, but it suffers the consequence of its form by making much of Hardy's work appear subjective and marginal. I find Millgate's earlier book, *Thomas Hardy: His Career as a Novelist*, 1971, a more interesting source of information.
39   *Life*, p. 172.
40   See Everett Knight, *Towards a Theory of the Classical Novel*, 1969.
41   Arnold, *Essays in Criticism*, Super, III, p. 123.
42   *Life*, p. 170: 'Evidences of art in Bible narratives . . . Their so called simplicity is, in fact, the simplicity of the highest cunning.'

Chapter 3   The Profitable Reading of Fiction

1   Gregor, *Great Web*, p. 115. On the question of 'realism' in this novel see George Levine's excellent chapter, 'Reversing the Real', *The Realistic Imagination*, 1981, pp. 229–51.
2   J. Hillis Miller: *Thomas Hardy: Distance and Desire*, 1970, p. 102.

Miller's book nevertheless ranks in my view as one of the most perceptive new readings of Hardy to emerge in the post-1968 period. The dialectic implied by the subtitle is structurally central to Hardy. Miller sees it, however, as reflecting Hardy's metaphysical alienation, whereas I think it is the product of a fully grasped historical situation.

3   It clearly echoes Arnold's ascription of energy as opposed to light as the major virtue of the Philistines. But Hardy makes very little of this. Henchard is more inscribed within the discourse of Positivism as a fetishist than he is within that of *Culture and Anarchy*. See A. Comte, *The Positive Philosophy*, 1974 (1855), trans. and condensed by Harriet Martineau, pp. 545–61.

4   Lukács: *The Historical Novel*, 1962, pp. 170–206.

5   Jakobson: *Selected Writings*, II, p. 255.

6   Showalter: 'The Unmanning of the Mayor of Casterbridge', in D. Kramer (ed.), *Critical Approaches to Thomas Hardy*, 1979, pp. 99–115. This is as far as I know the first modern article to suggest the possibility of a feminist interpretation of Hardy's novel. Obviously I agree with its general direction, though I think the novel comes to a more problematic conclusion than she does.

7   J. R. Brooks, *Thomas Hardy: The Poetic Structure*, 1971, p. 212. She does not notice that this poses any conflict in the novel. For a more developed analysis of narrative effect, see Showalter.

8   F. Engels, *Origin of the Family, Private Property, and the State*, with Introduction by Eleanor Burke Leacock, 1972, p. 129. Hardy has Phillotson make this point explicitly in *Jude the Obscure*. The whole of chapter II, section 4 is relevant to this novel.

9   See also my 'William Morris and the dream of revolution', J. Lucas (ed.), *Literature and Politics in the Nineteenth Century*, 1971, pp. 239–45.

10   See especially '*A Propos* of *Lady Chatterley's Lover*', *Phoenix II*, 1968, p. 513.

11   R. L. Stevenson, 'A gossip on romance' and 'A humble remonstrance', both in *Memories and Portraits*, 1912, pp. 151–82.

12   Leslie Stephen's editions of Fielding and Richardson were published respectively in 1882 and 1883.

13   See William Greenslade 'The concept of degeneration, 1880–1910', unpublished dissertation, Warwick University, 1982, pp. 121–34.

14   Walter Benjamin, *Understanding Brecht*, 1973, p. 96.

15   Gregor, *Great Web*, pp. 139–72; D. Lodge, Introduction, *The Woodlanders*, 1974, pp. 14–31. Boumelha, *Hardy and Women*, pp. 98–114. Lodge in particular doubly depoliticizes this novel first of all by claiming that Grace and Giles have only themselves to blame and secondly by writing about the novel as 'pastoral elegy'. Jacobus and Boumelha lay the foundations of an analysis which justifies Sherman's instinct that it is Hardy's most political novel.

16   Shelley, 'Laon and Cythna', IV. 1. 7; 'Witch of Atlas' IV. 1.

17   Greenslade, 'Concept of degeneration', pp. 135–43.

18   G. Stedman Jones, *Outcast London: A Study in the Relationship Between Classes*, 1971.

19 Jacobus, 'Tree and Machine', in Kramer, *Critical Approaches*, pp. 116–34.

20 G. W. Sherman, *The Pessimism of Thomas Hardy*, 1976, pp. 141–50. This erratic book is nevertheless very perceptive about the relationship between Hardy's 'worldview' and his social awareness.

21 Boumelha, *Hardy and Women*, p. 108. *Une Vie* is a key text in Vernon Lee's discussion of naturalism, 'A dialogue on novels'. Hardy made extensive notes on the first part of this which is another indication of how deeply at this time he was involved with theoretical discussions of fiction. See V. Lee, *Baldwin: Being Dialogues on Views and Aspirations*, 1886, pp. 187–245.

22 F. Engels, *Origin of the Family*, 1884, p. 126.

23 A. G. Cunningham, *The New Woman and the Victorian Novel*, 1978.

24 Howe, *Thomas Hardy*, p. 104.

25 Gregor, *Great Web*, p. 163.

Chapter 4   The Offensive Truth: *Tess of the d'Urbervilles*

1 St Jerome was, of course, notorious for his violent adherence to chastity. Hardy could have read an account of St Jerome in F. W. Farrar, *Lives of the Fathers: Sketches of Church History and Biography*, 1889, II, pp. 203–402.

2 J. Grindle and S. Gattrell (eds), *Tess of the d'Urbervilles*, 1983, p. 10. This is now the standard edition of the novel, and the kind of plurilingual text Hardy deserves. On the history of the formation of the novel and its entry into the public domain see also J. T. Laird, *The Shaping of 'Tess of the d'Urbervilles'*, 1975; and N. N. Feltes, *Modes of Production of Victorian Novels*, 1986, pp. 57–75.

3 The best is B. Paris, '"A Confusion of Many Standards": conflicting value systems in *Tess of the d'Urbervilles*', *Nineteenth Century Fiction*, vol. 24, 1969–70, pp. 116–46.

4 J. Hillis Miller, *Fiction and Repetition*, 1982, pp. 116–46.

5 Boumelha, *Hardy and Women*, p. 132.

6 Bakhtin, *Dialogic Imagination*, p. 49. See also S. Volosinov, *Marxism and the Philosophy of Language*, 1929, pp. 40–1.

7 D. Lodge: 'Tess, nature and the voices of Hardy', *The Language of Fiction: Essays in Criticism and Verbal Analysis of the English Novel*, 1966, pp. 164–88.

8 C. Darwin, Life and Letters of Charles Darwin, ed. Francis Darwin, 2 vols, 1896, 11. 105–6, quoted N. C. Gillespie: *Charles Darwin and the Problem of Creation*, 1979, p. 126. This is a very clear account of Darwin's own problematic account of the relationship between nature and ethics.

9 'Mental harvest' is a phrase from Mathilde Blind's Introduction to her translation of Marie Bashkirtsoff's *Journal*, 1890, I, p. vii. The use of language here thus firmly places the novel within the discourse of

contemporary feminism. Of course, this perspective does not allow us to marginalize the crime which is committed against Tess's body, but the victim of rape does not have to be treated as ruined forever.

10 Gregor, *Great Web*, p. 183.
11 H. Ellis: *The New Spirit*, 3rd edn, 1892, p. 9 (originally published 1891).
12 Arnold, *Essays in Criticism*, Super, III, p. 109. See D. J. Delaura, 'The "Ache of Modernism" in Hardy's later novels', *ELH*, 34 (1967), 380–99.
13 Bayley, *Thomas Hardy* p. 176.
14 Lodge, *Language of Fiction*, pp. 164–88.
15 Comte, *Positive Philosophy*, pp. 599–636. According to Comte, monotheism, which he identifies with Catholicism, elevated 'Morals to that social supremacy before accorded to polity' (p. 624). Moreover it was responsible for advancing the 'essential differences of the sexes' (p. 628). His remarks on the position of women here reinforce the irony.
16 Pater, *Renaissance*, p. 106.
17 Mona Caird, 'The morality of marriage, *Fortnightly Review*, 53 (1890), 329–30.
18 C. K. Hyder (ed.), *Swinburne as Critic*, 1972, p. 71.
19 Like Arnold himself, he moves precisely between 'Hellenism' and a tactical acquiescence in Christianity.
20 F. Engels, *Origins*, p. 128.
21 Boumelha, *Hardy and Women*, pp. 117–34; M. Jacobus, 'Tess: the making of a pure woman', in S. Lipshitz (ed.), *Tearing the Veil: Essays on Femininity*, 1978, pp. 77–92.
22 Cf. Mitchell, *Psychoanalysis and Feminism*, p. 30.
23 Unbelievably, Bayley tries to defend Angel's sense, see *Thomas Hardy*, pp. 170–3.
24 Caird 'Morality of marriage', p. 313. She goes on: 'It is idle to attempt to lure them back into the cage'.
25 I don't mean, of course, that only Christian male middle-class readers should read this novel. On the contrary, the novel constructs a 'virtual' reader as any text does, in order to elaborate the difference necessary to produce another 'ideal' reader which hopefully we are all on the way to becoming.

Chapter 5   Hardy's Fist

1 R. G. Cox (ed.), *Thomas Hardy: The Critical Heritage*, 1970, pp. 269, 283.
2 Cf. Eagleton, *Criticism and Ideology*, p. 131. I argue, however, that the strategy is less 'provisional' and more fully co-ordinated with the divided cultural situation it encounters.
3 'The Tree of Knowledge', *The New Review*, 1894, p. 681.

4   *Letters*, II, p. 92.
5   See Boumelha, *Hardy and Women*, pp. 63–97; and P. Ingham, Introduction and notes to *Jude the Obscure*, 1985.
6   Not that we should underestimate that observation. The novel is not a series of seemings in the sense that it deals merely with a world of consciousness. On the contrary it is difficult to find equally accurate and internal presentations of working-class life to compare with, let us say, the pig-killing episode, and indeed the whole 'world' of the novel.
7   T. Eagleton, 'Introduction' to *Jude the Obscure*, 1974, pp. 9–20; Ingham, 'Introduction' to *Jude the Obscure*, 1985, pp. xi–xxii. Ingham's edition is extremely valuable, as are her two articles on 'The Evolution of *Jude the Obscure*', *Review of English Studies*, 27 (1976), pp. 27–37, 159–69, which develop her theory about the allusions further.
8   2 Corinthians, 3: 3–6. The imagery has a clear bearing on the novel.
9   G. Wotton, *Thomas Hardy: Towards a Materialist Criticism*, 1985, p. 104.
10 L. Stephen, *An Agnostics Apology*, 1931, p. 58. The essay from which this comes, 'Dreams and realities', was first published in 1874, but the first edition of the collection appeared in 1893. The book as a whole is deeply relevant to *Jude the Obscure*. The word 'agnostic', which is one of the indicators of the date of the story, is made by Stephen to be the bearer of a legitimated obscurity: 'we can say, though obscurely, that some answer exists, *and would be satisfactory*, if only we could find it' (p. 2; my italics).
11 See Arnold, *Literature and Dogma*, Super, VI, p. 175.
12 E. Gibbon, *The History of the Decline and Fall of the Roman Empire*, 1897, II, p. 91.
13 Dowden, *Life of Percy Bysshe Shelley*, 1886; Arnold, *Essays in Criticism*, Second Series, Super, XI, p. 327. It is worth contrasting this with *Shelley's Socialism: Two Lectures*, by Eleanor Marx and Edward Aveling, to the Socialist League, 1888. Hardy's own ideas about Shelley are more likely to have been based on J. A. Symonds, *Shelley*, 1881, see especially pp. 182–3: 'The anomaly which made his practical career a failure, lay just here. The right he followed was too often the antithesis of ordinary morality.'
14 *Letters*, II, p. 94.
15 Ibid., I, p. 264.
16 Ingham, Introduction to *Jude*, p. xxii.
17 Pater, *Renaissance*, p. 187. The notorious 'Conclusion' from which this phrase is taken was restored to the text in 1893 after being omitted in the second edition of 1877.
18 Ingham, Introduction to *Jude*, p. xiv.
19 Gibbon, *Decline and Fall*, II, p. 437.
20 J. S. Mill, *On Liberty, Collected Works*, XVIII, 1977, p. 262.
21 Ibid., p. 263.
22 W. Morris, 'Misery and the way out', May Morris, 'William Morris, Artist, Writer and Socialist', 1936, II, pp. 150–64.
23 Ingham, Introduction to *Jude*, pp. xii–xiii.
24 Abbott and Campbell: *Life and letters of Benjamin Jowett*, 1897.

25   F. Temple et al., *Essays and Reviews*, 1861, p. 356.

26   F. H. Bradley, *Ethical Studies*, 2nd edn, 1962, p. 163. It is worth noting, with respect to my point about the topicality of Hardy's novel, that Bradley referred to this work in a note to a text that might seem directly related to *Jude, Appearance and Reality*, 1893; T. H. Green, *Prolegomena to Ethics*, 4th edn, 1899, pp. 60–1; cf. also pp. 296–7. A properly historical analysis of *Jude the Obscure* would have to take much fuller account of Green, who is relevant on a number of levels. His book on Hume is a radical critique of empiricism, his ethics provides a direct link between phenomenology and community, and his political influence reconstructs the principles of liberalism.

27   T. H. Green: 'Lectures on the Principles of Political Obligation', in F. Nettleship (ed.), *Works of Thomas Hill Green*, 1911, II, p. 428 (first published 1886).

28   This is another instance of the complex effect of the allusions. To do good cheerfully is a very weak translation of 'agere et laetere'. Had Jude really been able to read Spinoza he would have had a clearer idea of the relation of necessity and desire, as had two earlier translators, Eliot and Rutherford, neither of whom renders Spinoza like this. Hardy read a relatively perceptive article on Spinoza in *Chamber's Encyclopaedia*.

29   W. Pater: *Marius the Epicurean*, 1892 (1886), II, pp. 197–8, (ch. 25).

30   Ibid., p. 193. Hardy made extensive notes on this text and, like *Robert Elsmere*, and *An Agnostic's Apology*, it is consistently relevant to his novel. On the other hand, see Ryan, in Kramer, *Critical Approaches*, pp. 172–92, for a view that *The Well Beloved* is a parody of Pater's novel.

31   A. Schopenhauer *Essays and Aphorisms*, selected and translated by R. J. Hollingdale, 1970, p. 62. John Stokes reminds me that Schopenhauer did not advocate suicide, which substitutes an apparent redemption from misery for a true one (ibid., p. 78). But he did absolve it from condemnation, and in any case it is not entirely clear, that Hardy understood the distinction. See Hardy, *Literary Notebooks*, 1909.

32   The phrase is Scott Fitzgerald's. See A. Mizener, *F. Scott Fitzgerald: A Collection of Critical Essays*, 1963, p. 24.

33   J. S. Mill, *Autobiography, Collected Works*, vol. I, 1981, p. 139.

34   J. A. Symonds, *Essays Speculative and Suggestive*, 1893, pp. 266–7. Hardy took extensive notes on this: *Literary Notebooks*, 1846–1857. It is an essay on Whitman.

35   Pater, *Greek Studies*, 1895, p. 37.

36   Its original title. See Ingham, Introduction to *Jude*, p. xxiii.

37   *Letters*, III, p. 238, quoted in Ingham, Introduction to *Jude*, p. xxii.

38   Here again Spinoza seems to be relevant, but it is difficult to establish how carefully Hardy had read him. On the level of individual 'experience' Spinoza's seems to me the most nearly materialist account of the relation of structure to agency, and this explains to some extent his attraction for writers such as Eliot and Rutherford

who, without having recourse to historical materialism, understood the impasse of Cartesian dualism.

39 A. H. Nethercott: *The First Five Lives of Annie Besant*, 1961, p. 375. There is some work on the literary context of Sue, but the 1880s are marked by a number of very effective radical women, Beatrice Potter (Webb), Margaret Harkness, Olive Schreiner and, not least, Eleanor Marx. Annie Besant had already lead a remarkable career, braving the stigma of adultery with the wicked atheist Charles Bradlaugh, running a socialist journal, and organizing one of the earliest strikes of unskilled workers in 1887 at the factory of Bryant and May.

40 Wotton, *Thomas Hardy*, p. 102.

Index